COMING HERE, BEING HERE

A Canadian Migration Anthology

ESSENTIAL ANTHOLOGIES SERIES 8

Guernica Editions Inc. acknowledges the support of the Canada Council
for the Arts and the Ontario Arts Council. The Ontario Arts Council
is an agency of the Government of Ontario.

We acknowledge the financial support of the Government of Canada.

COMING HERE, BEING HERE

A Canadian Migration Anthology

edited by
DONALD F. MULCAHY

**GUERNICA
EDITIONS**
TORONTO • BUFFALO • LANCASTER (U.K.)
2016

Donald F. Mulcahy, editor
Michael Mirolla, general editor
David Moratto, cover and interior design
Cover image: Photo by Donald F. Mulcahy
Guernica Editions Inc.
1569 Heritage Way, Oakville, (ON), Canada L6M 2Z7
2250 Military Road, Tonawanda, N.Y. 14150-6000 U.S.A.
www.guernicaeditions.com

Distributors:
University of Toronto Press Distribution,
5201 Dufferin Street, Toronto (ON), Canada M3H 5T8
Gazelle Book Services, White Cross Mills, High Town, Lancaster LA1 4XS U.K.

First edition.
Printed in Canada.

Legal Deposit—Third Quarter
Library of Congress Catalog Card Number: 2016938892
Library and Archives Canada Cataloguing in Publication
Coming here, being here : a Canadian migration anthology / compiled
and edited by Donald F. Mulcahy. -- First edition.

(Essential anthologies ; 8)
Issued in print and electronic formats.
ISBN 978-1-77183-117-8 (paperback).--ISBN 978-1-77183-118-5 (epub).
--ISBN 978-1-77183-119-2 (mobi)

1. Emigration and immigration in literature. 2. Canadian essays
(English)--21st century. 3. Canadian literature (English)--21st century.
I. Mulcahy, Don, editor II. Series: Essential anthologies series (Toronto, Ont.) ; 8

PS8367.E46C66 2016   C814'.60803526912   C2016-902168-8   C2016-902169-6

Canadians are, after all,
as varied as pebbles on a beach.

Coming To Canada — Age Twenty-One

The postcard said: COME BACK SOON
There was a mountain, a faded lake
with a waterfall and a brown
sun setting in a tan sky

Aunt Violet's Canadian honeymoon 1932
It was swell and she
always meant to go back
but her life got in the way

It was cool and quiet there
with a king and a queen
and people drinking tea
and being polite and clean
snow coming down
everywhere

It took years to happen:
for the lake to fill up with snow
for the mountain to disappear
for the sun to go down

and years before COME
BACK SOON changed to
here and now and home
the place I came to
the place I was from

(Carol Shields, from *Coming to Canada*, Carlton University Press,
Ottawa 1995, reproduced here with permission
from the Carol Shields Literary Trust).

To all who came, are coming,
and will yet come to this incredible place;
to those among them whose goals remained,
or will forever remain elusive;
to those who needed to be here but never arrived;
to all who died trying to get to this safe haven called Canada.

Contents

🍂 🍁 Being Here 🍁 🍂

Going Back

COMING HERE, BEING HERE

*A Canadian
Migration
Anthology*

Introduction

In early 2003 John McLay and I discussed the possibility of a prose anthology, devoted to a common theme. At the time he was working on a sequel to *On Mountaintop Rock* and would be unable to participate as co-editor. We both felt that *immigration* would be a worthy theme, but concluded little beyond that. By September however I had rediscovered two elementary letters among the belongings of my late mother-in-law, Elizabeth Jones, written to her by a teenage friend who had emigrated from Wales to Canada in the 1920s. The letters, reproduced verbatim here in 'Letters from Ceinwen,' brought to mind the myriad other stories that must exist in a country where it is claimed that twenty per cent or more of the population are foreign-born immigrants. At that juncture I decided that the common, unifying topic should indeed be the inseparable themes of *emigration* and *immigration*, relative to Canada.

Although the initial intention was to create a *literary* anthology of works by established immigrant writers, the project's mandate soon morphed from strictly literary to all-inclusive, an outcome that was dictated not only by the collection's ongoing need for more writers, but also by the assorted variety of writers who showed an interest in participating. I eventually concluded that a more diverse roster of writers might well be seen as reflecting the diversity in Canadian society; might even be considered a metaphor of sorts for our complex multicultural population and its varied voices. Canadians are, after all, as varied as pebbles on a beach.

Despite everything, including my congenital pessimism, after three years the initial collection ultimately reached completion point—except insofar as the stories of immigration will never, ever be complete. The shared sagas of people coming here is sure to continue for as long as more are needed to populate this intriguing, gargantuan geographic space, that has become the final home and resting place for so many who have ventured here over the centuries.

I have served only as this anthology's coordinator. Credit for this volume must, naturally, be allocated to the publisher and the Guernica staff, for their belief in the project, and for their welcome refinements. But it is the authors themselves who created the very possibility of an immigration anthology, by placing the need for such a work above all material and other, less creative, more egocentric concerns. This is *their* book.

I am deeply indebted to Guernica Editions, and especially to Michael Mirolla, for recognizing the need for a book of this type at this time; to John McLay, for helping me to *hatch* the concept of an immigration anthology in the first place; to Iris Kool, for sharing her amazing computer genius with me; to Susan Ouriou for her invaluable translations from the French, and to my wife and primary editor, Iris, for her grit, patience and understanding throughout the multi-year bout of my chronic anthology obsession.

—Don Mulcahy
Strathroy, Ontario
Jan 8ᵗʰ 2015

Coming Here

Come from Away in Newfoundland

∽

Roberta Buchanan

(*Come from away*: a person "not from here," i.e., Newfoundland)

I Leave England.

It was 1964, the year of Shakespeare's quad-ricentennial. Here I was at the prestigious Shakespeare Institute, Birmingham University, where I had gone to do my Ph.D. After two years my fellowship ran out, and I still hadn't finished my thesis. I was hired as a research assistant, then promoted to research associate at a stipend of fifty pounds a month. I was employed in the menial but necessary tasks of checking quotations and bibliographical references, proofreading the Institute's publications, doing research for the Director, Professor Spencer; and, on one occasion, rewriting an article for *Shakespeare Survey*. When the librarian suddenly left, I was also asked to fill in her position, on a temporary basis. At the weekly seminars I made the tea and handed around the biscuits. For distinguished guests, wine and food were served. I bought the food, arranged tasty morsels on little crackers in an aesthetic way, and concocted porcupines of toothpicks bearing little pickled onions, olives, and cubes of cheese stuck into an apple. Mrs. Spencer told me I had a "talent" for this kind of work.

I was not Prince Hamlet, nor was meant to be, but one of the attendant lords, a useful tool, presumed to be deferential and glad to be of use, like T.S. Eliot's Prufrock.

At Birmingham University, the social and academic hierarchy was rigidly maintained. I found myself in a kind of grey area. I was neither student nor faculty. I was not entitled to eat in the nice Faculty Club; my place was in the cafeteria with the staff. I had my lunches and my morning tea with the secretaries, all perfectly good and kind people. All the same, I was given the message that my status was somewhat lower than a faculty member. I could babysit their children, but I was not their social or intellectual equal. There seemed no prospect of advancement. Young male graduate students were "mentored," as we say now, given some teaching experience; women students weren't. In 1964, the term "glass ceiling" had not yet been invented. It was more like a concrete ceiling. Glass at least suggests that if persistent you could smash your way through it.

I was unhappy in Birmingham. It was an interesting city all right, with two theatres, two excellent art galleries, nice shops, and a lively market on Saturdays. But I had no friends, no boyfriends. I lived in a room in a dreary red brick terrace house on the Bourn Brook, just opposite the University, a polluted trickle garnished with rusting bicycles, old paint cans and other urban trash. The Bourn Brook valley always seemed to be shrouded in industrial smog. Every morning I walked up the hill past the university gates to the Shakespeare Institute, a large rather gloomy Victorian mansion. By the time I got there I was wheezing and gasping for breath. Sometimes I was so ill the secretary had to drive me home. I became more and more asthmatic, more and more depressed. I had to get away—but how? Desperation gave me courage.

I opened *The World of Learning*, a huge compendium of all academic institutions in the universe, and began at A. I sent a letter to the University of Alaska—the farthest possible spot from Birmingham—asking them if they had any openings in their English Department and enclosing my CV. I got a polite but negative response: *"Thank you for your interest in the University of Alaska ..."* I scrutinized the weekly job ads in the *Times Literary Supplement.* Universities in Ghana, the Gold Coast, Khartoum, and Malta were looking for lecturers in English literature. I was interviewed for Malta, but the other candidate, a handsome young man from Oxford, got the job. Another ad: Memorial University of Newfoundland, in Canada. I sent off an application and my CV. One day a telegram arrived at the Stygian gloom of the dark-panelled Shakespeare Institute— immediate reply demanded, prepaid—offering me a job as lecturer in the English Department at the princely salary of $6,500 per annum—$500 above the minimum rate for lecturer. I was ecstatic and accepted immediately. "You're just the kind of person we need in Canada," said the young man interviewing me at Canada House for my immigration papers. I was staggered! I seemed to be superfluous in overcrowded England. As Professor Spencer so delicately put it at my farewell party at the Institute, I was part of the *"brain sewer."*

I sailed on the *Empress of England* from Greenock (my parents lived in Scotland) to Montreal, with my immigrant's suitcase—a heavy affair with a wooden frame and a tray inside. My journal at the time recorded my departure from the Old Country:

Bagpipes on the tender boat. Felt rather tearful, mainly because hadn't slept much last night, but went and had a lager and felt better. The virtues of alcohol proved once more. Ghastly feeling alone and knowing no one. Lots of smart Americans (Canadians, I suppose). Even the fattest-assed wears Bermuda(?) shorts—long shorts ending above the knee. Am in a cabin with three other ladies, all grandmothers. One is Irish and quiet, the other English and voluble, the 3rd Canadian, rather deaf and depressed and widowed with "a lovely little home." Had tea with the English and Irish, after a horrible solitary lunch with 4 deadly Scottish girls who spoke only to each other, and a deaf old man who spoke only to the waiter. Superb food, however, like a 1st class hotel, only more variety. Lackeys buzzing around the sauce boats like black bees. I wish I had gone on that cargo boat, however, with single cabin and "sharing private bath," and only 14 passengers [the Furness Withy Line to St John's; their passenger service ended that year]. One feels a bit lost among all these crowds, and no one speaking to each other. So tired I can hardly write. Canadian widow is dolling up in a chic écru knitted ribbon outfit. One dresses for dinner. It all seems rather archaic. (12 August 1964).

The voyage to Montreal, which took five days, soon became tedious. There was nothing to do except walk up and down the deck. One evening I was leaning against the rail in my golden Cleopatra sandals and yellow stretch pants—the latest fashion, contemplating the path of moonlight on the sea, when a man approached me. At last a flirtation! He was the boatswain. Socializing between crew and passengers was strictly forbidden, which lent an air of intrigue to the encounter. I had to hover near the connecting door to the crew's quarters. When the coast was clear, the boatswain beckoned to me and we had to slink furtively through the corridors to his cabin. Once there, he plied me with "seduction doses of gin and rum" (I recorded in my journal) and I was soon "swallowing alcohol and flattery alike in large and willing draughts" while soft music played on his record player. As we sat side by side on his bunk, he told me how he had once rescued a girl from drowning. What a hero! I murmured appropriate admiration. He took my hand and placed it on his fly. I felt something large and swelling. I felt very nervous and said I had to go. After that he took up with an American woman of uncertain age and possibly freer morals. I wrote to my friend in London that I had a new swain—a boatswain, which she thought very witty. Despite this brave face I felt I had made a fool of myself.

Now I sit here, an object of ridicule in the writing room, with drunken dancers staggering through, writing, to crown it all, my

diary like a schoolgirl. Work is the only thing, and that I avoid
like the plague. I must work and read. I am going to be pressed
for time as it is when I arrive there [in St John's]. Yet my eternal
frivolity, my vanity in my Cleopatra sandals, my avoidance of re-
ality, e.g. at this moment, I don't even know the value of a dollar.
Such is my ostrich-like ignoring of the Canadian realities soon to
hit me. (Journal, 15 August)

We disembarked in Quebec for immigration. After our documents
had been "sternly inspected" several times, "beaming officials" gave
us tea or coffee in paper cups—"Rather Alice-in-Wonderland-ish."
On the walls were photographs showing immigrants of every con-
ceivable nationality in "*Worthwhile Jobs*" (19 August). But I was impressed by their smiles and their welcome to Canada.

In the afternoon I took a tour of Quebec city. I was not impressed.
The atmosphere struck me as repellent: ... *antagonistically French*
—Wolfe's statue taken down—the whole town seems dominated by a
Plains-of-Abraham complex. Worst French aspects.

On the other hand, Montreal delighted me:

... Most beautiful city I've seen—clean and spacious. A lot of the
centre is very recent beautiful skyscrapers. But there is also the old
French and international quarters. Went on 3 hour bus tour with a
driver-guide not unlike a Richler character—very witty and amus-
ing, and obviously very fond of his city. He pointed out details
with loving care, and told us all about his marriage to an Irish
woman, and how she made him leave the French outside: English
inside, and how they adopted two children. I'm in love with Mont-
real completely. Re-read Duddy Kravitz. (Journal 19 August)

Mordecai Richler was one of the few Canadian writers to be found
in English libraries.

I had to wait four hours at the CN station for my train. Here I

witnessed my first bit of Canadiana: people eating turkey sandwiches smothered in gravy, and with salad! I thought this was the
funniest thing. The food was delicious—$1.95 at the Buffet de la
Gare for a Spanish omelette, chips, peas, salad, bread, coffee and
wine. Thus fortified, I boarded the train that was to take me to the
east coast. How superior the Canadian train seemed to the dirty,
shabby, overcrowded trains of England.

> *The roomette turns out to be a toilet with a let-down bed in it!*
> *Very comfortable seat for day. Iced water. Fan. Basin, wardrobe,*
> *shoe-locker. It seems a bit unhygienic to use the toilet, but I sup-*
> *pose that's what it's for.*
>
> *Everything is so convenient—the dial for heat, for the fan,*
> *bell for porter, thermos of iced water and paper cups, and even*
> *soap and matches! Negro porters, who come at a touch of the*
> *bell.* (19 August)

Revelling in this luxury, I woke up in my new country:

> *... to find myself in a beautiful little town, with wooden houses*
> *painted turquoise and lovely rich pink, the fields with long*
> *islands of boulders in the middle—what they've cleared when*
> *ploughing I suppose. The untreated wooden fences—beautiful*
> *silver weathered timber. The feeling that there's plenty of land.*
> *The little river solid with logs. Tears come into my eyes when I*
> *think of Birmingham—I feel I shall wake up any minute out of*
> *this pleasant dream and find myself there again. What a com-*
> *parison of filth and cleanness, crowdedness and space!*
>
> *Just passed a pink house with a blue roof—fabulous. Church-*
> *es like icing-sugar.* (19 August)

At length I arrived in Newfoundland, via the ferry to Port-aux-
Basques:

Everything so clean and pure-looking. Pure clean sands, utterly empty, bleached tree-trunks. Frame houses ptd heavenly pastel shades. Haystacks round as in Scotland with hairnets. Children's and animals' country—plenty of space to play and roam around in. Iodine-coloured streams. Not unlike Scotland but heavily wooded, bigger, more spacious.

Ferry—tho' sunny, pretty rough sea—dolphins—old lady being delicately sick in paper bag for "mal de l'air"—"motion sickness"—a peculiar way of putting it. Shocked by 2 teenage girls wearing curlers, in public, bobby-socks and trousers—the women not at all smart on the whole—tasteless clothes. Men have check shirts and unmatching ties—very far out. Close cropped hair—Beatles not caught on. Plenty of children, well treated. (Journal, "4ᵗʰ day in Canada")

I boarded the "Newfie Bullet" for the two-day trip to St. John's. The train, with its narrow gauge, was very slow and jerky, making me feel rather sick.

Arriving in St. John's on 21ˢᵗ August, 1964, my new boss, Dr. Seary, and his wife Gwen met me at the station and drove me to the Kenmount Motel. I found them *"very English, considering they've been here 11 years."* I had hardly ever stayed in a hotel before, and it seemed to me the height of luxury. I marvelled at the huge *"treble"* bed, all for me, and lovingly catalogued in my journal the features of my *"super room"*: two wooden walls and a wooden ceiling, *"very modern"*; my own private bathroom and toilet in one corner; towels, soap, matches, Kleenex, stationery and even a pen provided on the house; wall-to-wall carpeting, air conditioning, tourist information on Newfoundland, a picture of the landscape, and television.

I went downstairs to the dining-room, and had an expensive dinner of an enormous piece of fried salmon with *French fries*, which I carefully noted were chips. The waitresses were very funny-looking, dressed in white uniforms with white shoes, like nurses, except that they had little yellow aprons. I overheard one of the tourists saying: *The first time I went tuna-fishing I was six.* There was an air of unreality. Was it all a dream? I was brought back to reality with a bump—by cash. I had a hundred dollars, which seemed to me a large sum, and was dismayed to read posted on the door of my motel room that it cost nine dollars a night plus 5% tax. It took no mathematical genius to calculate that if I spent ten nights, with even minimal eating, I would be broke. And my first pay cheque was due at the end of September.

I was 26. I was in a strange country where I knew no one. I had no teaching experience. I was scared. In honour of my new country, I had bought a large bottle of *Canadian Club*, a 40-ouncer, at the duty-free shop on board ship. I had a pack of cards. I sat on the floor of my room, played patience, watched tearjerkers on television, and drank rye and ginger ale.

So began my new life in Canada.

First Impressions of St. John's

The next day was Sunday. The hotel room began to get on my nerves. I saw a notice in the lobby about church services. I hadn't gone to a church in years—but what else could one do on a Sunday? I took the bus to the Anglican Cathedral. The people in hats, the asking forgiveness for one's sins *"for there is no health in me"* did not cheer me up. After the service I walked down to Water Street, where some men whistled and shouted unintelligible remarks as I passed. A shop grandly called *THE LONDON NEW YORK AND PARIS* had the oddest models in the window dressed in strange outdated 1940s' clothes and hairstyles. There was a chill wind, laced with a whiff of fish; not many people about except a few lonely-looking sailors. I caught the bus back to the Kenmount Motel and sought the artificial comfort of my whisky bottle.

"The MUN"

On Monday, I went to the bursar's office to get a loan to tide me over until payday; they refused. (In England when one got a new job one could always get a salary advance). Here was a dilemma! How was I to manage? I must move out of the expensive Kenmount Motel at once. Most of the faculty were away for the summer, but fortunately I met a colleague in the English Department, Dr. Francis, a tall, red-bearded man (also English). He drove me around town and up Signal Hill in his red sports car, and told me I must *never* call *New-fin-land* New-*found*-land. Then he cooked me lunch in his apartment, and *"gave a long disquisition on the irrationality of women."* I summed up his character in my journal:

> *He is very dogmatic, in that he does not expect dissent from his opinions. I argue a little, but not much as it (argument) seems ultimately futile—altho' he thinks it changes all minds but women's.* (22 August)

Despite his odd opinions of women, Dr. Francis was kind and helpful. He found a widow who took in a respectable female boarder at a very reasonable price, breakfast and dinner included—more for the company, she told me, for she had been married to an American G.I. and had a generous pension. She showed me a room filled with an enormous double bed covered with a bright pink satin spread, and just enough space to cram in a large dressing table with mirror. I paid my *"astronomical"* bill of *"over twenty-seven dollars"* at the motel, and moved in immediately. (Afterwards I found out that Memorial would pay for my hotel as part of my moving expenses.)

Dr. Francis showed me around the university—"the MUN, as they call it here"—which seemed very small compared to Birmingham University. It was built on an exposed position on top of a hill

—"*winds wuthered outside—very clean and pleasant inside hw.—marble floors and all.*" I moved into my office on the third floor, with view of a ridgy hill covered with trees (Pippy Park), and laid out my textbooks on the empty bookshelves. Every day I took two buses to the university. It was very cold in my office, the wind howled and moaned in the roof, and the rain beat against the windows. I sat at my desk staring at Lily's *Campaspe* in *Five Elizabethan Comedies*. I was to teach three different courses: Elizabethan drama, English 200 (starting with Aristotle's *Poetics*!), and Bibliography and Research. Soon getting sick of *Campaspe*, I went over to the library (tiny, compared to the huge edifice of Birmingham University Library) and started looking at all the bibliographies of English literature in the Reference Section. At eleven o'clock I went for coffee in the coffee-room. Here, everybody—faculty, staff (even the janitors) and, later, students—had their coffee in the same place! The coffee room closed at 11:30. At twelve the Reference Section was locked, as if mad thieves might take off with its heavy tomes in the lunch hour. At noon everybody drove home and everything closed down until two—the reference section, the offices, even the switchboard. There was nowhere on campus to get lunch. I walked down to Churchill Square where I could get coffee and a sandwich in Ayre's Supermarket, then went back to the office later to try and make notes on the now detested *Campaspe*. At five, I took the bus back to my boarding house, where a huge meal awaited me: a large halibut steak, with potatoes, turnips and peas; Jello and tinned (*canned*) fruit for dessert, and tea. I ate alone, for my landlady did not eat with me. Then I went to my room and went to bed, since there was nothing else to do.

After a few days of sitting alone in my office, having lunch alone in the supermarket, and dinner alone in the boarding house, I became very depressed. Time was passing. I didn't seem to be making much progress with *Five Elizabethan Comedies*. I sat in my office in rising panic and thought of all the books I hadn't read. Soon the students would return and term would begin. How would I manage? One evening at dinner I could no longer suppress my anxiety and started to cry. My motherly landlady packed me off to bed.

My long-time dream was to have a place of my very own, instead of living in a room in someone else's house, as I had done in England. Dr. Francis took me to see an apartment (I learned not to call it a "*flat*") on Queen's Road. On the third floor, it had a large sitting room with a fireplace, a bedroom, kitchen with fridge and stove, and bathroom; hardwood floors. Best of all was the large window with a stunning view of the harbour, Signal Hill and the Narrows. All this for a hundred dollars a month, heating included. I could watch the sun rising over Signal Hill, shining on the sea, the ships sailing into the harbour through the Narrows. From that moment I fell in love with St. John's.

I found out that it was easy to get a bank loan in Canada, and borrowed $100 against pay day. I bought an iron bedstead from a friend of my landlady for $20. At a second-hand furniture store I bought a table, some chairs, and a chest of drawers for a very modest sum, delivered. (I grandly gave the men a dollar tip.) My crate of books and pictures arrived. I was delighted. The living room had not only the view of the Narrows but also of Prescott Street, which plunged steeply to the harbour, and I could look down into the tall row houses and see people washing dishes in their kitchens. The bedroom had a view of the Basilica with its clock, Queen's Road, and Rawlins Cross with its two drugstores and Murphy's Superette, which sold everything from plastic buckets to rabbits (in season), from coal to carrots. On Prescott Street there was a tiny basement Chinese laundry where I could take my sheets.

My spirits rose. I had a good job—University Lecturer—with generous pay of $400 per month. (I immediately put down $100 on a record player, to be paid in instalments.) I had an apartment of my own. Best of all, I had escaped from grimy old England with its wretched cold *bed-sitters* and dank bathrooms with wet towels, Birmingham with its polluted air, rows of grey dismal houses, and snobby university. Here wooden houses were gaily painted in different colours. The sun shone and sparkled on the sea. I had finally "arrived."

I Begin Teaching

Teaching was just talking about literature, wasn't it? How difficult could it be? After all, I loved literature! I bought a second-hand tape recorder, and attempted to practise a typical lecture—say, on *The Duchess of Malfi*, one of the four tragedies I would be teaching in English 200. Alas, after a few sentences and *ers* and *ums*, I dried up. I couldn't think of anything to say. I made several discoveries: I would have to write out all my lectures, and read them. And: it took me an hour to compose one page of lecture notes, not counting the preliminary reading. It took six typewritten pages (single spaced) for one lecture. That was six hours of writing.

My office mate, Dr. Elisabeth Orsten, arrived back from Oxford. She smoked a pipe, much to the horror of the President, who told her that it tarnished the image of the University. There were other young women among the faculty. Olga Broomfield, a Newfoundlander, kindly gave me her notes on the Bibliography course, which she had taken as a student from Dr. Story (famous as one of the compilers of the *Dictionary of Newfoundland English*). An Albertan, Diane Schlanker, of Ukrainian ancestry—one of the few "*Canadians*" (i.e., mainlanders) in the English Department—lived a few doors down from me on Queen's Road, and we soon became friends.

I grew more and more anxious as the beginning of semester approached. The students would soon find out that I knew nothing, and I would be ignominiously fired! I couldn't sleep, my stomach was in a constant knot. I went to Dr. Kennedy, just a few blocks down on Queen's Road, and asked him for some tranquillizers. He said he didn't prescribe tranquillizers. I was distraught—perhaps I cried. Anyway, he relented and wrote me a prescription.

Thus fortified, I went to my first class—Bibliography and Research. All I had to do was explain to the students what the course was about, and give them a reading list. These were all honours students, the crême de la crême. To my horror, my tongue felt thick, my speech was slurred, and I found it difficult to think! Tranquillizers were not the answer.

What a semester that was! I've never worked so hard or been under such pressure. It was worse than Finals. I had a nine o'clock class on Tuesday, Thursday and Saturday (English 200, 50 students); an evening class, Tuesday and Thursday (Elizabethan drama); and my bibliography class Monday and Wednesday. I had cut one hour of the bibliography class so that the students could go to the library and look at the bibliographies assigned for that week, and report back on them to the class. That still meant eight hours of lectures to prepare. After my nine o'clock class I rushed home to write the lecture for my evening class. This class had several highly intelligent teachers in it, and I was always crippled with nervous diarrhoea before it. Luckily, as soon as I started my lecture, it disappeared. On Sundays, I had to research and write the bibliography lecture on *The History of the Book*. And how I wrestled with Aristotle's *Poetics*—a difficult text that I could hardly understand myself and that was hell to explain to the second year students. No sooner was one lecture prepared and delivered than it was on to the next one. I was always in terror that some student would ask a question I couldn't answer, for a professor should know everything about her subject, I thought. I read as much as I could!

I knew what kind of professor I *didn't* want to be. I didn't want to be like Dr. H, at Keele, who looked over the students' heads at the wall behind us as if we were contemptible. I didn't want to be sarcastic and put students down. I would treat them with respect, always. I would never, ever say, like Dr. K, that Jane Austen was a great writer because she had a "masculine mind." And I was not going to treat Newfoundland with disdain, as the intellectual and social boondocks, as some of my colleagues did. After all, I was a colonial myself who had been born in South Africa. In fact I encouraged my bibliography students to choose a Newfoundland writer as the subject for their annotated bibliography, if they wished to do so. That was the smartest move I ever made, for it was in this way that I came to know something about Newfoundland literature.

My nemesis was teaching poetry on Saturday mornings to the second year students. My method was I.A. Richards, *Practical Criticism*: go through the poem line by line. Explication. We had a textbook that gave the poem, and then two critics' different interpretations of it. This confused most of the students, who thought there was only one interpretation—the teacher's—for every poem had a "hidden meaning," and it was your job to tell them what it was so they could write it on the exam. Since I was very bad at remembering names, and more so when I was nervous, I had the whole class sit in alphabetical order, so that I could call on them in turn and knew exactly where they sat. They hated this, as it separated friend from friend. Saturday mornings were poetry torture. I called on each student in turn to give their interpretation of a line or stanza. I didn't realize that some students were so shy that they never spoke in class. I was traumatizing them by calling out their name and insisting that they answer. In the other classes—Aristotle's *Poetics*, followed by four tragedies, I gave lectures. But it seemed to me that poetry was different and needed to be discussed.

Things came to a head with Wordsworth's "Ode on the Intimations of Immortality." Several Saturdays had been spent in trying to get through this long poem, line by line. On the third Saturday the students' patience snapped. I found written in large letters on the board: "*NO MORE IMITATIONS OF IMMORTALITY.*"

Poor students! How they suffered at the hands of an inexperienced teacher who was obliged to learn by her mistakes. I tried to arouse their interest. I remember asking the question: Why should we be interested in a play—Webster's *The Duchess of Malfi*—written four centuries ago? Does it have anything to say to us today? And trying to convince them that it did. It was a damned difficult play, too. At that time, the courses lasted a whole academic year, two semesters. So we were together for a long time. The students were very forgiving. At the last class, much to my surprise, they clapped. Apparently that was the custom at the time: that the students would show their appreciation in the last class. A very nice custom, for a new teacher.

In Newfoundland language holds many traps for the unwary. One of my students said he wanted to come and see me in the evening. I thought he was being fresh, or, as they say in Newfoundland, "*saucy.*" It was his turn to be confused—for weren't my office hours 2 to 4? How was I to know that in Newfoundland *evening* meant *afternoon*? I'm sure I committed many gaffes out of ignorance.

One linguistic difference I did enjoy was when the students called me "*Professor.*" "*Oh, I'm not a professor,*" I assured them, causing *them* to be confused. In England, *Professor* was a title given to only the most senior and distinguished academics, heads of departments and those at the top of the academic ladder. Here, anybody who taught at a university was a professor. How it would have annoyed my professors in England to have me, a lowly lecturer, called "*professor*"!

Come from Away

"*Where are you from?*" taxi drivers, complete strangers, new acquaintances, ask me. If I'm "*round the bay,*" I always reply, "*St. John's.*" They look puzzled for a moment, and then cunningly say, "*But you're not from here, are you?*" "*I've been here since 1964,*" I snap; probably a time before most of my questioners were born. "*But where are you from?*"

These questions always irritate me. Why should I have to explain to my interrogators the complicated details of my life? Sometimes I counter a question with a question: "*Where are* **you** *from?*" New-foundlanders love exchanging this information, and, if they are talking to a fellow-Newfoundlander, usually discover that they're related, perhaps by marriage, to a distant aunt or cousin, or that their next-door neighbour is a cousin thrice removed from some-one in the other's community. The best seller in Newfoundland is Dr. Seary's *Family Names of the Island of Newfoundland*.

I can never escape this question, "*Where are you from?*" As soon as I open my mouth, my accent betrays me. Yet if I try to change the way I speak, I sound phoney, especially to myself. Why can't I say *past* instead of *pahrst*? Or *can't* instead of *cahrnt*? I cahrn't do it. Yet when I go to England I sound Canadian. I say *candy* instead of *sweets*, and *sidewalk* instead of *pavement*, *French fries* instead of *chips*, and *chips* instead of *crisps*. My English friends think I'm try-ing to sound affectedly American. When I'm tired, I try to quickly translate from one idiom into another. *Where am I?* Am I on the sidewalk or on the pavement? Do I want a bag of crisps or a bag of chips? It's confusing. Some people in Canada think me snobbish for retaining my English accent instead of adopting a more decent North American one. "*You have an accent,*" they cry; as if they didn't. Others like it. One of my students admiringly said she could listen to me forever, for my soft voice and English accent lulled her to sleep.

So here's the answer to that irritating question: I was born in Uitenhage (Oiten-hah-ker), Cape Province, South Africa. When I was ten, my parents, who were themselves immigrants from Scot-land, decided to move back to England, or "*Home*" as it was called in the Colonies. I grew up in London. I went to university in the Midlands—first Keele, in the "*potteries,*" and then Birmingham. My accent is hybrid: a trace of Cape accent ("*feh heh*" instead of "fair hair"); Cockney (*Bloimey she's a loimey!*); Oxford, from my profes-sors at university; a touch of Birmingham; and a bit of Scottish from my parents. ("*It's a braw bricht moonlicht nicht tonicht.*") To the

scorn of Glaswegians (Glasgow was my parents' native town) I pronounce my name the *sassenach* way—*Bew*canon. In Glasgow they
say Buh*can*on, with the emphasis on the second syllable.

"Will you move back to England now?" people asked me when I retired. No way! I'm a Canadian citizen, and proud of it. And I never
fell out of love with Newfoundland.

They Left Their Homes with Nothing, and Made a New Life with Hard Work

Dana Borcea

This year marks the 25th anniversary of the start of the arrival in Canada of refugees the world came to know as the "boat people." In the years following the fall of Saigon, more than 60,000 Vietnamese refugees came to Canada. With help from the government and local groups, 6,000 settled in Edmonton. Here are some of their stories.

SITTING ON THE back porch of their north Edmonton home, Carol and Alan Kwok are sipping green tea and remembering a past they would rather forget. The couple are not usually mindful of anniversaries, but the weight of this one is too heavy to ignore. Twenty-five years ago, the Kwoks said goodbye to Saigon. Under the cover of darkness they climbed into a small crowded boat with their four children and a bag of clothes. So began their long search for a new home, a search that ended in Edmonton.

The journey across the South China Sea to a Malaysian refugee camp was supposed to last two days. Engine problems and poor navigation turned the voyage into a nine-day nightmare. "They told us we would have everything we needed on the boat," Alan Kwok said. He remembered his shock at seeing the boat he had risked everything to buy passage on. The Kwoks shared the 15-metre vessel with more than 150 people, desperate to flee South Vietnam's new Communist regime. They were among more than one million people from Vietnam, Cambodia and Laos who fled the region from 1975 to the early 1990s. Tens of thousands died. Many more braved harrowing journeys across rough waters to seek temporary refuge in camps inside Malaysia, Singapore, the Philippines, Hong Kong, and Japan. They became the "boat people" and were known around the world.

"There was no space to lie down and everyone had to squeeze in close," Carol Kwok said, bringing her legs up to her chest to demonstrate. There was little food and they soon ran out of water. Carol could do nothing when her children tugged at her sleeve and told her they were hungry. When it rained, they held a tarp above their heads and tried to wash themselves with the water. The stench in the boat was unbearable. Many boats got lost at sea and floated aimlessly for weeks, even months. In some cases, people who didn't starve or drown fell prey to pirates. In the overcrowded Malaysian refugee camp, the Kwoks suffered from stifling heat and boredom.

"I was thinking about the future," she says. "I didn't have any control in that life. I was always worried. Even at night when I slept, I worried."

When Canadian officials arrived in the camp a few months later, Carol began to hope. With a distant cousin studying in Saskatoon, she and her family were chosen to come to Canada as government-sponsored refugees.

When they arrived in Saskatchewan in May 1979, there was still snow on the ground. The children had never seen snow before, and loved it. Carol got a job in a factory and cleaned offices at night. Her husband found work in construction. They raised their children and studied English. Thirteen years ago, they moved to Edmonton and opened a convenience store downtown. Carol often worked 16 hours a day, seven days a week, but has since cut back a little. She works hard because she can. She likes the money and the security it brings her family. "If you want to come to a free country, you should do the right thing," she says. "Work, save money, be honest."

***

That work ethic was common among the boat people who settled in Canada, says Alice Colak, director of immigration and settlement services at Edmonton's Catholic Social Services. She was a front-line settlement worker during the late 1970s and early 1980s, when most boat people arrived in Canada.

"The research shows that the people who came in that period have contributed overwhelmingly to Canada, both economically as well as culturally," she says. "They have not been a burden on this society."

At the time, Colak heard complaints from people concerned about the large influx of refugees. "People were worried about the cost of allowing this many people to come," she says. "They worried about there not being enough jobs."

But many more welcomed the refugees warmly. Diane Bessai was one of them. As a young, widowed mother of four, Bessai opened her home to a family of four Vietnamese refugees. Members of her church, St. George's Anglican, pooled their resources to sponsor the Lai family, who arrived in 1980.

The Lais were among the tens of thousands of Indochinese refugees sponsored under the Immigration Act's new private sponsorship program. Under the new rules, any organization or group of five or more people could sponsor refugees by committing to their financial and personal support. Churches, ethnic associations, even bowling leagues across the country stepped forward in huge numbers. During this period, Canada accepted more Indochinese refugees per capita than any other country.

In her 30 years as a settlement worker, Colak has helped welcome waves of sponsored refugees from countries in Eastern Europe and Central America, and more recently from political hot spots such as Kosovo, Ethiopia, Afghanistan and Sudan. The numbers coming out of Vietnam were the largest she has seen. "To this day, there has been nothing like it," she says.

Like many other Canadians, Bessai remembers reacting strongly to the images of overcrowded boats full of people willing to risk everything for a chance at a better life. "I didn't have any money to contribute, but I had a big house and hospitality to offer," Bessai says. The Lais stayed with her for six weeks. To this day, their two sons, who went on to open a successful cabinet-making business, still call her "mom."

***

Hunched over a sewing machine in her cluttered dress shop, Tina Tong hemmed a pink taffeta bridesmaid's dress and remembered her escape from Vietnam 15 years ago. "We wanted to find freedom," Tong says—a frightened teenager when she and her brother said goodbye to her family to board a boat bound for Malaysia. "We wanted something good for the future and we didn't see anything good there."

Despite studying hard, Tong knew that with no money or government connections she would never be able to attend university in Vietnam. The night she left marked her third attempt. Her brother had already spent a year in prison for an earlier escape bid. After idling in a refugee camp for nearly a year, Tong and her brother were selected by Canadian officials to come to Edmonton, making them among the last of the boat people to settle in Canada as government-sponsored refugees.

They arrived in September, just in time to watch the leaves change colour. "All the trees were yellow and orange and I thought it was so beautiful," Tong says. "I liked the weather then, too. It was just a little bit cold."

The government provided Tong with a two-bedroom apartment downtown and free English classes. She soon felt lonely and estranged. "It was a sad time and a big life change," Tong says. Her lack of English proved to be her biggest hurdle. "You don't know how to write, how to talk or how to listen." Her first job, baking desserts in a mall bakery, forced her to learn. "It was my first job and very exciting. It was hard to understand my boss at first but he never got mad, even when I made mistakes. The customers were also very nice. It made me want to learn (English) faster." Over the next decade, she worked various jobs and had four children. Her English improved.

Just over a year ago, Tong realized her dream of owning a business when she bought a dress shop on the corner of 105th Avenue and 97th Street. A Beautiful Angel Fashion is full of bright, modern fashions and traditional Asian dresses. Although she is still losing money on the store, Tong has always wanted to be an entrepreneur. In Vietnam, that wasn't possible. "What's yours is yours here," she said. "You don't have to worry about a knock on the door." Tong often works late, doing alterations while her children play in the back of the shop. Many nights the phone rings constantly. Most of the calls are for her nine-year-old daughter. But Tong doesn't seem to mind. She says she's here for her children. "They can do anything they want now," she says, handing her daughter the phone.

Prejudice

୬

Anton Capri

I PICK MYSELF up and try to act unhurt. The bully, I still don't know his name, sneers at me. "You dumb fuckin' DP. Go back where you came from." I only understand some of what he is saying, but recognize my label: I'm a DP. My parents too are DP's, displaced persons, people without a country. But Canada has accepted us—my parents have been accepted as farm workers for a year. After that we can live anywhere in Canada, and after four more years become citizens. By 1954 we will be citizens, and will have a country.

After the harvest we move to Toronto. The farmer that my father works for says that he cannot pay him during the winter. We can stay on the farm, but we will have no money to live on. It's not legal for my father to work in the city. He's supposed to work on a farm for a year. My mother gets a job in a clothes factory.

In Toronto the school is much bigger, and already my English is quite good, although when I speak everybody can still tell that I'm a DP. But I now have a friend, Dave. It is spring now and this is my first game of baseball. When it's my turn to hit the ball I go and stand on the plate, but the boy throwing the ball throws it straight at me. Then Dave comes up to me and explains that I have to stand beside the plate and the pitcher will throw the ball over the plate. Everybody, except Dave, laughs at me. This is how we become friends. I want to play well, so I watch how the other players run hard and slide into the bases. Later I hit the ball and slide into first base. Again, everybody except Dave laughs, and he comes over to me and explains that I don't need to slide into first base. Now I know that you can run past first base and that this is faster than sliding.

Dave has these really tight little curls that he keeps cut very short. I get a brush cut that's as close as I can get to what his hair looks like, but it doesn't look as good. His hair looks neat even when it's ready to be cut. I wish I had hair like that. I also wish I had dark skin like him.

Dave's mother is dead and his father travels a lot, talking to groups of people. I haven't quite understood what he tells these people even though Dave has tried to tell me. It has to do with something called *prejudice*, which is a word I don't yet know, and Dave doesn't bother to explain it to me in a detailed way. But my English is getting better all the time. Dave lives with some people who are not related to him and he comes to our house quite often. At first my mother, who doesn't earn very much in the clothes factory, is not too happy that Dave comes for supper, but she is happy that I have a friend. Later, she gets to not mind at all. My father doesn't pay much attention to us and reads the paper all the time when he is home. He says he is trying to improve his English, but I notice that he is always looking at the part of the paper where jobs are offered. He doesn't have his unemployment book yet because we haven't been here for a year. When he gets a job he works until they ask for his unemployment book. After that they will allow him to find another job. This is all very hard on him.

One day I see something that makes me feel less unhappy about being a DP. I'm on the Queen Street streetcar near the rear exit and a couple of men in heavy coveralls and boots covered with mud stand beside me, speaking English with strong accents. That is when another man says in a very loud voice, so that everyone can hear: "Those goddamn DP's. We won the war, now they come here and take our jobs. Why the hell don't they go back where they came from?" One of the two men becomes a little flushed, but says nothing. At the next stop he steps on the stair, so that the door opens, then he reaches in and grabs the loudmouth by the jacket and lifts him right out of the streetcar. He then steps off the stair, the door closes and the streetcar moves on. I notice that quite a lot of the people in the streetcar are smiling.

Dave is my best friend. He is helping me in school with all the subjects except math. I am quite a bit ahead of everyone in math, as I had learned a lot about it at the school in the DP camp. Dave has also got me to join the Glee Club. He has a beautiful voice. It's funny, when I sing I don't have much of an accent. We travel to some of the other schools in Toronto and sing there. Next week we will be going to a festival in Kingston. We'll be there all weekend. Dave and I are going to share a room.

The festival is great. Our school comes second, but I notice that the other boys, and especially the girls, don't like to sit with Dave and me. I think it's because I'm a DP and he's my best friend. I'm beginning to understand the meaning of *prejudice* now. Maybe if I lose a bit more of my accent they won't have this prejudice, and then Dave won't be hurt for being my friend.

I'm getting quite good at baseball. I usually get to play right field and the other day I caught a very long fly ball for an important out and I also hit the ball very hard. Some of the other boys actually came over afterwards and slapped me on the back. I haven't been called a DP for quite some time now.

I finally get to meet Dave's dad. He's back home again, and this time he's giving a talk in a church, and even though it's not a Catholic church I go with Dave. I don't tell my parents. There are a lot of people there, and I think I'm the only DP, because everybody else seems like a real Canadian. It's easy to tell because they're all coloured. Dave's dad talks about their brothers in the south and the day when they will all be free, when there will be no more prejudice, and people will live as brothers. There is a lot more that I do not understand. Later Dave introduces me to his dad and I shake his hand. "So, you're the young man who has befriended my son. I'm very pleased to meet you. Dave has told me many times about you and your family." I don't know what to say. Surely it's Dave who had befriended me, not the other way around. So I just say: "Yes, sir. I'm very pleased to meet you, sir."

Later I ask Dave what his dad had meant. "After all, Dave, you are the one who became my friend when nobody else wanted to have anything to do with me because I'm a DP." Dave looks at me long and hard before he answers: "I'm coloured."

I know that. It's obvious. "Yes, you're coloured."

"Well, that's it. Now, you're accepted, your accent is almost gone, and pretty soon nobody will be calling you a DP any more. But me—I'm going to be coloured for my whole life."

My First Day in Canada

Chung Won Cho

It was Christmas Eve 1953 in Toronto, and my very first day in Canada. The memory of what happened that evening at Malton Airport is still vivid among all the other hazy, fleeting recollections of my journey, which had started in the war-torn country of Korea. There had been a one-month stop-over in Tokyo, and I had flown over various U.S. cities before arriving in Toronto, my final destination, where I planned to live and study. It now seems so very long ago.

The propeller-driven Trans Canada Airlines plane from Chicago had landed, and taxied to the terminal at around 11:30 pm that December 24th. Of the passengers entering Canada on that plane, I seemed to be the only one with a visa of any kind. The immigration officer asked me to wait a while, and offered me a chair. He then proceeded to locate a medical officer who was required to examine the chest X-ray film and health certificate issued by a doctor in Seoul. This medical data, which had accompanied me on the entire journey from Pusan, Korea, throughout all the airports, stopovers and transfers, had been guarded by me as though it were the most valuable thing in the world.

The wait seemed endless. In reality, it could not have been more than 15 minutes, but it certainly felt much longer. All the other passengers, having been checked through, were long gone now. Eventually the immigration officer reappeared and told me that he was unable to locate the medical examiner, suggesting that he might be out *merry-making* since it was Christmas Eve. Without any hesitation, he then let me through without the customary medical check.

By the time I walked out of what was then a very small terminal at Malton Airport, it was past midnight; Christmas Eve had now become Christmas Day. No member of my family had ever belonged to a Christian church during my time in Korea. I'd had considerable exposure to the traditions of Christianity however, but to me Christmas Day was just a day like any other. I'm not sure if there is any significance in the fact that I chose to arrive in Canada on Christmas day.

Outside, the airport seemed deserted, but for a large bus waiting at the curb-side to transport people into the city. I decided to take the bus, and approached it slowly, cautiously, with a piece of heavy luggage in each hand. The winter night sky was clear, the temperature cool but tolerable, the general atmosphere very quiet. I do not remember seeing any special Christmas decorations; the commercialisation currently seen in Canadian cities had not significantly affected Toronto's Malton of 1953.

There was no one present to greet me, or welcome me. Nobody there to tell me where to go. To any onlooker noticing me, I would have appeared utterly lonesome.

Suddenly, however, I experienced an entirely new sensation: a violent outburst of pure joy; a strong, uncontrollable emotional uprising within. My whole body seemed to be resonating with pure happiness. My inner voice wanted to shout: *"Freedom! I'm free at last!"* I was totally surprised by this ability to generate such explosive emotion over sensing freedom.

During my years in Canada those meaningful words have continued to periodically flash through my mind. In retrospect, it is unlikely, considering my limited English on arriving here, that my inner voice would have been able to articulate those words ... in English, that is. It is likely that, through frequent recollections of the event over the years, I have subconsciously translated them from the native Korean in which I functioned mentally. Regardless, I remember those words as clearly as if I had actually uttered them.

I could not get over the fact that officialdom would never bother me again. Would never stop me in the middle of the street and ask me to show identification papers. Never question the *raison d'être* for my existence in this world. In future I would be left alone. Those were the sources of my joy on arriving here.

In those days, my younger days, I was always the introvert. Some interpreted this as a reflection of emotional frigidity, and that I was incapable of ever externalising strong emotions. My early experiences here in Canada were unique, to me anyway. Arriving as a somewhat serious graduate student, I was at a loss to explain the powerful emotional experience on my arrival. I had reassuring expectations of success in pursuing my studies here, without interruptions, like the Korean War had been in my homeland. I was about to embark enthusiastically on what was just one more challenge in life. I felt convinced that my emotional arrival held a deeper meaning, was related to something more complex than my merely arriving in Toronto as a new graduate student.

On climbing the steps of the shuttle bus, which had few passengers on board, I asked the driver if he could direct me to a reasonable downtown hotel—one that a poor foreign student like myself could afford. He said he knew of one and would take me there. During much of the bus ride to downtown Toronto my mind was on my dramatic emotional response following the realization that I was now in Canada.

But there were other thoughts, a panorama of other events, unfolding too on that bus ride: like my brief loss of freedom during passage through U.S. airports without a U.S. transit visa; countless incidences of street corner harassment by Korean wartime security checkers; the difficulties I faced in the process of obtaining my travel documents; all those years of *refugee* student life in the southern city of Pusan, estranged for the first time from my familiar native city of Seoul; those experiences of the suffocating urgency of war. That expression of emotion at the airport might merely have been a reaction to the cumulative effect of three full years of war. I thought also of my childhood, and pleasant memories of my parents.

The first stop for the bus was outside Toronto's Royal York Hotel. The driver told me to remain on the bus, and he later drove me to the Walker House, almost directly across the street from the Royal York. I thanked the driver as I got off the bus with my luggage, which contained two pairs of socks suitable for Canada's severe weather, given to me by my Korean friends.

At the hotel I rang a bell and waited a good five or ten minutes before anyone appeared at the front desk to register me and give me my room key. A bellboy with a hint of alcohol on his breath helped me with my luggage. No one asked about my ability to pay for the lodgings. It would be a few years yet before the appearance of credit cards.

When I woke up in the hotel room, it was 2 pm on Christmas Day, and I felt the need to let someone know I was actually in Toronto. The only person I knew in the whole city was Dr. I..., the professor who had first informed me by mail of my acceptance into graduate school. That, plus my appointment as demonstrator, would enable me to continue my study of physics. His letter, in response to my initial written inquiry to his department, had become the sole official document around which my journey had taken place.

It was Christmas Day now, and a national public holiday. It would be useless to try to visit or contact anyone in the Physics Department. Fortunately, my month-long stay in Tokyo had taught me to use the telephone as a convenient tool to contact people in their homes. For me, this was a newly acquired skill of modern living.

I searched for Dr. I... in the Toronto telephone directory available in my hotel room, and, fortunately for me, found only one listed under that surname. Gathering all my courage, I dialled his number. After a brief wait, Dr. I... came to the phone and identified himself.

"*Dr. I...,*" I said, "*this is Chung Won Cho ... from Korea. I arrived here just last night.*"

A friendly conversation ensued from that point, with the professor telling me that the hotel I was staying at was the one he chose when he first arrived in Toronto from the U.K. as a student. He said he was currently resting after his Christmas dinner, along with his family, and he unhesitatingly invited me to supper later that evening.

My very first day in Canada had now begun; a day to be followed by many more, and many more years even. After a month I felt as though I had lived here for years. Changes in my life began to develop rapidly, and my outlook changed with similar amazing speed.

That original intention, of a brief temporary stay in Canada in order to obtain further training in physics, is but a distant memory now. I studied diligently, worked hard, and Canada provided for me. I ultimately became a permanent resident, and citizen. I met my wife Joyce in Toronto, and we raised a family together. And now, following many twists and turns en route getting to this juncture, and following a highly emotional arrival here, my roots are set down very deep, and very permanently, into Canadian soil.

Secrets, Lies,
and the Call to Reconciliation

~

Joan Clayton

("If we lose our memory, we lose ourselves." Ivan Klima)

IN A SMALL Ontario town a man stands in front of his mother's grave, alone. He is tall and well built with an unusually kind face—and eyes like the sea; an indescribable blue-green colour that changes with his moods, and perhaps the seasons. Down the hill are row after row of white crosses, and the wind blowing through the old willows creates a shadow play that he finds oddly comforting.

"Jonas?" he hears a voice say and he turns towards it, not having been called this since he was a child. An old woman in black, her face hidden by a lace head covering, is walking towards him, a bouquet of lilies and roses in her arms. He does not recall her from the funeral, and in the weeks following this encounter he will wonder if he had imagined her, if it was all a dream. Her words had pierced his feeble sense of closure.

"Your mother isn't who you thought she was," the woman had said, handing him one of the flowers. "She'd been married before wedding your father—to someone who was murdered. Is that the correct word in wartime? Murder? After his death she walked by herself across Europe, leaving it all behind, taking on a new language, identity and culture. I think she would want you to know now that she is gone, and there is nothing more to fear."

This revelation happened in November, 2004, and I was given the story two years later. The remarkable journey of the dead woman, who I call Eva, has been shrouded in mystery, silence and a wish to forget. Her son John recalls his childhood confusion: his father's sharp words correcting his mother's grammar as if she were stupid; their constant moving—as if there was a gun somewhere seeking them out. There was so much in his childhood that he did not understand, which began to make sense after that disclosure. But there were still many questions he was afraid to ask.

His mother had always been perfect to him, absolute in her love, and yet often he would watch her staring, unfocussed, as if remembering something she could not put words to.

Secrets often come out after someone has died. I think this is an important layer of the immigration experience for many who lived through the Second World War, especially so for survivors of the Ukrainian Genocide of 1932-33. I have spent many years trying to understand Eva's experience. It began as a dialogue with John, who has found it difficult to imagine the world as it was during the eras of Stalin and Hitler. This was the world that his mother grew up in; the time that she fell in love and made unimaginable decisions that altered the course of her life.

Eva was born in 1923 in a small village in Western Ukraine close to Ternopil. Her early childhood was simple and carefree—a world of small farms, orchards of apples and peaches, and a lake nearby where she liked to swim. John told me many stories, like the one about his mother heading out at night with her sisters, searching for old bits of scrap metal to fix a leaky roof. Like ghostly figures, they went home under a full moon, but not before Eva lay in the grass for a while, thinking that she wanted more than a bare subsistence.

Always inquisitive, and with a fierce determination, Eva was encouraged to read philosophy and the great poets. She would be seen walking in the early morning, memorizing passages which may have helped with her survival, later. These brief anecdotes have helped me to construct the character of this woman, who left her village when she was in her early twenties to follow a lover of questionable origin.

I wish to understand. *Ya khochu shcob.*

The pastoral existence she lived with her family and community started to change radically when books became contraband, and a brutal attack on the Ukrainian Soviet Socialist Republic was instigated by Stalin. The Holodomor, which means 'death by hunger,' has only been recognized internationally since 2008, and it is still controversial. For this reason I will say little about the many factors that might have been part of that genocide, but will focus on it, rather, as the first stage in Eva's development, and how it may have planted the seed for her to leave the past behind.

She was ten years old when millions of people died of starvation in her country. Stalin's henchmen were told to burn the wheat fields, and shoot anyone trying to hold on to a piece of bread. Fortunately, there were no roads into her village, so the soldiers had no ready access. With their isolation, small gardens, and ancient traditions, there was more food for them than for many other communities, especially those in Eastern Ukraine. Still, there were shortages, and soup kitchens were set up in the schools, and an extra potato or water would be added to make sure that everyone had a share. News travelled, however, about the people starving; about the cadavers that lined the sidewalks; and the wagons of emaciated bodies that were left to rot.

A large part of my research was through the local Ukrainian Club and my interviews with people there who had survived the Terrible Famine. They welcomed me and taught me embroidery and dancing. I attended festivals where girls danced in high red boots and long hair ribbons—elderly men played haunting melodies on the *bayan*, which told stories of loss and tragedy. Every Easter, I painted *pysanka*, the beautiful eggs renowned as a Ukrainian cultural treasure, and was told by our teacher 'never to waste a drop' of the coloured dye. People at the Club spoke of the time when there was little to be had, and of the suffering that persisted over time, and through the generations. The commemoration of the Holodomor takes place in November, and it is a solemn event. Black pins with five sheaves of wheat are given out and small loaves of bread broken into thin pieces so that people never forget; never forget what it is like to be starving.

Ukraine had always been Europe's bread basket, with always enough wheat in the fields. The villagers were rugged people who knew how to work the earth. They rose early in the mornings, as the wind blew over the mountains and across the wide open steppes. To have no food was a startling reality; and people remember children being put on trains to Kiev by parents hoping their progeny might find a better existence there, though fearing they might never see them again.

Last summer I met with one of the last survivors of the Holodomor, and reviewed my findings and the threads of the story I was putting together. He felt that my understanding was thorough and gave his blessing to the project. He has since died, peacefully, of old age, and the need to tell the story and remember is even more fully entrenched within me now.

A couple of years into the research, I was given Eva's passport. It is a small red document—for *Persons of Undetermined Nationality.*

The countries in Eastern Europe have been referred to as the *Bloodlands,* whose borders were constantly shifting in the 1930s and 40s. Eva had to learn many languages along her journey, and she became a nurse, as many women did, by simply helping out in field-hospitals and makeshift surgical facilities.

I slept with her passport under my pillow for a couple of years, as I tried to make sense of what I knew, as well as the many voids and enigmas that remained. This is not uncommon when people try to make sense of their parents' stories, for example. An important element of the Ukrainian experience was the shame that lingered after the brutal atrocities which occurred during the man-made famine. Starvation affects one's mental processes, which can contribute to wrong, even inhumane decisions and behaviour.

Eva walked to the Hill of Crosses in Lithuania. This is a sacred site where people bring crosses and crucifixes—huge effigies that seem to rise to the heavens. The tradition of bringing symbols of peace and spirituality to this shrine has existed for over a century, and several times the Soviets tried to bulldoze the area, but always, within days, all the crosses, icons, and Statues of Mary were brought back.

We do not know exactly the path that Eva walked over the couple of years that she was on the road. From the disclosure at her gravesite, and following discussion with various European scholars, the most likely explanation for her secrecy and ongoing fear here in Canada was that she was part of the Resistance Movement. I have also been led to believe that the man she married was involved in various underground organizations, and was possibly one of their leaders. A likely scenario is that he disappeared and was never heard of again. At that time, bodies were being thrown in rivers and into mass graves, with no markers.

Other factors for concern are the difficulties inherent in grieving and obtaining closure when you never see the body. It leaves you wondering if the person is really dead, especially during wartime, with so many conflicts and opposing factions—with people doing whatever they must do to survive. When one doesn't see the body there is always a possibility that they might show up somehow, or be heard of in a letter found at the bottom of a trunk.

Eva married a Lithuanian man, who migrated to Canada before she did. New immigrants were given five dollars and a train ticket when they arrived in Halifax, if they were lucky, with the understanding that they would work merely for room and board for at least a year. Eva herself emigrated from Bremen, Germany in 1951. During her time in Germany, she worked as a nurse in a military hospital and lived in a transit camp where people from various countries stayed before they left for a new life overseas. Ten percent of people did not pass the immigration interview, and I wonder if this worried Eva as she waited to be processed—a displaced person with untold stories. On her transatlantic voyage, there was plenty of cheap vodka and cigarettes—and people throwing up the whole way over.

She settled with her husband in a town in South Western Ontario, where he started a business and worked long hours. She lived as if she was of Lithuanian heritage, and they spoke Lithuanian at home. John recalls going to school where the other children had Canadian names, like Peter and Mark. He asked that he not be called Jonas anymore, but rather, John, and this hurt his mother.

As with any secret, those about the past can leak out in interesting ways. This reality has convinced me that who we have been, and what we have experienced, always find a path of return, demanding our attention and asking for reconciliation. And it can take decades. This might not happen until after someone has died, when the bones speak and the spirit is given its last chance to have a voice.

John's father would correct Eva's language as if she were stupid, and I think now that this created a tension that lived like a ghost in the house, to keep her past hidden, and repress her personality. As a teenager John finally challenged his parents, and it was disclosed that she had been originally from Ukraine, but then that reality was again brushed aside.

Eva's past was never a topic that was allowed to be discussed at any length, again—an indication that there were powerful reasons to keep her history hidden. Although she lived a quiet life in an area of Canada where there was little crime or reason to worry, John said that they moved many times as a result of his mother's fear and anxiety.

Trauma, and an existence which threatens our basic survival, become embedded deep in the psyche. We know that people who have lived through severe deprivation and loss continue to horde and engage in other behaviour to protect themselves. Eva had clearly been afraid during her long walk, and this fear lived on during her life here in Canada as a wife and mother. Through unusual circumstances I also learned that Eva had told one friend here about her Ukrainian background, but again, she asked that it not be revealed.

When John was nineteen, he returned to Ukraine with his mother for a visit. There was still no road into her village, and he recalls getting off a bus and walking through unmarked land, past a forest, and beside a meadow—his mother knowing exactly where she was going. There were red poppies and blue cornflowers in the fields, and wild roses grew up and over the abandoned buildings all summer long.

The villagers welcomed them with open arms, and of the first evening there, John remembers drinking unfermented vodka, and the explosive reaction in this gut later, which led to many laughs ... as his mother relaxed into the old rituals, songs and stories.

Druze me. Vse bude dobre.

Eva embraced the people as old, familiar friends, with a shared history, as if all was now fine. Her life in the village had been a simple one, and the age old traditions were still the same. Little had changed for the village people.

Another clue to his mother's true identity occurred one afternoon in Kiev. As the country was still under Communist rule, there were soldiers everywhere and one of them confronted John and grabbed his passport. His mother stepped forward and John then saw a side of his mother that had never surfaced in Canada. She stared down the soldier, with fire in her eyes, as she drew herself up to challenge his arrogance and misuse of power—her words fierce and threatening—and the man immediately backed down and returned the vital document.

That trip had a profound impact on John, in terms of understanding his mother, but when they returned, her Ukrainian heritage again went underground. It was not to be spoken of, and there were no reminders or symbols of it anywhere in their house. She never connected with anyone in the Ukrainian community, or acknowledged this part of her lineage in any overt ways.

John lived his adult life knowing that this part of his mother was not to be discussed or honoured. After the disclosure at her grave, he was inconsolably upset over all the questions he had been afraid to ask. Later he became fascinated with European history throughout the 20th century, and began to read voraciously about the resistance movements, as they existed in France, Poland and Ukraine.

Eva's story highlights the complications that children face in asking about parts of their parents' stories that are woven with profound grief, fear and shame. Even after death, the bones may call out to be known for all that the person had experienced, and for reconciliation.

Eva has been a hero to me, and as I explored the history of Ukraine and the Resistance, it became clear that her life had been full of unfathomable decisions, bravery and determination.

She died over ten years ago. She was in her early eighties then, and is buried in a Catholic Cemetery. There is still no headstone at the gravesite, for reasons I do not understand. I can only imagine that it is symbolic of the need for secrecy and privacy that she carried after her long walk during the Second World War. It was a walk that began because she would not submit to tyranny; a walk to fight for justice and dignity, within an arduous journey that came at great personal cost.

The Phoenix

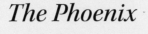

Thuc Cong

IN ANCIENT MYTHOLOGY the phoenix was a magical bird with the miraculous power to regenerate itself by becoming reborn from its own ashes.

In my own mind, I have come to identify with that bird. In 2005 I will celebrate the 20th anniversary of my arrival in Edmonton, an event that seems to have turned the ashes of my previous existence into a splendid phoenix.

In 1982, a high school science teacher, seeking freedom, escaped from South Vietnam, a communist country in Southeast Asia. With a well-focussed sense of direction, but no navigating knowledge, he led a small boatload of 15 starving and frightened people to the safety of Malaysia. There, he was detained in Pulau Bidong camp for two months, after which, under the sponsorship of a church in Barrhead, Alberta he made his way to Edmonton. Immediately after his arrival he found work as a janitor at the International Airport. With very little knowledge of English, he struggled to cope with his new life in Canada. His most prized companion was his English pocket dictionary. He eventually advanced from the janitor's position to that of a restaurant chef, and then finally decided to quit work and return to school. In time he became a certified engineering technician, and now there is considerable demand for his skills in the glass industry. That boat person was my husband, Sonny Nguyen.

In turn, through Sonny's sponsorship, in 1985 I was able to follow him to Edmonton. Arriving here was an amazing experience; I felt like a blind person who had suddenly regained sight. The magnificence of the landscape, the friendliness of Canadians, the freedom, all made the effort of escaping worthwhile.

I have always retained a high degree of respect and admiration for the boat people, and the difficult decisions they had to make. They risked their lives for a great cause—freedom; a cause that inspired them to work extremely hard to cope with settling into their new countries and overcoming language barriers.

I found the cold of Edmonton's winters to be a serious challenge. But even while gripped by such intense cold, I was sustained by that vision of a phoenix, rising from its ashes, becoming a gorgeous new bird.

I was being reborn here in Canada. My life seemed to be starting all over again from the beginning: a new language to learn; a new career to pursue; new friends to make—a new mortgage to carry!

Having made the decision to emigrate, I had to accept every new challenge that came along. Everything was *possible*, but not necessarily *easy*. Patience seemed to be the most important requirement. Working at all kinds of odd jobs, including daycare worker, I was able to support myself while going through school. To climb from the very bottom of the social ladder to somewhere around its middle took me six years. The job I currently hold could only have been acquired by hard work and patience. Lots of patience! Abandoning my dream of remaining a teacher, I embarked on a new career. I now enjoy my new career, but once in a while miss teaching in that rural high school in South Vietnam.

In 1988, a beautiful girl came into our lives. Her name is Tu. This gifted child brought me lots of hope. Having been born in a free country, she has a bright future. My husband and I both work hard to rear her in decent living conditions, to guarantee that bright future for her. She is worth every minute of our efforts. I believe it was God's plan for us to have this wonderful child.

In 1991 we bought our first condo—a place of our own, and privacy at last. After several years of living in apartments, we decided to buy a place that could be called *home*. A place with a fenced yard in which my daughter could play; somewhere that allowed her to cry when she was ill or upset, with no complaints about the disturbing noise.

On my 20th anniversary, I, this virtual phoenix, will spread my wings and thank Canada and its people for accepting me, a strange bird, as a family member. I am proud to be Canadian, and will do whatever it takes to improve our country. I have been a guest speaker at many special occasions, such as graduation ceremonies for English-as-a-Second-Language students, and Canadian Citizenship Ceremonies. I am well received by my audiences, and I really believe their acknowledgement relates largely to me being an honest, hard-working Canadian.

Having lived here for 20 years, I have concluded that this country is so wonderful, a paradise for people who merely want to live a peaceful life. The happiness that I have achieved here intensifies my belief in Buddha. As a Buddhist, I try to be more generous, to be a good citizen, and to make everyone happy. I also try to gradually reimburse Canada for the debt I owe this beloved place. I get more involved in volunteer work. I donate blood on a regular basis, God having created me with O-positive blood, something I must share wisely, beneficially with others. On watching my blood fill the bag the other day, I was reminded that *all* blood is red, regardless of its source; and that its universal redness seems to symbolize the sense of equality that prevails in this multicultural Canada of ours.

When I eventually become a grandma, I will tell my grandchildren the story of this phoenix, and perhaps the story will be passed on for many generations. Of course, before I tell them the story, I will sing along with them clearly and proudly: "Oh Canada, our home and native land ..."

Carlo and Andrea

(From a memoir in progress)

⌒

Antonio D'Alfonso

CARLO D'ALFONSO AND Emilia Salvatore, my parents, were born in Guglionesi, Molise, situated on the Adriatic coast of Italy. Molise used to be part of a region best known as the Abruzzi. Such is what it was known as until 27 December 1963. As late as 1970 this small plot of land officially became the youngest region of that Mediterranean boot-shaped peninsula. As kids, we proudly identified ourselves as coming from *the boot*—how else to label ourselves, we various peoples born or raised there by men and women who enjoyed an existence riding in caravans on that wide European highway used by pluricultural and plurilingual conquerors and merchants?

Although there is an obvious sense of pride about being Abruzzian-Molisan, these nomadic peoples were not necessarily patriotic. Their identity kept changing from one thing to another, transformed by politics, celebrations, and disasters. Many Italians abroad seem to originate from this region (or the other region emptied by emigration, Calabria). This mountainous stretch was home to the Samnites, who were not at all interested in joining the Roman federation. Three bloody wars—in 343–338 B.C., 304 B.C. and 298–290 B.C.—fought between Rome and the Samnites, came

to an end with a Roman victory. A slow-won triumph; and a con-
quest that left these nomadic peoples void of the written history of
this central part of Italy.

Italy: the etymology of the name remains uncertain. The term
Italia, some believe, derives from *víteliú* (land of the veal), from the
Oscan, a language spoken by the Samnites. In the Umbrian lan-
guage we find *vitlo* (veal) and in Latin *vitulus.* A coin discovered in
Corfinio, Abruzzo, directs us to the 91 B.C. meeting created by the
Italic League, charged with the task of demanding, from reigning
Rome, legal and civil rights for these Adriatic peoples. Poet Ovid
and statesman Pontius Pilate were Samnites who spent their lives
abroad. *Italos,* interestingly enough, also appears in an ancient
Greek dialect. Clearly, the Bull became the symbol of the Samnites,
who had to defend themselves bravely against the all-devouring
Wolf, symbol of the Romans. Finally, some scholars claimed that
Molise gets its name from a Norman lord of the 11th century, Gui-
mond de Moulins (Guidomondo De Molisio). Its origins continue
to be a mystery, much like the language spoken by the nomads who
crossed its lands. The few surviving inscriptions indicate that the
peoples wrote in a Cyrillic-based language, moving from right to
left. It may take decades before further clarification is discovered
among the piles of history books written by the victors.

The Abruzzo-Molise, with its less than 1.5 million inhabitants,
occupies the landscape spread out between the Apennines and the
Adriatic coast, south of the Marche, north of Puglia. Our family
grew up Abruzzese, and gradually adapted themselves to the noun
Molisani, inevitably forgetting the fact that one is the other. Such
subjects made their way into our conversations and arguments
around the kitchen table. The political separation artificially divided families, histories, and cultures that had previously been
united. This simplistic classification of nationalities might please
centralized governments, but it creates unnecessary wreckage in
the minds and hearts of people. The only good thing that came out

of this traumatic split was the ensuing anti-nationalist feelings that emerged in these broken families. Let us be clear, if I sometimes use only one of the words, Molise or Abruzzo, bear in mind that I am speaking of both places as an un-torn entity.

My father's name is Abruzzian, originating most probably from the region of Pescara, perhaps from a town called Lettomanoppello, where many families with the surname D'Alfonso seem to have aggregated; D'Alfonso: with the capital D, a capital A, separated by the apostrophe, not with a small 'd', which would endow us with aristocratic leverage which we do not possess. No 'ph' instead of 'f', not with the minuscule 'a', not with the 'z' instead of 's'. D'Alfonso. To this day, rarely does a person pronounce my family name as it really is. They call us Dalphonso, Dalonzo, Alfonso, Alfonzo, or worse Dalphonseault.

My paternal grandmother's name, Di Salvio, is certainly Abruzzian in origin. My mother's parents also come from the Abruzzi: my grandfather from Lanciano, my grandmother from Vasto (city of the Rossetti family of great poets). That is as far back as we can go with some sort of precision. Before that, names and dates get blurry. Why finding one's origins should be complicated, I still do not know. A family tree should normally be quite easy to trace, but Italians can rarely climb up the genealogical tree without losing their way into a complex network of strangely-tied knots. Having participated in the Genographic Project, led by Dr. Spenser Wells at *National Geographic,* I have witnessed how complex origins are. On the paternal side I belong to the N269 group, whereas on the maternal side to the V Haplogroup. Not being able to etch with clarity the faces of my great-great-grandparents is a source of mystery and pride. My families, collectively, are an enigma of diversity, division, displacement.

If I reveal with imprecise details the faces of my family, I do so with tongue in cheek. For simplicity's sake, calling myself an Italic from "America" will have to suffice. The language I grew up listening to and speaking is an intricate, sophisticated combination of Latin, Umbrian-Oscan, Tuscan, Serbo-Croatian, French, Greek, German, and Arbërech. This impure hybrid of languages is the melody my being continues to sing.

My sister, Angela, and I grew up in an environment that never looked at the past as a depository of possessions and ruins. There never was nostalgia for what unfolded as a foil for a better life. Italy remains a point of reference, but not a place to return to. Though my parents never became Canadian citizens, and never considered a change of religion, they are happy to be living in Canada. They did not feel the need to alter their identity to assimilate into a fictitious lifestyle. They travelled the continent with the knowledge of their dialect; no matter which town they visited, my father and mother in their car were greeted by a welcoming stranger who answered in Italian. From a distance the political climate of Europe influenced my parents' thoughts, but so did the catastrophes and glories on the American continent. Injustice was criticized equally. My sister and I were taught to fight for our rights, as our parents fought for their rights. Nationalism, anti-Semitism, and racism were strictly forbidden in our home. Our parents showed us how to balance ourselves in various places. They like living in Montreal, happy to be able to eat the vegetables they grow in their garden during the couple of summer months. They go dancing once a week, and love one another dearly. At lunch, every day, my mother raises her glass of red wine (she does not drink white wine) and thanks my father for their shared love. For our parents, emigration was a choice, a lifestyle, in a metaphorical way an extension of the ancient cultures they carry in their heart and mind. Emigration is not an exception, but the rule.

What is the exception is staying put in one location year after year.

The father of my mother arrived in Halifax in 1913, as a seasonal worker for the Canadian Pacific Railway. He was 17. During my visit to Pier 21, I found his entry document. The customs officer had assigned number 555 to him, and recorded that the boy had 15 dollars in his pockets. Filippo Salvatore did what one out of two immigrant Italians do: after amassing enough money, he returned to Italy, where he met Lucia Tana, married, and had six children (one of whom died). Filippo never came back to Canada, though 'America' would emerge from his lips in his old age. On numerous occasions I have heard it said that Montreal and Conshohocken, Pennsylvania, are cities with a large contingent of Abruzzian-Molisans.

My paternal grandfather Antonio, known as Nicola to everyone, though no one knows why, was a good-looking man, who worked no more than he had to. Marrying Angiolina Di Salvio, an educated peasant, was perhaps a conscious and brilliant move on his part. Nicola did not know how to read and write, but Angiolina did; and she was hardworking too, and a practicing Catholic.

Nicola spent most of his adult life abroad, first in Africa, fighting for an idiot invader in Ethiopia, and then in South America. Benito Mussolini's National Socialism was an ideology that did not sit well with our family. My grandfather wore a moustache that Charles Chaplin had made famous, and which Hitler later plagiarized. Nicola escaped to Buenos Aires where he lived for five years. Fascism was not a lifestyle my grandfather appreciated. The 1939-45 War thrust Molise into upheaval and emotional havoc. Many betrayed German soldiers, who expected Italians to serve them. Both my grandfather and my father had to hide for months after having misled the occupiers into alien territory, and my maternal grandmother was locked in a prison for half a year for refusing to hand over vegetables and bread to feed the Germans.

Resting on a summit on the western part of Molise, Guglionesi was a perfect viewing-point overlooking the Adriatic. Fifteen kilometres below the hills, Termoli sits, as an ideal gate to the Eastern front, and across the sea is Croatia. There was a lot to do, and courage was not lacking. Although not organized formally as a resistance group, men and women in these villages and hamlets made it difficult for soldiers to manipulate civilians. Hundreds of years of serfdom had taught the art of resistance to the hard-working agricultural 'princes' and 'princesses' who ploughed those fertile vegetable-and-fruit slopes. At the end of the war, towns were reduced to detritus.

The soil was tainted with the blood and limbs of young men from both factions. There are no winners in war, only victims. The only way out of the quagmire was departure.

'Emigration' resounded from the mouths of those hurting inhabitants. Paradoxically, during that undoing Italy moved into a financial boom that for obscure reasons never reached Southern Italy. Right in the midst of what Federico Fellini ironically labeled La Dolce Vita, more than 14 million men and women embarked on an exodus that has been denied to this day the shortest of footnotes in the history books of Italy. Children and adults were encouraged to leave their homes so that those who stayed behind could enjoy whatever crumbs could be found beneath broken stone and bone.

My father never mentioned his father's escapades in Argentina. That exile is a secret he will take with him to the grave. I have begged him numerous times to speak about his father's Argentinean sojourn, but to no avail. My father preferred to praise his father's brother, Giuseppe, who settled in 'America' at the beginning of the 20th century. Unlike Filippo Salvatore, Giuseppe D'Alfonso did not go back to Guglionesi. He had come over with his Italian wife, Teresa Bevelacqua, and purchased a tiny house on rue des Belges, a few steps from Jarry Street, in Francophone Ahuntsic. Giuseppe and Teresa would never travel back to Italy. Their first child had died in Italy before they became permanently established in Montreal; their four children—Antoinette, Joseph, Antonio, Pasquale —were born and educated in Canada. This side of the D'Alfonso family constitutes the first French-speaking Canadian Italians of our extended family.

My paternal grandmother, Angiolina, lost, I believe, six children between 1914 and 1939. From World War I, through the terrible 1918 flu pandemic, to World War II, death made its way into our residences. My father was 11 when he became an only son, sole bearer of his family's emotional crest. Andrea, the older son, died in 1939. Rumours circulated about him being the victim of some sensational romantic story turned sour. The 18-year-old man was pushed over the balcony railing of a school built to accommodate the Fascist Youth. Andrea's passing became a dark cloud over our family that would never dissipate. At the time, young men and women who were present with my uncle reported possible foul play.

No one knew for sure. At sunset, at the end of the school day, on the fourth-story balcony, Andrea held his girlfriend in his arms. Other couples were laughing nearby. It was then that the lights went out, and suddenly, in the darkness, Maria let out a scream. When the lights came back on, Andrea, no longer beside Maria, had turned head over heels a few times before crashing to the ground. He did not stand a chance. He died in his mother's arms. Maria grieved, paid her respects to our family, and eventually got pregnant with another man, whom she married, though he repeatedly expressed his doubts about being the father of their child. My father, adamant, reassured the future spouse of his dead brother's integrity; he would not have touched Maria.

How I would have cherished spending an hour with Maria. What sort of man was Andrea? No one remembers what he looked like. The single image of Andrea that hangs in my room is an etching by an artist who sketched the semblance from a photograph of my father. My grandmother Angiolina complained up to the day she died, in 1980, that Andrea's wide smile was not Carlo's reserved smile. I can imagine how a fine writer could turn this event into the beginning of a novel or a film. But this tale is not romantic at all. My grandmother wore black for the duration of her life. Long-lasting are the existential consequences of that young man's brief presence on earth. Engraved on his tombstone, misspelled, is: Andrea D'Alfonzo. 2nd February 1921–13th December 1939.

Andrea has become a family myth. 'Lulucc.' This is the appellation Andrea is best known by.

'Andrealucc.' 'Lulucc'—'Young Andrea.' The *praenomen* appears later in other members of the extended family. What used to be a large family eventually became a small tight and unbreakable unit.

Giuseppe, my great-uncle, the brother of my grandfather, would play the paternal role my father required. Giuseppe was the reason why my father ended up in Montreal. Before moving out of Italy, Udine was my father's intellectual haven. Northeastern Italy was where he had been drafted during his military services. Friuli, Trieste, the Italian border to Slovenia, continue to be a leitmotiv in my father's life; that northern country spread prolongs memories of the Adriatic seascape he enjoyed as a child. In other words, his coming to Canada was a secondary choice; Carlo did not want to leave his ageing parents behind in Guglionesi. His father, after having worked in Argentina, returned to Italy pretty much without a penny to his name. Though 'Argentina' made its way onto the lips of Nicola, and Angiolina, and clearly for different reasons, one negative, the other positive, Carlo accepted Giuseppe's invitation.

My father lived with Giuseppe's family for a couple of years before asking his girlfriend Emilia, our mother, to join him. Emigration, immigration, the journey, the absent father, the powerful mother, work, success, failure, death: these themes haunted my father's evenings once he returned home from Notre-Dame Street to Jarry. Thanks to a distant uncle, Raffaele Tarasca, a very knowledgeable man who had come to Canada from the U.S.A. in the early 1900s, Carlo was able to find a job as a welder at the shipyards located along the Montreal shoreline. A 50-year story: my family's story is composed of letters and postcards sent from many cities to various other cities, written by individuals who came and went, nonstop. Brothers, sisters, cousins dying too young, their lives are recalled only if the younger generation asks about them. Without curiosity, the lives of emigrants/immigrants are nonexistent.

Without the inquisitiveness of the younger generations the emigrant will never become an immigrant, no matter how much time passes. I listen. It is my turn to speak their stories.

He Was One of Eight

Irene Gargantini

Strathroy, Ontario, 2004: Dinner was over and my guests, each carrying a glass of wine or a mug of coffee, moved their chairs to form a circle on the veranda. *Storytelling time*, I mused instantly. The group included the Strybosch clan, and the Strybosches always liked talking, singing and entertaining people as they recounted stories about their home country, Holland. Even though I was a late addition to the family, I'd heard these stories many times over.

And so it began.

"I was cheated and abused by my brothers," said Tony, one of the eight Strybosch siblings who had immigrated to Canada in the early 1950s. He looked around to see if he had an audience, and he did, so he continued. "I was five years old, still in kindergarten, when late one afternoon my brother Martin called me from the backyard. His hands were full of black cherries—cherries so big that I drooled at the sight of them."

"Martin said: 'I helped a farmer pick cherries, and he rewarded me with these. They're juicy, and can be yours ...' He stopped then and gestured, inviting me to join him on the nearby bench. I followed him sheepishly and sat close to him, my eyes focussed on his hands. 'They can be yours if we can strike a deal,' Martin said. I was anxious to hear what my older brother had to say. 'Here it is: you get my cherries, I get your pup, Loekie.'

"I hesitated. Loekie was my playmate, the only living thing on earth who listened *to me*, who came when *I* called him, who was *there for me*. Loekie was my dearest possession."

Tony wetted his lips with red wine and looked straight into the eyes of his brother Martin, now over 70 years old. Tony seemed to search for empathy, but there wasn't any. Martin remained silent, staring into the distance.

Tony continued. "Some of the cherries hung from between Martin's fingers; they looked *so* good. Then Martin said: 'Not to worry, little brother, the dog stays in the family, right? You can play with him any time you want. I just want to train him, to make him do things—guard our home, refuse food from the *Mof* (the Germans), but accept it from the *Tommy* (the British) ... those sorts of things.'"

Then Tony stopped and took another sip of wine.

"It was wartime," he said. "Holland was under German occupation, but soon the Allies would move in, parachuting their soldiers down at night. Our hometown, Liessel, was about 60 kilometres from Nijmegen. You've all heard of the famous bridge, right?"

The audience, consisting mostly of people old enough to have heard of or witnessed the horrors of World War II, nodded their agreement.

"But I should go on with the story about the cherries—a story I won't forget," Tony said. "So, my brother Martin gave me a captivating smile. 'You have nothing to lose,' he said. 'You'll only gain these wonderful cherries.' The odour of the freshly picked fruit reached my nostrils. 'Deal,' I mumbled, and held out my hands. 'Wait, get a bowl from the kitchen,' Martin said, 'Your hands are too small to get them all.'"

Tony pointed a finger at Martin in mocking accusation. "That brother of mine is sitting there, behaving as if nothing had ever happened."

"Not a fault of mine if you weren't too bright," Martin said, shrugging.

"See! See what kind of brother I had to grow up with? And wait until I tell you the story about the horse and the fence." His vivid eyes scanned the group, creating in them an expectation that we all knew he would fulfill.

***

Tony is now 66. The abuses he claims to have suffered make great stories and he knows it; but there is no trace of resentment in his heart. He is well aware that his older siblings had to face a difficult task, and he was part of it.

Little Tony's trouble with his dog was only the beginning; there were bigger troubles to come. Two years later, in 1946, the four Strybosch brothers—John, Martin, Bill, Tony—and the four sisters —namely Nellie, Josephine, Antonia and Ricky—lost their mother to a heart attack. Then, one year later their father died from cancer. At that juncture the siblings' ages ranged from eight to 23 years.

At the age of 23, John already exhibited a remarkable ability to elicit consensus. Under his guidance, for a few years the eight orphans managed without a parental presence. They owned a farm situated in Liessel, North Brabant—a 24-acre cultivated field —double the size of the average Dutch farm. They worked their land with horses, gathered milk from farmers to deliver to the local co-op, and threshed grains for other farmers. Martin was a hard worker. At six o'clock in the morning he left on the milk route, and for the remainder of the day he ploughed the fields, then later he taught tricks to his dog, Loekie. But horses were the love of his life. He rode them in country races and trained them patiently, for both work and leisure. One horse, Voske, was his favourite. Voske listened to each of his commands and jumped like a champion. And he didn't need even the smallest word of encouragement. If Voske saw a fence, he would go for it, even jumping a foot higher than was necessary. But this was 10-year-old Tony's misfortune.

The storyteller resumed his narration.

"That day things were grim: 'Do this, do that.' Bill, then 13, was ordering me about. 'Pay attention! Don't do *that*!' Martin, 16, screamed next. I was their little slave, that's what I was. So I cried aloud: 'I'm old enough to work, but not to play with the horse! It's more fun!' It was then that Martin said: 'Okay, okay, want to ride? Sure, here is the horse. You can go and ride. Take him for a run on the road.' He gladly helped me onto the horse."

Tony paused.

"You know what those two terrible brothers of mine did? After I had a little ride I then turned the horse around to take him back to the stable. Martin and Bill put up a fence, about a metre and a half high. That's what *they* did!"

"You should have seen that horse," Martin said. "With no hesitation he broke into a gallop and ran toward the fence, regardless of being able to just go around it. When Voske needed more bridle poor little Tony didn't hesitate to loosen it. Then, as Voske arched his forelegs upwards Tony flew in the air, flipped around once and then fell on the ground, unconscious."

"See how *he* tells the story," Tony said. "Like it was fun!"

"It's fun to remember it," Martin said, laughing. "I admit it, but I can assure you that both Bill and I got the scare of our lives. We rushed to you, and took you into the house. We stayed with you until you reopened your eyes. Fortunately there were no serious injuries."

"How in the world did you know that?" Tony asked.

"Well, you appeared to be the same silly little brother after the fall as you were before."

***

Eventually a careless financial investment left the eight orphans with few resources. They decided to search for better living conditions abroad. In 1950 Josephine got married and immigrated to Ontario with her husband Harry. A year later the seven siblings flew to Montreal, each with only a 100-dollar bill in their pocket. At the railway station they immediately lost one of those precious bills to an unscrupulous porter who didn't have any change, but who made up for the lack of it with repeated, deep bowing. Not speaking a word of the local language they were unable to negotiate in any way, so they had to take the loss in their stride. A few hours later the seven orphans boarded the train, ultimately arriving in London, Ontario, where they were met by their sponsors, the Van Den Boomen family. Another short drive to Strathroy followed, and then the Strybosches were ready to begin the adventure of life in their new country.

That new life started in a big house on a Caradoc concession road, where searching for work, learning the language, buying a car, and finding Tony a school were the most urgent necessities. A couple of months later the family rented a farmer's house on Highway 22. Then, later, Nellie got married. John and Bill shared a 1940 Dodge to get to work at a glass factory; Martin picked tobacco, corn, and sugar beets; Antonia ran the household, and Ricky helped a nursery owner with household chores. Little Tony went to the local country school, which was one big room that children in various grades had to share. The difficulty of following what the teacher had to say in an unfamiliar language, and Tony's impatience for action didn't create the best atmosphere for learning.

When the family moved back to Strathroy, teenaged Tony made his first attempt to explore the world all on his own. He played hooky and frequented places that he was not supposed to. The family worried; none of them had any experience of parenting, so they had to improvise. After a quick democratic consultation, the emerging consensus was to take Tony away from all temptations of the city (the *"metropolis"* of Strathroy at that time boasted of 3,000 souls!) and send him to work on a farm in Lambton County, 20 kilometres away. The farm's owner was Elgin Vilancy Fuller, a shorthorn cattle breeder who took an immediate liking to young Tony. And as he worked beside the farmer Tony gained invaluable experience. He learned about crop rotation and fertilizers, how to harvest using a combine, and how to repair farm machinery. Tony felt good, and fulfilled now; he could earn more than his keep and thus contribute to the family in a concrete way.

In the early and mid-50s events moved fast for the Strybosch family: John, Antonia and Martin got married; the siblings called Tony back from his exile; and in 1956, four members of the family, including Tony, bought a 150-acre farm in Kerwood. Tony became a full participant in the affairs of the Strybosch family.

And then he figured he should look for a girlfriend.

Tony recalls the difficulty, even then, of breaking loose from the family's supervision. He loves to prove it by mentioning the following episode. I leave it up to Tony to report it in his usual colour-ful style.

"I was sitting in the back of the car with my new date. I had al-ready surpassed myself trying to create a romantic atmosphere. I had praised the young woman for her lovely dress and told her she had a wonderful smile, and I was waiting for the proper time to get a bit closer. I hoped for some *necking*—that's the word we used at that time." Tony burst out laughing then. "And you'd never guess what happened next!" He chuckled.

"Ricky, my youngest and very religious sister, was sitting at the front, and her husband was behind the wheel. As I moved closer to the girl, Ricky began reciting the Holy Rosary—softly at first, then louder and louder. That was bad enough, but things became much worse when she turned sideways, with one eye on the beads, the other on me and my date." Tony focussed his eyes on Ricky, now seated opposite him.

The sister didn't deny the fact; she merely ignored Tony. Her face wore a smirk from ear to ear.

But Tony was a resourceful young man. He soon found his soul mate in Dianne Elaine Cattrysse, a beautiful woman who shared his love for the land and for animals. In 1964, Tony and Dianne got married.

Later, when all the other siblings sold Tony their shares in the farm, he and Dianne became involved in a very promising venture. Over the years they gradually expanded their business to make it a 650-acre farm—the *Lysel Holsteins*—and made the transition from a part-purebred grade herd to an all purebred herd, consisting of about 60 milking cows and a 100 young head. In the 1980s and 1990s they became recognized as the owners of one of the best Canadian herds. In those years, three *All Reserve All American Cattle* champions were from their herd. They won numerous prizes, including, in 1987, an *All Canadian Breeder Herd* nomination.

Family life blossomed too, as five handsome children filled their home with laughter and joy.

The little boy from Holland, who had lost his parents at the age of eight, who had moved to a foreign country without knowing a word of English, and without having any idea of what to expect, had made it with flying colours. Close to retiring from farming at the time of writing this, my brother-in-law Tony is currently chair of the board of directors of the St. Willibrord Credit Union, a financial institution originally founded by Dutch immigrants—to help newcomers from Holland settle in Ontario.

Tony had succeeded as an immigrant, and as a Canadian too, as did the other members of the Strybosch family of Strathroy.

No Return

∾

Tchitala Kamba

(Translated from the French by Susan Ouriou)

Nakozonga mboka ééééé
Nakozonga mboka aaaaa
Nakeyi éééé
Naza na nga, nalikambo na moto tééé!
Nakeyi ééé
Mobembo ézali liwa téééé.

They came by the thousands, the TV anchor says
Made their way through the Strait of Gibraltar
Penniless, paperless, each and every one
Half-starved and exhausted from the journey
Nothing but a dream—a dream—to urge them on
The West they thought
And a better world

Strait of Gibraltar
Through your port they made
Their way from the black continent
On to their dream of the West
Europe, the U.S. of A., Canada
Braving seas, then oceans
Won't you tell me though
Have you seen my father?
Have you seen my brother?
Have you seen my sister?
Have you seen my children passing through?
Sole mute witness, unmoving, unmoved
Your indifference spurs me to revolt
Speak to me, whisper the words you've kept secret
Have you seen my loved ones passing through?

Among their ranks were the best we had
Executives, engineers, physicians, teachers
And many, many more
Such a crying shame
The men in power close their eyes
Block their ears, scratch their skulls.

Strait of Gibraltar
Do you know they left their homes
One drought-filled morning, hearts soaring
Softly singing
Nakozonga mboka, mobembo ézali liwa téééé
But now, their hopes are gone
Their bodies unknowable
Washed ashore with the tide
Or floating to the rhythm of the waves
Disfigured or petrified
Could these be the bodies of my loved ones
In piles on the wharves of Gibraltar
Like fish caught forever in a net?

There lie the bodies of the many
Executives, engineers, physicians, teachers
All our own
Such a crying shame
The men in power close their eyes
Block their ears, scratch their skulls.

Strait of Gibraltar
I beg you. My father
My brother
My sister
My loved ones
Give them back
You were wrong
Your friends all gone
Once we loved you
Praised your bounty
Dreamed of travels through you
And of journeys in return
To our motherland

Do you remember the soft song they hummed?
Nakozonga mboka ééééé
Nakozonga mboka aaaaa
Nakeyi éééé
Naza na nga, nalikambo na moto tééé!
Nakeyi ééé
Mobembo ézali liwa téééé.

The Music of Small Things

~

Monica Kidd

I.

I T WAS THE picture of that little boy. Swept from his father's hands and washed overboard, destroyed in an act of desperation and courage few could comprehend. I still can't look at it for more than a few seconds. I was driving back to Calgary from my parents' place in rural Alberta listening to Cross Country Checkup and the outpouring of compassion for Alan Kurdi and all those he came to represent, and as I peeked at my own three kids sleeping in their car seats—my youngest, the same age as the boy—something crystallized. Maybe I was taken in by spin, or just caught up in the worldwide wail of grief. Or maybe I was purple with rage at my government's dismantling of my country's international presence and plain *goodness.* Either way, I knew, with a sense of calm, that I needed to do something. If my Prime Minister was misrepresenting me, then I would go all Margaret Mead on him: *Never doubt that a group of committed citizens,* etc. etc. I worked up the courage to talk to my husband and found he had been thinking along the same lines. We lived privileged lives in a wealthy country and would find a way to sponsor a refugee family.

Refugee sponsorship is long and dull and sometimes Kafka-esque. Much of the how-to story has been revealed as thousands over the last year have spoken publicly about their own journeys —the catalyzing moments, the delays, the loopholes. We joined a Group of Five[1] and decided to work with the Mennonite Central Committee—none of us is Mennonite, but they have a track record working with refugees—and on a Sunday night in October we pored over a stack of descriptions of travel-ready families from conflict areas around the world. It read like a list of the damned. Having the power to choose another's fate so arbitrarily weighed heavy on our group, though all of us are accustomed in our personal and professional lives to heavy responsibility. No one should be able to choose like that, and yet there we were.

The file that caught our eye was a family of seven (a couple with five children, ranging in age from four to sixteen), originally from Congo, and living in a camp in Tanzania. There were few other details: their main languages, the basis of their refugee claim. We told the MCC that's who we wanted, and a few days later we were told we had been matched to them. Then came the fundraising, finding them a place to live and the stuff to fill it, the impossible work of trying to predict and prepare for their needs. Garth made a website; Mark handled the accounting; Jenny and Jess worked their connections with aid societies in Calgary; Cat, Aaron and Joe kept us on track legally and wrangled in-kind donations; Steve and I considered their medical needs; Amy figured out everything we needed to do and held it all together.

We had no way to reach our family in the camp, so we couldn't ask them basic questions about their literacy or even their shoe sizes. We spoke to other sponsor groups, we watched documentaries about Congo, we stayed up far too late watching YouTube videos posted from the Nyarugusu camp to get an idea of what their lives had been like; four of the children had been born in the camp and had known nothing else.

On February 15, Family Day in Alberta, we got word that they were coming in two weeks; six months after coming together as a group, this had become an old refrain. We'd had an apartment rented and fully furnished for three months already, based on the promise that they were coming any day now. But this time there was a flight number and an arrival time at the Calgary airport. Those of us who could booked time off work, and started putting together last minute details.

II

Back up almost a year to the day.

It's a Wednesday morning, and I'm driving to a clinic on the Siksika Nation east of Calgary. It takes about an hour to get there, and the road is long and empty. The radio is good company. I listen to the CBC as the sun comes up, following fence posts as I used to do on my long bus rides to high school about two hours north of here. On this particular morning there is a documentary about the artistic collaboration of Guillermo Galindo and Richard Misrach. Galindo is a sound artist and composer, Mexican by origin. Misrach is an American photographer concerned with life along the US/Mexico border. He documents the small things left behind by illegal migrants from Mexico—toys, backpacks, shoes, fragments of letters. Some things he collects and sends to Galindo, who turns them into musical instruments. What he makes from them is nothing short of elegiac.

As an old radio person, I too collect wild sound. I listen for the soundtrack behind the burble of life and write poems about it. It grounds me. Listening to Galindo's haunting soundscapes while driving through all the open prairie to work in a place so estranged from the mainstream privilege I represent, guts me. I write to Galindo to tell him so. He graciously responds, and invites me to a show in San Francisco he and Misrach are working on for February 25, 2016. I tell him I'll try to make it.

Then comes our call. Our family will be arriving on *February 25*. I will not be going to California. Instead, I will be at the airport, waiting for seven displaced souls to walk through a set of sliding glass doors and into a new life.

Each time I drive to Siksika, I think of Galindo and all of those small things left behind in the sand.

III.

February 20th: Steve and Garth go over to the apartment and set up the second bunk bed—there will be two sets in the children's room—and make sure the washing machine is working. They find a dryer on Kijiji and go to pick it up. Turns out the owner's parents were refugees from Vietnam. They are only too happy to let us have it for free.

Our babysitter comes over to watch our collective five children while Jenny and I go shopping, first to an African food store where we find fufu and cassava flour and maize, and then to a supermarket to pick up peanut butter, salt, maple syrup. Toiletries and cleaning supplies have already been donated. By the time we get to the apartment with a carload of groceries, it is time for our babysitter to go home, so Steve leaves to spell her off and make pizza with the kids while Jenny, Garth and I set up the kitchen, organize the furniture and dress the beds. The littlest girl will sleep in her parents' room, and the other four will sleep in the room across the hall. The little bed has a green duvet cover with stencils of animals; it's the most beautiful thing in the apartment.

I become unspeakably sad putting sheets on the bed, and the few clothes we have for them in the closet.

When we are finished, we three walk the garbage around to the dumpster at the back of the apartment building. The sun is setting, casting an amber light over the downtown skyline and Nose Hill.

Our family will soon be on the road from the camp to Dar es Salaam. The light is like sunset on the African plains.

February 21st: I email a bunch of women on my street, sending out the call for food to put in the family's freezer. I tell them I know nothing about what it is like to feed five children, cooking over a charcoal fire in a refugee camp, but ask them to make something nutritious. The email gets forwarded to people around the neighbourhood, and soon the promises of deliveries come flying in.

February 22nd: At work on Monday, I apologize for being distracted, and tell a colleague I don't even know that well what is happening this week. She insists that she post, on our unit's Facebook page, an appeal asking for clothing. I get an email from someone else at work; she has two friends, originally from Congo, who are willing to interpret for us over the phone.

February 24th: After work, I go to the mall and pick up a cell phone. The woman behind the counter tells me that, when she came to Canada seven years ago, she didn't speak a word of English. She tells me what we are doing is good. I save my own number in their address book and send them a text. The message sings in my pocket.

At home, I find that friends have dropped off bags and bags of stew and soup. One neighbour tells me her husband's friend works for the United Nations in camps around the world doing nutrition work; he would be putting me in touch with her. A colleague of my husband comes by with five garbage bags of clothes. A friend drops off two more bags on the step and runs away when she hears the general chaos of me trying to put the kids to bed. I now have nine bags of clothes piled in my living room, five pots of stew in the freezer, plus the one I made; Jenny next door has the same number also.

All day, I've been bursting to tell people. We've compared these last minute preparations to having a baby, to Christmas Eve, and to the night before your wedding. They will be here tomorrow and I cannot sleep with nervous energy.

IV.

When we were at our most discouraged about finding a family of seven an affordable place to live in one of the most expensive cities in Canada; after more than two dozen places had fallen through; after a guy told us we ought to contact the health department because it was probably illegal to have "so many people" living in a circa 1905 bungalow that had probably seen a whole lot more in its day, I took my kids to a birthday party. There was a woman there I recognized; our kids go to the same school. She didn't seem to know many people, so I wandered over to chat with her. I asked her if she worked outside the home. "Property management," she said. I stopped, dropped all pretence of small talk, and asked point blank whether she had anything for rent. Two units, she told me. I spat out our story as quickly as I could, before she might recoil and start to explain why her apartments would not work for our needs. Instead she said: "I would love to be part of that." I went weak in the knees with gratitude.

Her parents-in-law, who own the apartment, came to Canada as refugees. She rents it to us for half of what the market would normally demand.

V.

I could tell you about all of the last minute messages about early flight arrivals and van rentals and stocking the apartment that morning with yet more groceries. I could tell you about their faces when they finally came through the doors, and about the goose bumps and tears when it was finally true. I could tell you about our fifteen children, who shyly circled each other until the smiles came. I could tell you about showing them to their new apartment, then going home and staring over a beer into middle distance, emotionally and physically spent. But all of that is better left to your imagination. I will not tell you the details of their lives as we are coming to understand them, or talk about the potholes we hit as the family grows accustomed to life in Calgary; that is their story to tell, if they ever choose to. I hope what they've arrived to find is better than what they've left behind. I hope they are happy, though I cannot say for sure.

Now that this chapter is over, I think of Galindo and his music of small things, how it is a kind of witness to the largest of all human stories: that of finding a place in the world. We began with a small step and collected a mountain of things. Our family is here now and what will happen to them is anyone's guess, but my hope is that the music we made will continue to softly play.

Notes

1. One of the three main ways refugees may be settled in Canada is by being sponsored through the Blended Visa Office Referral Program. Sponsors form a "Group of [at least] Five" Canadian citizens and work with a Sponsorship Agreement Holder, often a church, that helps to provides settlement support. The Group of Five raises enough money to support the refugee(s) for twelve months and agrees to help with language, education, vocational training, with a goal to helping the refugee(s) achieve independence within one year.

Excerpts from *Not One of the Boys*

(An autobiography in progress)

∼

Christopher Levenson

From 'Coming to Canada':

As a boy and young man I never thought that I would come to live in Canada, and yet in some ways it seems to have been preordained. When in 1940, at the height of the Blitz, my father's school in central London was evacuated en masse to the ancient and non-strategic city of Lancaster in northern Lancashire, my parents, my younger brother and I soon found ourselves sharing a house with the Brands, a Canadian family from Alberta. Mrs. Brand's two sons, Robert and Brian, were almost the same ages as Geoffrey and myself, but their father was away serving in the Merchant Navy.

Some time in the next few years my parents gave me a 'young adult' novel, *Chris in Canada*, which I enjoyed and doubtless identified with, but probably more important for my involvement with Canada were the two or three weeks in the Fall of 1943. Because my parents were unable to return immediately to our own house in Edgware, a suburb in northwest London, I was sent to stay with the family of one of my father's colleagues in Leatherhead, Surrey. A unit of the Canadian Army was stationed nearby, probably in preparation for D-Day. With other local kids I was happy to hang around the soldiers, who fed us 'cookies,' a word unknown to me before, and chewing gum and occasionally took us for short, doubtless highly illegal rides in their jeeps, which stank invitingly of hot oil and cigarette smoke. Later on, in high school geography classes, I recall gazing at dreary black and white textbook photos of prairie wheat-fields and at the distant view of Edmonton, a city which at one stage of my adolescence, why I do not know, was where I had de-cided to settle if ever I did emigrate to Canada.

However, for years after that, as an undergraduate at Cam-bridge and, subsequently, for a year teaching in the Netherlands, and for three as English Lektor at the University of Muenster, West Germany, I never gave Canada a further thought, assuming that after a few more years of travelling I would settle down to an aca-demic job in the UK. It was not to be. In 1964 at the suggestion of three poets whom we had invited to dinner—the American Donald Hall and his British fellow-readers Christopher Middleton and Charles Tomlinson, I applied to several universities in the States that they had recommended in order to work towards a Ph.D., in-itially in English, though this was later changed to Comparative Literature. In the end I was accepted by the University of Iowa with the additional benefit of a three-year writing scholarship from the International Writing Program.

Despite meeting the novelist Clark Blaise and other Canadians through the poetry and translation workshops that I attended there, it was still my intention, once I had my Doctorate, to return to the UK. I remember that one of my fellow students was con-stantly singing the praises of the Royal Winnipeg Ballet and of Winnipeg as a whole, as a cultural centre. However, I am embar-rassed to confess that, when our local student-run radio station WSUI relayed 15-minute news items from Britain, France, Germany and Canada, I listened to the first three but switched off when the Canadian segment, called 'Over the Back Fence' was being broad-cast. Somehow I had got the impression that Canada was British suburbia writ large.

What changed my mind was necessity. After blithely assuming

for three and a half years that on my return to my home country I would be instantly employable, I discovered late in 1967, when I started applying for UK university posts, that because of massive cuts in government spending, universities that had planned to hire, say, eight new faculty members could only afford two or three. I applied for every advertised post in English, German and Comparative Literature—a grand total of 20—but since my name was not Northrop Frye or Marshall McLuhan, I could hardly expect to be flown over to England for an interview. By Easter 1968, returning to Iowa City from California on what had been intended as a farewell-to-North-America trip, we realized that, with three young children to support, we would have to fall back on Plan B. Except that there was no Plan B.

With the help and advice of friendly faculty members, my wife and I decided to apply to selected U.S. colleges and universities where we knew someone, and to a large number of Canadian universities; to all in fact that were not either Francophone, since French was and alas remains a poor third among my foreign languages, or to religious ones, because we were not religious. Nor did we contact those situated in the prairies, since we had only recently survived four years of prairie in Iowa. That cut down the numbers significantly, but in that pre-computer age, it was still a lot of typing at a time when I should have been concentrating on my Comprehensives. So we were relieved when in May we finally received two positive replies, one from Goddard College in Vermont, where we had good ex-Iowan friends, and one from Carleton.

Thus it was that on 1ˢᵗ June 1968 I flew up to Ottawa from Iowa City for my interview at Carleton.

***

Although in most respects my professional 'Bildung' was as complete by the time I reached Canada in 1968 as it was ever likely to get—I love a bumper sticker I once saw which read "Real students never graduate," I have now spent over half my life, and nearly all my working life, in Canada, so that it would be unfair to omit so much. In any case I do believe that, whatever that elusive term 'Canadian' means, I have become one. So what I want to do now is simply summarize some of the major events in my life here, and explore how they tie in with my earlier experiences.

When I flew up from Iowa City on 1st June 1968 for my two job interviews, it was only my second experience of flying, the first having been the very brief trip from Hanover to Berlin and back in the fall of 1953. It was a fine, calm day and the short flight to Chicago on a high-wing prop plane did not seem to rise above 8,000 to 10,000 feet, so that from my window seat I was able to look down at the vast patchwork of mostly rectangular fields and barns and small farming communities of eastern Iowa and Illinois. There was something reassuring in their sense of order.

Soon though it was to be shattered. Chicago's O'Hare airport, America's busiest, where I had to change onto an Air Canada jet, was lively, raucous, and full of bustle, and en route for the departure lounge I ran an intriguing gauntlet of smells from the various cafés and fast food outlets. When I reached Toronto two hours later and passed through Canadian Customs, I was immediately struck by an almost Scandinavian calm and coolness. No one seemed to be shouting; whatever rushing there was seemed discreet; the air-conditioning and the tinted glass seemed to envelop everything in an odourless white noise. Many times since then I have arrived at or passed through a much expanded Pearson International Airport with very different impressions, but that first contrast did then, and still does, seem to embody a national difference, something that can be felt also when comparing, for instance, the highway restaurants along the 401 and those on the New York Freeways.

Ottawa too, when I arrived, seemed quiet, well bred, civilized.

My potential future colleagues took me to dinner at Madame Burger's on the Hull side of the Ottawa River, one of about three high-class restaurants in the city at that time. They showed me the recently completed National Arts Centre and put me up for the night at the nearby Lord Elgin Hotel.

My sense of quiet, well-bred calm was again to be short-lived. At six the next morning, I turned on the TV to scenes of the desperate chaos following the assassination of Senator Robert Kennedy, until that time the Democratic front runner in the forthcoming U.S. presidential elections. I watched, horrified by images of Kennedy being shot, slumping to the floor, and being rushed on a gurney into a waiting ambulance en route for desperate but unsuccessful surgery. (Incredibly, one of the commercials airing between these tense and historic moments was for an exterminator!) This further evidence of the essential violence of American civilization brought home to me yet again why I should not allow myself to be lured into a longer stay there. After the assassination, and the collapse of so many hopes on the American left (and indeed among progressives around the world), everything else that day seemed anti-climactic. But I had to go through with my interview.

Carleton University, which had achieved university status when the previous Carleton College moved to its present site in 1957, was suburban in its setting but well-treed and attractively landscaped, on a wedge-shaped lot between the shallow but fast flowing Rideau River and the now purely ornamental canal, built in 1819 by Colonel By to enable Canadian goods to be transported by water from Montreal to Ottawa without coming in range of U.S. cannons on the far shore of the Saint Lawrence.

The 22-storey Arts Tower, in which I was to spend all but the first three of my 31 years at Carleton, was still only on the drawing board, and if I had had anything to do with it, that's where it would have remained. In my second or third year, before I had tenure, when architects' drawings of the proposed building were published,

I rashly and, despite a large number of signatures, unsuccessfully launched a petition against it. But too late, of course. The building was erected and, while affording excellent panoramic views of Ottawa from its upper floors, its squat upthrust bulk spoilt the view for most local residents. The remaining buildings on campus, except for the School of Architecture, were pleasant but unspectacular, as were most of my colleagues ...

My Grandmother
and The Gold Mountain

Ian Mah

My grandmother, Suey Woon Quon, was born in the Toi San district of Guangdong, China in 1909. The youngest of five children, she grew up in Toi San with a close-knit group of immediate and extended family members. Her family's livelihood was based on hard work, farming the land upon which they lived.

At age 16, she met Jock Mah, whom she would eventually wed in an arranged marriage. In 1921, shortly after their meeting, Jock immigrated to Canada to pursue the dream of riches in what was known to Toi San residents as "Gold Mountain." My grandmother would tell me stories of how her friends "back home" would refer to Canada as Gold Mountain, because of the vast riches and prosperity available to all who would pursue them. Many Chinese people came over to Canada to work hard, become rich and bring their families over, but some had no intentions of staying here permanently and would later return to China with their pockets stuffed full of "gold."

Four years after his arrival in Canada, Jock returned to China and married Suey Woon. It was his intention to bring her back to the Gold Mountain after they married, but he was prevented from doing so by the Canadian Government's Chinese Immigration Act, also referred to as the Chinese Exclusion Act, passed in 1923. Jock kept sending her support money from the Gold Mountain along with promises that he would get her over there one day soon, but she was prevented from coming to Canada by the Act. In a trip back to China in 1932, their only child, Vince, was conceived, but Jock was still unable to bring his family to Canada.

Living in China, my grandmother gave everything she could give to caring for their only son, nurturing him and raising him with strong values, integrity and honesty. They continued to farm the land to earn a meagre living, but during the drought that struck the region in the early 1940's, and during the Japanese occupation of the area during WW II, starvation took hold of a wide region of Guangdong. Grandma used to say that she would cook up the small amounts of rice they had available and give that to her son for lunch when he came home from school, which often meant that she had to go without food for that day. In some instances it would be several days before she had a meal of her own.

Eventually the drought ended, but then the area became flooded by endless rain. Nothing would grow, and without food to eat it would have meant certain death. Unable to walk due to weakness caused by not having anything to eat for several days, she sent her son to his aunt and uncle's place, five kilometres away, to get some rice. Grandma said the water was so deep that it reached her son's waist, and she was worried that he might be swept away, drown, and never get back. His aunt told him to take as much rice as he could carry, so he loaded up the basket that he was carrying and eventually made it back home. It was that food that saved her and her son's lives. As we grew up, she told this story to us kids several times, attributing her and her son's survival to the kindness and generosity of her brother's wife.

In 1950 her son immigrated to Canada, but she was unable to follow because the Communist government of China had enacted a ban on emigration. Unable to join her husband and son in Canada, she lived on her own in China for the next seven years, occasionally receiving some money sent back from the "Gold Mountain." In 1957, her son paid a group of people from Hong Kong to smuggle her out of China and transport her to Canada. When they came to get her, she quietly left her life behind, abandoning her house and belongings in China for a long-awaited reunion with her family at the Gold Mountain.

Her arrival in Edmonton, Alberta was a particularly difficult time for her, because of the racism that was so widely prevalent at the time, and because her inability to speak English was compounding the other difficulties involved in integrating into Western life. At the age of 48 this transition into a new way of life must have seemed a daunting task, because everything she knew about life in China was suddenly no longer applicable to life here in Canada. The winters were harsh, but the hard impact of culture shock and non-acceptance by others was even harsher.

Everywhere she went people stared at her, and occasionally somebody would yell something at her. She didn't know what they were saying, but based on the tone of their voices it must not have been good. She eventually learned that "Chink" was not a flattering label. Being an outcast from the predominantly white society, she found comfort in spending time with the few Chinese women who had come to Edmonton at around the same time, and like her, were living in conditions of extreme poverty. It appeared that there were no job openings for women who did not speak English, and also happened to be Chinese. Although she tried to learn the English language, she had such a difficult time with it that she was never able to become fluent. She reverted to spending time with her Chinese friends and playing the game of mahjong to pass the time.

She told me stories of how she had come over with no money and had to live in "Camelot," a rooming house in what is now the drug-infested, seedy part of the inner city. Finally however, after 25 years of forced separation, she had been able to be with her husband, only to learn that he had suffered a debilitating stroke four years earlier and was in a state of declining health. His inability to work for so many years had drained him of his savings, and he was now completely dependent on their son Vince for the support that would enable them to pay their rent and have food to eat. All the talk back in China about how good life was at the Gold Mountain didn't seem very credible after all. Until her husband's death in 1962, she spent virtually all of her waking hours by his side, taking care of him as his health deteriorated.

After her husband passed away, she found comfort and acceptance in her group of mahjong-playing friends. She passed the days by playing the game and sharing stories of cruel treatment by the people of the Gold Mountain. She later found out that her husband had paid a Canadian government *head tax* of $500 in 1921 in order to gain entry into the country, an amount that was crippling to most people. Even more humiliating was the fact that the tax only applied to Chinese immigrants. It seemed that Canada was not a very hospitable place for the Chinese at that time.

Her son Vince married a girl from Hong Kong in 1965, and after their first son was born Grandma moved in with Vince and his family to take care of her subsequent three grandchildren. By this time, life was slowly becoming more fulfilling for her. She had immense pride in her grandchildren and devoted her life to caring for them and teaching them to respect others and to always live with a wholesome set of values, including honesty and integrity.

Slowly, over the decades, white society became more tolerant and accepting of people of different races, and she finally became more comfortable in venturing out of the house and taking the grandchildren to public places without the fear of being called names and being teased. She took her grandchildren to Klondike Days, the park, shopping, for walks around the neighbourhood, to the museum, the library and many other places. Grandma always had a smile on her own face whenever her grandchildren were smiling and having fun.

She would never let us forget her stories of how rough life was for her because of the injustices heaped upon the Chinese immigrants by Canadian immigration policies. In fact, she never became comfortable enough with Canada to call it *home*. Even at the age of 86 she still referred to Toi San as home. Grandma passed away in Edmonton on October 25, 1995.

Canada, Papa's Land of Opportunity: Memories of My First Year in Canada

Theresia M. Quigley

CANADIAN WINTERS WERE not as cold as we had been led to believe. Papa had written to make sure we packed warm coats, mittens, and hats. We were expected to arrive in Canada at the end of October, with winter just weeks away. While he himself had not experienced a Canadian winter as such, friends had told him to be prepared. He had come over on *The Homeland* out of Hamburg, and docked at the now famous Pier 21, in Halifax, in late March. He wanted to find a job and make a home for us before we followed him six months later.

I remember his letters, so full of enthusiasm. In Canada, it seemed, everyone owned a car. He had worked for a few weeks as chef in the house of a wealthy family in Montreal, and the kitchen appliances were beyond anything he had ever imagined. You simply pushed a button, and all was done for you! Montreal even had a church on a mountain, with escalators to accommodate the faithful. So much for igloos and ice and Mounties in red coats riding beautiful horses!

Papa told us that Canada had two official languages and had given us a choice of either living in a totally French area or in one that was largely English. It made no difference to him, since he could converse fluently in at least five languages and had by then found a job with the Canadian National Railway, where he was given a choice of settling in either Quebec City or Montreal. Since, after the war, we lived in a French-occupied area of Germany, where French was an obligatory subject in all schools, we thought of all the reams of boring vocabulary and incomprehensible grammar and immediately decided that English had to be easier to learn. Our decision was no doubt influenced by some good-looking boys from England who were on an exchange trip to our city and whom we had found rather interesting, what with their school uniforms and some of the older boys even smoking long pipes. We had communicated in sign language, but by the time they left we could say "*good morning*," and "*how do you do?*"—words that rolled off our tongues and made us feel rather important.

But to get back to Canadian winters: either the winter of 1952/53 was a particularly mild one, or we simply had imagined such bone-chilling weather that anything could be considered relatively mild in comparison. Papa had found temporary accommodation for us in a boarding house along the Montreal waterfront, and we had to take a bus to school in Lachine. In our dark-blue duffel coats, which Mama had sewed just before leaving Germany, and the red woollen hats and mittens that Oma had knitted for us, we would trudge through the snow to the bus stop. We had rubber overshoes too, something we had never needed in southern Germany, where snow was reserved for the mountains and was a rare occurrence in the city, where it would usually disappear within a few days. It had always been an exciting event to see the world around us dressed in white, and we would get out our sled and hurry to a hill near the house to take advantage of what we knew would be much too short a time for sledding and snowball fights, and rolling in the snow. But here in Canada, everyone expected the snow to last till April and, somehow, after the first little while, it didn't seem so special anymore.

Our boarding house was a square, two-story clapboard place with a veranda in the front, which we were not supposed to use, since our rooms were at the back. Papa had rented a large bed-sitting room that led to a narrow kitchen that we shared with the landlady, Mrs. Refuse, a rather large woman with an astonishingly high voice. Mrs. Refuse also had three cats, who loved to sit on the kitchen counters hoping for scraps, something Papa detested. We girls slept in a small adjoining bedroom, just big enough for a double bed, with shelves along the wall over the bed for our clothes. For some reason I always landed up sleeping in the middle between my two sisters, Hannele and Bärbel, which meant elbows from two sides during the night. Papa and Mama shared the pull-out couch, which served as a sofa during the day as well as seating for meals, homework and other activities. At the far end of the room was a door that led to a small cold pantry that had shelves for canned goods, potatoes and a few dishes, but was too cold to be used for anything else.

We shared toilet facilities with Mrs. Refuse as well, while the only full bathroom in the house was on the second floor and was used by all the boarders in the house. Unfortunately, the hot water situation in the house was somewhat precarious and, when the boarders complained that they could never have a full bath, Mrs. Refuse calmly told them that she always heated two kettles of water for herself and found that that was sufficient for a lovely re-laxing bath. I remember the three of us giggling at the thought of the rather buxom Mrs. Refuse actually fitting into the bathtub, let alone having a relaxing bath, whenever we saw her make her way up the stairs in her long, pink satin housecoat, carrying her two kettles of hot water.

Thinking back to those days, it seems hard to believe that we lived in those totally cramped conditions and yet were so happy. We had, of course, experienced the war, under much worse condi-tions, separated from Papa, who had been imprisoned in Dutch and English prison-of-war camps throughout the war, while Mama, Hannele, Bärbel and I were living as German war refugees in Japan and did not know whether Papa was alive or dead. Now we were together again as a family, and in a new country that welcomed us. And Papa never stopped reminding us what a wonderful country Canada was. A country of opportunity, he said, a place where we could be whatever we wanted to be.

He was so enthusiastic that we simply could not envision being anywhere else. And, indeed, our love for our newly adopted country found firm roots when, three days after moving into our new lodgings, the son of one of the other boarders knocked on our door with a bowl full of candies. We could hardly believe our ears when he told us that on a certain day in October, every year, Canadian children were allowed to dress up and go from house to house and ask for candy treats. No such day existed in Germany!

Papa had enrolled us in an English Catholic school in Lachine, run by the Sisters of Saint Anne and an order of religious brothers, where we were allowed to follow instructions at the level we had left in Germany. What amazes me even today is our classmates' total acceptance of three foreign girls who could hardly speak one word of English. They simply took it for granted that we would soon learn, and I cannot remember even one time being laughed at or ridiculed for pronunciation or incorrect syntax, which surely must have been rather funny at times.

By late March, the weather had become much milder, and Papa, always wanting to fill our childhood with adventures to remember, since he had missed so much of it because of the war, decided that the weather was surely warm enough to breakfast outside on the small screened-in porch at the back of the house. It was no use trying to tell him that it was really a bit chilly out there. He had this vision in his head of breakfast in the healthy Canadian outdoors, and that was that. He would cook us a wonderful breakfast of French toast or scrambled eggs with mushrooms and serve it to us himself, completely oblivious of the fact that we were desperately trying to keep from shivering and were only pretending that we were enjoying this new experience in order not to disappoint him.

During the summer that followed our arrival, we concentrated on improving our English. Every morning our new German friend, Beate, whose family had come to Canada the year before, and who was already quite proficient in English, came over to our house and we would read English stories together. Bärbel and I also found employment across the street from our boarding house, where a wealthy doctor had a beautiful house and grounds that led all the way to the shore of Lake Saint Louis. We had heard that he was looking for someone to weed his flowerbeds, so we walked across the street, knocked on his front door and told the maid that we were looking for work in the garden. Somewhat taken aback by these two young girls with their long pigtails and strange accents, she gave us a puzzled look and then went in search of the doctor. I can imagine his surprise when we told him that we would like to weed his garden. I remember Bärbel poking me in the ribs when I rather awkwardly asked whether he was the old man who owned this house and was he looking for someone to do some gardening. The *"gentleman,"* she hissed at me, and he had a hard time hiding his amusement. He hired us for fifty cents an hour to come every morning and weed his flowers as well as mow the smaller patches of lawn. Since our Oma had had a large garden in Germany, where we often helped her weed and water, this was not a difficult job for us, and we earned enough money to buy bicycles for each of us by the fall.

By that time, Papa had also found larger accommodation for us in the upper flat of a house on a quiet street in Dorval. It was a cosy place with panelled walls and a bright kitchen. Papa was travelling frequently by then to such places as Detroit, Chicago, Halifax and Vancouver, and he brought household items back from each trip, which, under Mama's guidance, soon converted our place into a comfortable home.

We did well in school, though we had to study hard in our new language. We made friends and got involved in school activities and church events. Father Latour, the *fire and brimstone* priest of our parish, often came by for a visit. He seemed fascinated by our family for some reason, although Papa always appeared a bit nervous whenever he dropped by. We girls found that rather amusing and, after one such visit, we laughed at him and told him that he had said "I see" at least 23 times while Father was holding forth.

It seemed as though our ship of life had finally reached a safe and calm harbour after the storms of war and years of separation—until one day in October, just one year after our arrival in Canada. Papa had not been feeling well and a visit to the doctor revealed swelling of the prostate. The doctor suggested a "simple operation" which would take care of things.

When the phone call came, Mama was alone at home. "I am afraid I have some bad news, Mrs. Fiand," the voice on the telephone said, "you had better sit down. Your husband has cancer, Mrs. Fiand. Very advanced cancer. There is nothing we can do for him now. We will send him home. He has only a short time left."

"Cancer?" she said. "Cancer?" She went down to the English lady who lived in the flat below. "What is cancer?" she asked.

Papa came home then. The family doctor visited and administered morphine. He became thinner by the day. We girls watched in silence. We prayed and believed in a miracle, but it was not to be. Even today, when I see cyclamen blooming in the stores at Christmas, I think of our living room that year, where a lovely pink flower bloomed the day he died—Christmas Eve 1953.

The doctor whose flowerbeds we had weeded that summer sent a big Christmas turkey, fully cooked. The Sisters sent baskets of food to last all winter. Neighbours were kind, and Father Latour paid the rent. There was no social welfare net in Canada at that time, and Papa had not been working long enough for any kind of pension. Mama sewed, and Hannele went to work as soon as she turned 16. Bärbel and I cleaned houses for extra money during weekends and holidays. We survived.

Canada was good to us, and has been ever since. Despite hardships and sorrow, Papa's *land of opportunity* made it possible for us all to achieve what we wanted to achieve. It has become the place we identify with, the place we love, our country, our home.

Land of Milk and Corn Flakes

Carrie-Ann Smith

CANADA IS, AND was historically, a land of opportunities. A quick word-search of Pier 21's story collection database reveals that over a dozen alumni stories include the oft-heard, well-loved and somewhat misleading phrases "land of milk and honey" and "streets paved with gold." The extent to which Canada perpetuated this myth of prosperity, in that it was an overflow of the United States mythos or that it sprang from the letters home of earlier immigrants eager to be joined by their friends and relatives, cannot be known. Suffice to say, people had high expectations, and this is reflected as immigrants tell their stories. Strangely, a term just as commonly recalled is the unlikely "corn flakes." It is not as odd as it might seem at first; if you landed at Pier 21 in the 1950s, you had to walk a floor covered with corn flakes to get to that street paved with gold.

In a 1980 oral history interview with Therese Lamie, retired Pier 21 Immigration Officer Frank Wright explains: "After the people were examined, given their papers, given their money advances, they would pick up their baggage. The customs officer would examine their baggage, and they would go down to the end of the ramp where they would go to the second floor. They would exchange requisitions for their tickets. So, they had their ticket, immigration papers, went to the immigration doctor and received immigration papers, and on their way down the ramp they were given a package of corn flakes, a package of cigarettes or tobacco and cigarette papers. They didn't know what corn flakes were, and by the time they reached the second floor the corn flakes were usually scattered all over."

That smell is connected to memory, is almost as hackneyed as the idea of "streets paved with gold," but it is undeniable. The aroma of well-trodden flakes combined with that of confiscated meat, cheese, and hundreds of bodies in one room had to have made an impression. Other senses also came into play; the sound of crunching underfoot, and the unique taste, helped keep corn flakes alive in the memories of former immigrants as well. In the following story excerpts, Pier 21 alumni recall their introduction to the breakfast cereal, and whether aware of it or not, their words reveal how corn flakes helped shape their first impressions of Canada.

The memories of W.A.T. Van den Byllaardt of the Netherlands and Andolfatto Severino of Italy fall into the *'mixed message'* category. Mr. Byllaardt recalls that his family was, "presented with a box of 'ready to eat bowl' of Kellogg's Corn Flakes and a Bible." For Mr. Severino it was, "a small bag containing a booklet with health tips (VD), some chocolate bars and a small box of cornflakes that nobody knew what to do with." Welcome to Canada, gentlemen!

In the *"I think I'm going to like it here"* category are the memories of two young girls. Cecile Bacinski had been in a displaced persons camp for months preceding her arrival, so her sentiments should not come as a surprise. She wrote: "Everyone has memories of that time, new land, new life; what I do remember mostly was the food, especially 'Kellogg's Corn Flakes.' To this day I have yet to eat them and not think of the cafeteria there on Pier 21. What an impact it left on this young child ... nothing more than Kellogg's Corn Flakes. After all it was the most delicious food after the hunger of past years. As they offered the second helping, I 'abused' that generosity."

Cathy Bos wrote: "We had our first corn flakes and potatoes with the skin on. Bacon and eggs, Canadian style, went down very well. My mother insisted we eat all the food, to show our appreciation."

The Hungarian revolution led to the arrival of Yolan Bencsik, whose story is an amazing drama of failed revolution and heroic escape. His first peaceful moment in months may have been the one that he describes here: "We were then ushered into the immigration building to be examined by doctors. We watched TV and ate corn flakes for the first time without milk as one would eat potato chips." Eva Kende also left Hungary after the revolution but she wouldn't notice the proliferation of flakes until her family had boarded the train in front of Pier 21: "The train was fabulous. We have never seen anything like it. Luxurious plush seats, friendly black porters in crisp uniforms and boxes of Kellogg's Corn Flakes in every nook and cranny. We have never seen corn flakes before and never had cereal for breakfast. Tasting this freebie, we decided it was a Canadian equivalent of potato chips and snacked on it during the whole trip."

Some people loved them, some people hated them, some were struck by the novelty of the box. Ole Falkeisen from the Netherlands wrote: "My first recollection of a good Canadian meal came in the form of Kellogg's Corn Flakes served in a mini-box. Never having seen this before, l wondered in amazement if everyone in Canada ate out of little one-meal boxes!" Estonian Aljas Peep writes that she was, "highly amazed at the way Corn Flakes was packed and served in individual cut-open boxes."

The history of the corn flake itself is an interesting one. Though the details of exactly how the invention occurred vary, the story essentially goes like this: While running the Sanitarium a.k.a "The San" in Battle Creek, Michigan, Dr. John Harvey Kellogg, a Seventh Day Adventist who advocated a strict vegetarian diet for his patients, was experimenting in an effort to invent a breakfast alternative to meat and eggs. He baked boiled wheat on a tin pan and left it out overnight. When he rolled it out the next day the individual grains fell into flakes. Dr. Kellogg was religious about all of his beliefs but not commercially minded, so he sold the rights to the product to his brother Will, who, much to the displeasure of J.H., sweetened the flakes and formed the Battle Creek Toasted Corn Flake Company in 1906.

The charm of this 'American Dream' story and the fondness of the quotes from Pier 21's alumni mask the tremendous irony implicit in the provision of Kellogg's Corn Flakes to new immigrants. Dr. Kellogg was a strong proponent of Eugenics; he blamed immigrants for society's ills and actively promoted diet and exercise among America's educated and wealthy as a means of strengthening the 'superior' Anglo-Saxon/American race.

Sir Francis Galton had coined the term Eugenics in 1883 to express the idea that science could help give the more suitable races or strains of blood (i.e. white) a better chance of prevailing over the 'lesser' races. This fundamentally racist theory gained popularity in Britain, the United States, and Canada. In his work "Plain Facts for Old and Young," Kellogg wrote: "Through complete submergence into another race the American race was fast dying out, its place being filled by emigrants of different lineage, religion, political ideas, and education." (Burlington, Iowa, Segner and Co., 1889)

What would such a man have thought upon seeing his flakes strewn about the Immigration Hall of Pier 21, or being raised to hungry foreign mouths? Were the marketing team at Kellogg's in the 1950s fans of irony, or just ahead of their time in the area of branding and the merits of customer loyalty? Their success is beautifully illustrated in the excerpt below. Of all the Pier 21 corn flakes stories (and there is a perforated box full), none match Mary Caravaggio's memories for detail and affection:

We sat in the Reception Hall and waited for processing. As we waited, a gift was given to us. We were so happy and excited. It was a small box, which read "Corn Flakes" on it. I started opening the carton, not knowing what was in it. We were all

curious. We opened the inside wrapper and took a few Corn
Flakes to taste them. The flavour wasn't what we expected.
It didn't taste very good. It had very little flavour and it was
an odd texture. We had never eaten anything like this before. These weren't Frosted Flakes, which were not on the
market yet. Looking around, children and adults alike were
making faces to express their dislike of the Corn Flakes. The
adults were putting the boxes down but the children began
tossing the rest at each other and in no time the flakes were
covering the floor. We were tired, restless, and weary from
days spent on the ship and the thought that we still had days
to spend on a train sitting on hard wooden seats until we
would reach the place we would call home ... obviously our
manners were forgotten. As I moved around the Reception
Hall, I felt the crushing of the Corn Flakes under our feet.
The crunching sound under the feet of others is imbedded
in my memory. Even today the crackling sound brings me
back to that day, the memory forever in my mind and soul. It
didn't take long to get accustomed to Corn Flakes. After the
two-day ride to Toronto, we met with family and settled into
the home we shared with cousins. Morning breakfast con-
sisted of cereal; Corn Flakes were always on the table. To my
aunt's surprise, two large boxes weren't enough and she
would grudgingly go and buy more. Corn Flakes have become a staple in my life in Canada. It is always available in
my kitchen. I thank Canada's immigration system for intro-
ducing us to Corn Flakes.

As for Dr. Kellogg, we will never know whether the colourful
scenes at Pier 21 had him turning in his grave, or if the intervening
years would have seen his views alter. All we can know for certain
is that whether you are talking about cereal or citizenship, you
can't buy the kind of loyalty that Mary Caravaggio describes—you
have to give it away.

Being Here

No Country for a Master Race

Henry Beissel

I'M AS SURELY and as firmly part of Canada as any of you. I made it my home from the moment I arrived in 1951. Indeed, the world of my childhood quickly became so alien to me that it seemed to belong to another life, and I dated it BC, *Before Canada*. My immigration here was, in a profound sense, a rebirth for me, and measuring my age from the year of arrival was more than vicarious rejuvenation. English became my mother tongue —though my mother didn't speak it—and I acquired a new self.

And yet I'm an outsider. Like it or not, we are each the sum total of our experiences, even though we all have some that we would prefer at least to forget, if not to undo. There can be no sanity without the acknowledgement and integration of every aspect and phase of our lives. For years I wanted to forget my childhood, but my childhood would not forget me. Night after night I woke up in a sweat from nightmares filled with the horrors of war.

You see, much of my childhood was spent in air raid shelters, praying that the bombs would miss our house, watching the city of my first birth—Cologne, Germany—slowly turn into a heap of rubble under which thousands of people, some of them friends and family, were buried, crushed or burnt to death. Most of those who were not killed fled the horrors of continuous aerial bombardment. Of Cologne's original population of 800,000 in 1939, there were 40,000 left at the end of the war, most of them living like rats in underground shelters and smouldering ruins, pounded day and night by British and American bombers. I still cannot hear certain alarm sirens without my nervous system going into mild shock along the scars of my war memories.

There was also the shock and shame of coming to consciousness in 1945 with the realization that I was born to a civilized nation that had committed the atrocities of Auschwitz and Belsen. I felt those who were charged with my education had betrayed me, and I wanted to get away from them, indeed from all things German; to put as much distance as possible between such incomprehensible cruelty and myself. Because I worked for the American and British Occupation Forces, I managed to get to London (UK) on a student visa. There, I met a Canadian student who persuaded me to abandon my plan to emigrate to Bolivia and come to Canada instead. He probably saved my life because, given my romantic revolutionary spirit, I would have joined Che Guevara's ragtag rebels and perished with them.

What I needed was a place to escape to, a space in which to reconstruct myself. Europe seemed doomed, and I wanted a future. Canada was just the place for me. In its calm social and political waters my wounds healed, and my childhood has become an integral part of myself. The process of reconciliation was painful, but it has provided an optic that has made some hidden patterns of history visible.

I have indulged in these personal remarks not in order to inflict on you my biography, but because I regard my own case as archetypal of the Canadian immigrant. Change the names and faces, substitute dates and places—and you have the portrait of millions of people who have come here, and are still coming here, to escape —escape harsh economic conditions, intolerable social restrictions, political terror and persecution, or just a soulless existence without hope. To them, to us, Canada is the land of opportunity—the opportunity to live creatively, in freedom, with dignity, and to shape a future for our children.

You might ask: "Who in the world needs Canada for that?" Well, there are millions around the world who need a country that keeps its doors open to those determined to escape inhuman conditions. Today more than ever. Ours is a time of unprecedented barbarities. The planet is rife with genocide. Persecution on grounds of race and religion, to say nothing of political ideologies, is the norm rather than the exception in many parts of the world now.

As for the war to end all wars, there is no such thing. In the past four decades of peace, there have been over 150 wars around the world in which more than fifty million people have been killed. Add to this, famine in parts of Africa and India, natural and man-made catastrophes, and you understand why this is the age of mass migration on a global scale. Everywhere there are overcrowded refugee camps where millions of men, women and children, desperate and homeless, subsist on handouts in a world that no longer wants them. As the song says, tears are not enough. What they need is a country with a large enough spirit and geography to offer them the opportunity of a new life. They need Canada, as I did—a country with a generous immigration policy.

In return for the luxury of freedom and economic security, our immigrants contribute something to this country that the world needs at least as badly as an open door. It grows from seeds packed away inside them. They all carry it—that invisible package marked P-A-S-T, filled with, among other things, the pains and sufferings that drove them from their homes and homelands. It's been part of the meagre belongings with which every settler has arrived on the shores of this land. By coming here they broke with their past, and many tried to forget it in exchange for a commitment to the future. But the past won't let go of you until its lessons become part of your life, and the lessons of suffering are compassion, tolerance and humility.

It could not be otherwise but that this gigantic legacy of suffering should have had a share in forging our national character. For we are a nation of immigrants. They ... we ... have imported the experience and knowledge of man's inhumanity to man to this country for three or four centuries now, slipped it unnoticed past immigration and customs officials, and deposited it in the collective unconscious along with the determination to temper the cruel and destructive impulses in the human heart and create a more peaceful and more just society than the one left behind. The shared pain and despair that brought our immigrants here is the soil in which those softening agents grow, without which it is impossible for people of different temperaments and talents, different persuasions and pursuits, different languages and lifestyles, different races and religions, to live together harmoniously and productively—as they do in Canada.

If, then, it is in the very nature of immigration to act as a selective process that assures the birth of a pluralist society, is what I've claimed for Canada equally true of that other great immigrant nation in our hemisphere—the United States? The answer is Yes and No. Of course, the United States constitutes a pluralist society in which all the creeds and colours mingle, as in Canada. But there is a difference, and I regard it as fundamental. It surfaces in many ways. It's commonplace, for example, to say that as a social entity the United States is a 'melting-pot' and we are a 'salad-bowl.' Leaving aside whether or not the metaphors are correct, it is significant that so many embrace them. A 'melting-pot' is an image of homogeneity; it reflects the desire for conformity. And that, in turn, is a manifestation of what one might call ideological singularity—the idea that there is, or the wish that there be, a single social scenario superior to all others and therefore morally binding on all people. Alas, idealism always turns into dogmatism. It is no accident that

the McCarthy witch-hunt of yesteryear, which dramatically demonstrated the narrow limits of political tolerance south of our borders, was, unlike a lot of other things, unable to spread northward
into Canada whose 'salad-bowl' image implies a greater tolerance
for divergences of viewpoints and lifestyles.

Every immigrant brings along hopes, aspirations and expectations. It is, in fact, the belief in the possibility of a better world that
prompts people to immigrate in the first place. This belief can take
two basic forms. One is the conviction that, with effort and understanding, human suffering can be reduced, and the quality of life
improved. The other is the belief in a paradise on earth—the belief that with enough intelligence and application everything is
possible and that history is the slow path of humanity towards an
ultimate state of absolute justice, freedom and equality. This romantic idealism is the loom on which the social fabric of the United
States is spun. It's the source of its splendour and its strength—the
ebullient spirit of enterprise and optimism, the creative vitality and
energy as well as the magnanimity of its moral commitments—all
qualities that have made the U.S.A. the great nation that it is. But
it's also the source of its weaknesses and failures—the bigotry of
fundamentalists, the naïve ruthlessness of its economy, its super-
man complex, its messianic delusions and its military prowess. Although such weaknesses and strengths are not unknown in
Canada, they are alien to our national character.

The reason is that immigrants to Canada generally arrived with
more modest expectations and ambitions. They were not looking
to recover a lost paradise, but were content to live in the freedom
of open spaces, earn a living wage, enjoy a decent standard of living
and know that they were working for themselves and their children, who, in turn, could be expected to have a brighter future.
The selective process that sent the immigrant with utopian baggage south of the 49th parallel, and led the ameliorist to Canada, is
rooted in the history of the settlement of the two nations: the one

propelled by· the Pilgrim Fathers syndrome, that made colonization a struggle of the forces of goodness against the forces of evil, at the end of which lay the promise of the City of God which, for less pious minds, became a city of gold; the other laboriously following the retreat of the beaver, in the service of distant kings, whose pragmatic and mundane objectives militated against grandiose schemes and called for men willing or forced to serve in the winds of shifting loyalties and betrayals at English or French courts.

But there has to be another factor to account for the difference in mentality between Americans and Canadians; otherwise it would be impossible to understand why we, unlike our neighbour, never shook off the colonial yoke. We outgrew it, perhaps; or it became too troublesome for the masters to maintain and they took it off us, but we never revolted and conquered our freedom. The reason is our climate. There is a tendency to underrate the effect of the climate on the character of a people. I'm convinced that Canadians are what they are substantially because of our winters, and that, if the United States as a whole experienced the same winters as ours, they wouldn't have gone to Vietnam, they wouldn't be financing the overthrow of the government of Nicaragua, and they wouldn't be preparing for the Armageddon of Star Wars.

For about six months of every year, nature in most of Canada is, to all intents and purposes, dead. Frozen rigid or buried under half a continent of snow, it stares at us with bleak, expressionless eyes. The animals have gone south or underground into hibernation. The human animal falls back on survival strategies that tax its capacities to the limit, and sometimes beyond. For more than half of our lives we are obliged to confront daily the fragility of life, our own perishability, the merciless indifference of nature, and the futility of grandiose ambitions in the face of the eternal return of the same seasonal cycle of birth and death. Not even to the wildest imagination can our winter wasteland resemble paradise, or sustain the hope that it might ever be turned into one. Isolated in a

cocoon of fur—boots, hats, coats, mittens, ear-muffs and nose bags
—we are left alone with our mortality to contemplate the vanity of
all things.

Thus the annual and visceral experience of the Canadian winter reinforces the very traits in our character that the immigrant
smuggles into the country under cover of the painful memories he
wants to forget. Winter makes Canadians more compassionate,
more tolerant and more humble. By the same token, the more ami-
able climate between Florida and California encourages the hubris
of a superpower and its peoples' Cinderella dreams. The movement
of American thought is linear and progressive. It sees time as an
ascent to some ultimate ecstasy or apotheosis. Canadians, as a
whole, don't share such delusions. For us, the mythic pattern of our
experience is the Homeric circle: life is a journey that returns to its
beginnings. There are things to be righted on the way, as Odysseus
did when he returned to Ithaca, but there is no place for utopias
here. Or as I put it in my *Cantos North*:

> *This is no country for a master race. Here*
> *rivers run immemorial with the explosive*
> *energy of glaciers, dwarf us even in our dreams*
> *and sweep away the vain. Niagaras of sunlight*
> *have pounded this rock into a shield to crush*
> *pride by sheer weight and volume.*

Here the joys of life are in the living: the journey is what matters,
not the destination.

The traumas of the immigrant's life *BC* (Before Canada), re-
inforced by our severe winters, are the source of our weakness: they
make us conservative, often un-enterprising, over-cautious and
under-confident, passive, perhaps cynical at times, and even dull.
But our traumas are also the source of our strengths: we don't consider ourselves superior to anyone, individual or nation; we distrust

evangelists, be they of the religious, the political or the commercial kind. We lack the sense of messianic mission that continues to delude many nations, and always leads to bloodshed. We don't have any truth we consider binding for all, no Canadian way of life to export, no designs on anyone's economy or territory. Experience teaches us that there are many different and valid ways of looking at the world, that one must be sceptical of absolutes and generous with compromises, that survival calls for mutual assistance and cooperation, and that we must respect and cherish the differences between us because they constitute our true human wealth. In other words, we are temperamentally and ideologically committed to pluralism. We practise it at home and abroad, at least collectively, though we may sometimes be found wanting individually. And, I submit, this spirit of tolerance, compassion and cooperation is what the world needs more than anything else today. Given the lunacy of our nuclear arms race, it may offer the only hope for our species to survive.

You will not have missed the irony of my standing here, a Canadian voice, holding up for emulation by the whole world the virtue of humility. A very un-Canadian posture, I grant, and I should apologize profusely for the contradiction. But I'm unrepentant. After all, I'm not suggesting that our country is a model of perfection. I'm not naïve enough to think that there is no racism or discrimination here. I have experienced some of it myself. Our native people, and people with easily identifiable racial differences, know how discriminatory we can be. But the treatment of our First Nations people is now acknowledged for the shocking and shameful disgrace that it was, and every effort is made to redress their suffering. Such racist conduct is uncharacteristic of the nation today, and unequivocally condemned both by the courts and by the general public.

For all our shortcomings, Canada can be an example to the world. From coast to coast, people of every imaginable race and religion, colour and custom, ethnic and national origin, language and loyalty, live side by side as friends and neighbours. In the Franco-Scottish setting of my Glengarry (Ontario) abode, my pharmacist is a Pakistani married to a Greek; my doctor is from Trinidad and his wife from the U.K.; my neighbour in one direction is a Dutch painter, next door to a Hungarian couple; in the other direction, across the concession road, lives a German with a wife from Quebec; next to them an extraordinary couple, the husband of Italian/Welsh origin, who have adopted some 19 children from as far away as India, Korea and Malaysia, making my rural route a miniature United Nations. That's what Canada is: a United Nations in action, a concave mirror of the Human Family on its best behaviour. And we mean to keep it that way.

We may be the only nation in the world with a Ministry of Multiculturalism, whose function it is to foster the various cultures of which our country is composed. That's a far cry from the homogeneity of a melting-pot. Ours is the only nationalism that may still be justifiable in the emerging new world order—because it is really a commitment to internationalism. Nothing is more badly needed today than the lesson that, like the individuals in a society, the nations of the world can coexist and survive only on the basis of compassion, tolerance and humility. Perhaps we should start exporting the Canadian winter.

—*(Dunvegan, Ontario, 1985)*

Postscript

Thirty years have passed since I delivered the above (slightly edited) essay under the title "Canadian Pluralism: The View of an Outsider Inside" to the Couchiching Conference in 1985. The world has changed dramatically since then, and these changes cannot but influence my views on immigration to Canada.

I can only list a few of the main changes which directly affect immigration, and I'd start with the growing impoverishment of billions around the world as a consequence of the rapacious manipulation of financial markets by bankers and brokers. This is creating multitudes of destitute people in the so-called Developing World anxious to emigrate to the more affluent, capitalist countries where, ironically, the number of poor is also increasing as a consequence of the same unconscionable financial practices.

The second major change is the fall of the Berlin Wall and the subsequent unravelling of the Soviet Empire. The result is large-scale emigration from all of the Eastern European countries. This flow of emigrants is mostly directed at the First World countries of Europe.

Perhaps the most profound and troublesome change was initiated by the Bush family—both father and son: they unleashed two brutal wars against Iraq under patently mendacious pretexts, wars that have killed well over a million Iraqis, half of them civilians, which has disastrously destabilized not only the Middle East but the whole Western world. One of the consequences has been a mass migration on a global scale not seen since WW II, some of which is now reaching our shores.

Then there is Climate Change, which was not yet part of the public dialogue in 1985, largely because international corporations spread misinformation on the subject so they could continue to pollute the atmosphere to maximize profits. The recent 196-nations UN conference in Paris has demonstrated that the world is finally waking up to the serious threats of Climate Change. Time will tell whether or not it's too late to avoid cataclysmic disasters.

Already, extreme weather patterns are devastating many parts of the world, glaciers are melting at the poles and the oceans are rising, inundating low-lying land. It is a matter of speculation how high and how quickly water levels will rise, but it is likely that within the 21st century hundreds of millions of people will be forced to seek higher ground, and for most of them that means emigration.

Last but not least, there is the continuing population explosion. In 1985, 4½ billion of us populated our planet; today the number is close to 7½ billion. It took 150,000 years for the human species to reach a population of three billion; the second three billion has taken a mere 30 years. It doesn't take a mathematical genius to figure out where this is leading. If you're interested in looking into the implications of this development, I recommend William Catton Jr.'s *Overshoot* (1982). He shows us a pattern that is quite common in nature: a species that suddenly has access to an abundance of food will immediately multiply in numbers that inevitably exceed those the habitat can sustain; when the excess passes a certain critical point, it is followed by a die-off. Catton's study cites some typical cases of species and cultures that have disappeared as a consequence of superabundance.

In the meantime, such rates of population growth produce waves of refugees and migrants. There simply isn't room for them in their native land, as China and India demonstrate. Or take a more contemporary example: Nigeria had a population of around 80 million in 1985; today it has over 180 million. Nigeria has more than doubled its population in 30 years. This means that there will be half a billion Nigerians by mid-century. Mass migration will be the inevitable consequence.

I've listed five major developments that have begun to significantly impact immigration to Canada. To examine and elaborate the precise effects of each is beyond a "postscript". Besides, the conclusions of such a study would remain speculative because the future doesn't show its hand until we're in its presence. This much is certain—the Canada to which I swore loyalty in 1956 is quickly changing.

The hasty decision of Prime Minister Trudeau to bring 25,000 Syrian refugees here within 6 weeks, illustrates the problem. While the PM's gesture was both generous and politically astute, it was also logistically misguided, and the time frame was quickly extended by a couple of months which in turn prompted the government (for reasons we can only speculate on) to double the number of Syrian refugees it would accept by the end of 2016. The haste with which these decisions were made suggests a serious disregard for security issues and for the demographic consequences. To bring such a large, homogenous group of immigrants all at once to a country whose official languages they don't speak and whose dominant traditions are alien to them, means to create ghettos. And ghettos are the breeding ground of discrimination and racism.

Some of the forces dispersing populations across the globe and pushing for heterogeneous societies everywhere are beyond our control. All the more reason to revisit and rewrite our rules of immigration to bring them in line with contemporary global realities, and with the kind of country we want Canada to be. We no longer have a real winter to export!

—*(Ottawa, December 2015)*

Writing in French in Alberta

Laurent Chabin

(Translated from the French version by Susan Ouriou)

IN AND OF itself, writing in French in Alberta is nothing out of the ordinary; a writer can work anywhere, in any language. However, writing is one thing and publishing quite another. Going from the act of writing—a resolutely solitary activity —to practicing a writer's profession in a language other than the language of the place one lives in can give rise to all kinds of questions. Writing professionally in French in an Anglophone province could be interpreted as an act of protest, born out of a desire either to prove its feasibility or that one is entitled to do so despite all opposition ... but opposition from whom? ... and to what?

In my case, there is no protest involved. I do not write in French *despite* opposition from anything or anyone. I write in French because French is my mother tongue and, even more importantly, it is the only language in which I am able to write properly. So the choice is a natural one that is unrelated to the place in which I write. I do not write based on geography or where I live, nor do I serve as a historian for the region (even though I did make the choice to live here), or to be its flag-bearer. Regionalism as such has nothing to do with literature, although it can at times be one of literature's components.

Although Alberta appears in many of my young adult novels, it is as a necessary scene, a setting that serves to anchor the story in concrete reality more than as the heart of the story. The province has figured more largely in my more recent adult novels. Once again, however, historiography does not enter into the equation. Alberta and the prairies represent a broader imaginary space in my fiction. They do not just serve as background to the story but are a representation of reality, in short the raw material of any novel.

Choosing to write in French in Alberta might seem to make the writer part of a community, striving, in one fashion or another, to resist the "allophone" pressure designed to obliterate it. Once again, that has not been my experience. What pressure exactly? And from where? I have never come up against any such pressure; to be clear, *writing* is what makes me a writer, whatever language I choose to write in. Writing in French could, it's true, make me into a de facto member of the francophone community, if the latter were simply defined as all those who read and express themselves in French. Such a community, however, is quite virtual. Those who speak, understand and/or teach French in Alberta—and especially in Calgary, where I have made my home for over ten years—come from different cultural communities whose connection to the French language is not necessarily the same.

My potential readers, the ones I sometimes have in mind without being able to actually visualize them, are part of the same diversity. I do not have a target reader for whom I write. I write *in* Alberta, I may write *about* Alberta, but I do not write *for* Albertans. That is, not specifically. I am not even writing for Francophones, wherever they may come from, since several of my books have been translated. In my eyes, it amounts to self-mutilation for an author to target a specific audience. Why would a writer voluntarily restrict his or her readership? Faulkner didn't write for Americans in the southern States, any more than Beckett wrote for Irish immigrants in France or Kafka for Czech Jews. The very idea would be seen as ludicrous by pretty well everyone.

A culture must not retreat into itself. The French fact—in Alberta as elsewhere—can only be vibrant if, instead of reducing itself to what amounts to a more ethnic than linguistic element—for survival purposes—it accepts its multiplicity and opens up to others. I have no interest in being part of a community that defines itself as a minority. It would be tantamount to putting my own self in a minority position, which is not my experience. I refuse outright to be confined in a self-proclaimed ghetto to which certain special rights would accrue due to one's position as a survivor. I make no claim to any special rights based on the language in which I express myself and work.

As a citizen, all I ask is that I not be granted fewer rights than other citizens. And I have not. No one has ever prevented me from speaking or writing in French in Alberta. The fact that I express myself and write in French has never been a hindrance to me or closed any doors. On the contrary, all the support I have received over my writing career has been provided by provincial institutions for which my language was never seen as an obstacle.

Whether it be the University of Calgary, immersion schools, the Alberta Foundation for the Arts, the Young Alberta Book Society, the Word on the Street festival or the Banff-Calgary International Writers Festival, each organization has provided assistance without discriminating in any way. Their only consideration has been my work's worth, independent of political or linguistic considerations.

Yet I have never gone out of my way to attract attention. The various institutions came looking for me. Generally speaking, in Alberta society there is a keen interest in, even a demand for, what is called the "fait francophone," that, unfortunately, is not always either recognized or understood.

Advocating for a language—whatever language that may be—does not entail protesting for one's right to use the language when nothing stops you from doing just that. The best—and simplest—advocacy is that of practicing one's own language, through the arts, for example. No one threatens a language that is freely used, and there is no reason to invent enemies when all one really needs to do is practice and write in one's own language.

A language does not die because of efforts made to kill it. Centuries of oppression and linguistic imperialism were not able to do away with Basque and Catalan in Europe. On the contrary, those same languages are flourishing more today than ever before; what's more, without the benefit of external assistance since they are spoken nowhere else in the world. But those languages are the pride of their speakers who have continued using them in the face of adversity. The only thing that can kill a language is for it to be abandoned by its own speakers, or to have them retreat into themselves, eventually smothering it.

Finally, my situation vis-à-vis French in Alberta is best summarized by an aphorism from Emile Cioran, himself a stateless man: *One does not live in a country, one lives in a language. One's homeland is that and nothing more.* (Cioran, 1999)

So that is where I live: in the French language. As for Alberta? All the better ...

A Simple Wedding

(From *To a Brighter Future*)

~⌒

Ursula Delfs

Somewhere between Woking and Edmonton, the swaying railroad car made its way past miles and miles of bush and muskeg. The tall, broad-shouldered young man found himself restlessly pacing up and down its aisles. He should have been very tired, nearly exhausted, for the last week of long days had been spent putting many finishing touches on his log cabin. This first home in Canada had to be made as inviting as possible for the coming of its first feminine occupant. It is understandable that this impending event was constantly on his mind, and though physically spent, Günther was much too keyed up to sleep.

He tried to put himself in her place. *What a lot of impressions my little bride will have to absorb*, he thought. First, the trip from her home in Cranz to the seaport at Bremen; days and nights aboard ship on the long ocean voyage; the tedious train ride across Canada; then the wedding, under such unusual circumstances, and the new challenges and duties of a housewife on a Canadian homestead. What must she be thinking, as she too, sat on a train, hers coming from Halifax to Edmonton?

It was a proud feeling, Günther wrote to Tante Anna, that he, as a man, would have the privilege of guiding, helping and protecting this young woman who had been willing to put her life and future into his hands. He knew that in this foreign country he would have to take the place of parents, siblings and friends—even her home. That was a tall order, but Günther felt confident. Had he not faced and overcome many difficulties and challenges since he arrived in Canada two years before? He had grown, not only in physical stature, but also in experience, competence, patience and confidence. In this positive frame of mind, he watched the lights of Edmonton come into view.

The next day, on the evening of April 24th 1930, Günther stood expectantly at the trackside, his heart pounding. As the train slid into the station, he spied his beloved! The months of longing and waiting came to an end in one long loving embrace. The so-often-dreamed-of reunion had become a reality!

By previous arrangement, a German acquaintance, Erwin Deimling, had come to the station with his car. This man had an insurance business in Edmonton, and had been a helpful facilitator to many German immigrants upon their arrival in the city. Now he took the two happy young people to his spacious home and introduced them to his wife. Else was tucked into a cozy bedroom for some much-needed rest, and Günther tried, without too much success, to get a little sleep on a makeshift sofa in an adjoining room. Only later, over a late breakfast, could they fully believe that they were truly in Canada, together.

That afternoon the Deimlings took them to the Department of Vital Statistics to get a marriage license. Later that same day, April 25th 1930, they stood before Pastor K.W. Freitag in a German Lutheran Church in Strathcona. He solemnly declared: "I pronounce you, Günther John Pankow, and you, Else Gertrud Gesien, man and wife." His words echoed in the large empty church, for the only others present were Erwin and Margarethe Deimling, who served as witnesses. It was a strange wedding, in this respect, but these circumstances were unavoidable. They were strangers in Edmonton and thousands of miles separated them from their families. But they had each other, and at this point that was all that mattered. For a few days they remained guests of the Deimlings, who took them shopping at Eaton's and showed them the city.

Soon they were aboard the northbound train, which carried them in the direction of the Peace River Country, and home. To Else, it must have seemed like an interminable distance, with nothing but miles and miles of bush. She would have had good reason to ask herself: "Where is Günther taking me?"

Finally, the train pulled to a stop in Spirit River, the address she had so often written on her letters. For the first time in many days, Else saw a familiar face, for there, greeting them warmly at the station, was Horst Anders. He had come with a team and wagon to pick them up. Soon, settled among boxes, trunks, crates and suitcases, the threesome began the wagon trip—the last leg of Else's long journey. The first several miles went quite smoothly (though that may be an exaggeration), but as they neared the notorious mud-hole near McArthur's, they could see that more horses had come to meet them. Fred Egge and Herman Wulf hitched on their animals for extra horsepower to drag the heavily loaded wagons through the quagmire. Again, Else must have wondered. With the many new impressions, and all the excitement, her fatigue was now forgotten.

In late afternoon, as the last rays of sunshine peeked through the trees, Günther pointed to the south: "There it is—our home, our land!" And Else gazed in wonder at the log cabin nestled in the trees. It is hard to imagine the variety of feelings that must have overwhelmed her as the tired steaming horses stopped at the cabin door. The entrance had been decked with a frame of evergreen boughs topped with a large hand-printed placard which read: "Herzlich Villkommen" (Hearty Welcome). Some 20 neighbours had gathered, including the only three women resident in the area at the time, and each one of them gave the young bride a warm welcome. She experienced the true hospitality of a German pioneer settlement, as they visited, made music, sang folk songs and enjoyed cake and coffee. The young couple could not have imagined a warmer or more delightful reception deep in the Canadian wilderness.

Many hours later they waved goodbye to their neighbours, as the wagons rumbled away on the bush trails. The lovely scent of wood smoke filled the air. The fire crackled as a dim soft glow emanated from the coal-oil lamp. At length there was just the dark, and the warmth and the quiet, with the music of the wind in the treetops.

Hundedagene and
The Foxtail Phenomenon

Vivian Hansen

MR. SLYK'S ACCORDION bleats gaily through the dog days of late July 1964. He has no idea that his music will travel beyond his bedroom window, or that his accordion melodies will ricochet off prairie poplars to become the echo that impresses howling coyotes, and will journey through time to lodge in my memory. Alfie Slyk and I lie in the grass outside our homes, mesmerized by the accordion rhythm and the stars shimmering through a black sky, in a quiet elocution of time. Alfie says: "I will always remember this night."

"Det er langet over vort Sengetid," I tell Alfie. *It is long past our bedtime.* "Når vid bliver ved med at ligge hende og lytte til din Far's accordion, så kommer vi jo aldrig I Seng!" *If we lie out here and listen to your dad's accordion, we won't ever have to go to bed.*

Alfie giggles, recognizing the truth and futility in my words. Here on the lawn we are friends in Danish. In school, we ignore each other. But neither of us will ever turn off this night, or forget that it is about dog days, that help our parents remember the land of their birth. Mr. Slyk's accordion calls to me now. The music conjures the goose-down Danish words of my childhood, and the Foxtails.

***

127

I am standing outside our new back door, knee deep in foxtails, pleased with their tickle. They are like kittens, curling around my small legs. Wading through their bursting sticky burrs, they play with me. I love their name.

"What happened to all the foxes?" I ask my brother. "Why would they all run away and leave their tails behind?" I am prepared to believe any story he tells me, for this is Canada, and our new home looks out on a dried-up prairie slough and wilderness. He answers me in Danish, chuckling: "Når rævene løber for hurtig gennem blæsten taber de deres haller." *If foxes run too fast through the wind, their tails fall off!* He is teasing me, but I'm not sure of the truth. I scan the flat prairie horizon and the sea of foxtails, trying to imagine the great fox herd that galloped through here. I can see the ferocious wind that surprised them, snatching and combing their tails into restless, leg-clinging awns.

The wind on the Calgary prairie in August 1961 was a relentless cloud that could lose a small girl, and my mother didn't let me go far outside without my brothers. Nor was she as pleased as I was about the foxtails. For weeks into that fall, she complained that they attacked her every time she opened the door. I told her they wanted to come inside to get away from the wind. "Hmmph," said she. "It's Hundedagene. You never know what to expect."

Hundedagene is the Danish word for dog days, the enchanted summer nights in the 30 days between the full moons of July and August. It is a hot, clammy month when heat waves slow time, and logic retreats into shadows. In Denmark, Hundedagene will launch treacherous climatic change. The fickleness of Hundedagene was cast in my mother's primal Danish tongue, which clung to her throat like a burr. These words persisted in honouring old Viking knowledge, the pagan sense of life—animate and inanimate. When leaves or snowflakes or foxtails 'fall,' in English, this translates to *dale* in Danish. Each foxtail that flies through the air knows itself as a distinct life force.

I caught my mother's nuances of imminent danger, of trying not to rile the uncanny forces of nature. Awareness of earth's fickleness was particularly critical in this new country, on this new street, where we would build our lives. The foxtails were a flurry of Hundedagene, the residue of dried-up sloughs.

I was five years old when we moved into our new home on Blakiston Drive in Calgary. The peculiar migration of foxtails to our back door is my first memory of the Alberta prairie. This road was named after Capt. Thomas Blakiston, British gentleman and explorer with the Palliser Expedition. My family was flanked to the south by the Slyks, and a Dutch family next door. Some Germans, Italians, Ukrainians, Irish and Czechs made up the rest of the cultural mosaic. They were all happy to buy a house with $500 of government incentive, and they didn't care whom they lived beside as long as they could live.

The Czechs grew potatoes in their front lawn after the wind blew the foxtails west. We pondered the craziness of this strategy, but their reasons for planting potatoes were the same as ours: cheap food to survive a brutal Calgary winter. For about five years after the foxtails left, the inhabitants of Blakiston Drive grew potatoes in every square inch of dirt they found. Should Hundedagene blight the potatoes in this new country, we would all starve.

In 1961, the immigrants on Blakiston Drive were trying out their destiny, their energies directed solely towards survival. Most of us were Caucasian, and like foxtails, destined to disappear and settle into the expansive gold of the prairie. We were unaware that our whiteness carried an invisible badge of privilege. Only the diverse accents of our European parents gave us away. It was difficult to be invisible enough, to disguise who you were, when your parents pronounced 'butter' as 'buddah,' and you had to translate at the restaurant. Those were the shameful moments that I analyzed many times over in my life, trying to flog my own shame, trying to find a smooth road through the ambivalence. I became Canadian:

a hybrid foxtail that clings tenaciously to roots, and a language other than English.

By the time I started school in 1963, the foxtails had long since flown, and the City of Calgary was actively attempting to tame its prairie. The dust that was riled by clearing land for the new University of Calgary caught in the wind and rebelled against the taming, blowing a grey sheath over everything.

The British flag blew at Brentwood Elementary School. In Grade One we began the long-term assimilation process that was the gauntlet for all colonials. We sang 'God Save the Queen.' Teachers read from the Bible every morning. We recited the Lord's Prayer before we began arithmetic.

Some of us continued to speak our mother tongue at home, but it was easily forgotten at school. The Slyks spoke Danish with us, and would do so until reaching the borders of our front lawns. We had an unspoken rule never to allow any language but English to pass our lips at school. We were intent on becoming invisible; white enough to be indiscernible from English-speaking schoolmates.

In 1966 the flag changed: two red side bars with a white centre, and a maple leaf smack in the middle. Now we were truly Canadian, but it would take years before we could speak the words that honoured and cherished our primal cultures. It would be years before we could remember the magical, fickle time of Hundedagene, to trust the capricious wind of change.

These ephemeral things that *daler,* complete their own small destiny, not unlike the immigrants on Blakiston Drive who became invisible in the gold blanket of the 1960s prairie. They claimed their place during Hundedagene, the dance of *Dale* felling them into a honeyed gold over a summer slough.

"Attention Mr. Inglewick"

(aka: Ecclestein, Engilvices, Englevicf, Englewitz,
Englhiciz, Englibicks, Lglovicz, Inceclevics, Ingelevres,
Igngivard, Inglebick, Inglevics, Eaglevitch, Ingleview,
Inglewick, Inglewood, Ingllenics, Ongelevics etc., etc.)

~~⌒

Vid Ingelevics

MY FATHER PASSED away on March 30, 2001 at the age of 71. During the unsettling process of going through a lifetime's worth of collected material, I came across one set of items that I immediately recognized as a posthumous gift from my father to me. During the late 1960s to early 1970s, unknown to me, my father had created a personal archive consisting of misspellings of his name on correspondence addressed to him at his workplace. In this archive—a large envelope stuffed with other envelopes—were 84 examples of how his surname had been mangled in the course of his business correspondence with a wide range of Canadian companies. The perpetrators even included his own co-workers at various branches of Smith Transport, a transportation company now swallowed by Canadian Pacific, where he was entering mid-level management during those years.

This collection has significance for me, in several ways. First, of course, it is deeply personal as it was obviously my father's private joke, and now reminds me of his sharp sense of humour. But, at the same time, given the extreme nature of some of the "mistakes," I sense that his humour may also have functioned as a kind of defence against what must have seemed at times as intentional acts of misreading and misspelling. Some of those misspellings went well beyond simple and understandable errors of omission or the substitution of a couple of letters, becoming wholesale cultural transformations of his Latvian surname. In most cases, his correspondents would have had easy access to the correct spelling of his name, as they were responding to his initial letters or were in regular working contact.

What struck me, as a carrier of the same surname a generation later, was that I have rarely experienced such wildly inaccurate misspellings of my name. Yet, given the tight chronological clustering of postmark dates on the envelopes, it seemed to often happen to him. This made me think that perhaps his little collection has a wider social import and may tell us something about the life of a young post-war refugee trying to "make it good" in Toronto. In reflecting further on this, I have come to suspect that the nature and frequency of the mistakes can be read as one of the ways in which a resistance to a changing cultural landscape was being expressed in the everyday working world of Toronto in the 1960s, a once very monocultural city then being transformed by the effects of post-war immigration.

At that time my father was one of a growing number of young former refugee/immigrants who had fled their war-ravaged or occupied Eastern European homelands and had begun to work their way into the Canadian business world. On first arriving in Canada (which only grudgingly began to accept refugees several years after the war's end) they found that the term "D.P." (displaced person) was often used as a derogatory term by Canadians. The D.P's were blamed for stealing jobs that, in truth, no one else wanted to do. As these "foreigners" began to move from the margins towards the centre, an act of petty thoughtlessness like misspelling someone's name was one form of banal humiliation that was socially acceptable. After all, it was just a mistake. But we know what Freud said about such mistakes. My father's archive offers evidence of just how frequent and wilful these "mistakes" actually were.

However, even as he collected his envelopes, his own position in this process of literally being re-written by others was not completely unambivalent. A few years after my father's arrival in Canada he had given up using his real first name, Brunoslavs, in favour of "Barney" just as I myself "lost" my own Latvian proper name, Vidvuds, when I first started public school in the 1950s—becoming Vid.

I realize, of course, that other immigrants have suffered far greater humiliations and injustices in the past, so it is not to seek redress or revenge that these excerpts from my father's collection of misspellings are offered. Instead, I would say that their value resides in the ability of these small stings and trivial cruelties to reveal to us something of the texture of the everyday Toronto of 50 years ago; a particular texture that would be inaccessible without my father's quirky envelope collection. Perhaps their publication can stand as a kind of unsentimental "counter-monument" that allows us to contemplate the social realities in which the day-to-day working lives of my father and other new immigrants to Toronto were entangled.

Mrs. Lukasiewicz
and The Winter Boots

Barbara D. Janusz

THE OLDER WOMAN sitting across from me looked frightened, so frightened that I held off asking her to disclose the nature of the matter that had brought her to my office. I inquired instead about her arrival in Canada.

Nodding, as though in acquiescence of my intentions, Mrs. Lukasiewicz began by explaining that she and her husband had just arrived three months earlier. "We left Poland almost two years ago for Italy, where we were in a refugee camp. My son and his wife and our two grandchildren live here in Calgary."

Rather than setting my new client at ease, my avoidance of the matter at hand had provoked Mrs. Lukasiewicz to the brink of tears. Despite her crestfallen spirits, she flashed me a broad smile. I surmised that, over the years, she'd acquired the heavily etched laugh lines around her wide mouth as a defense mechanism to hide her true feelings. I quickly changed the subject and asked her why she needed my legal advice.

Unzipping the main compartment of her purse, she retrieved a folded pink legal form that immediately alerted me to the fact that she'd been charged with a criminal offence. Unfolding the Promise to Appear, her right hand shaking slightly, she pushed the paper towards me across the polished, wooden surface of my desk.

Zeroing in immediately on the short rendition of the offence —theft under $200—and the date that she was to appear in court —October 22nd, I then turned my attention to her date of birth —1927, and calculated that she was 63 years of age.

"This is all a mistake!" she blurted out. "I didn't intend to steal those boots!"

Her voice, when she became excited, had a screeching pitch that made me wince. I dreaded the thought of her losing control in court when testifying, and the trial Judge suffering the same reaction. Glancing back at the summons, I confirmed that indeed Mrs. Lukasiewicz was alleged to have stolen a pair of boots from Woolco.

"What happened?" I asked, lowering the tone of my voice in the hope that she would follow suit.

With much animation, using her hands for emphasis, she proceeded to relate her story.

"I couldn't decide on which boots I wanted to buy. I first went to Bata and tried on a few pairs there. Then I went to Woolco and tried on some more. I wanted to compare the heel of the pair that I'd chosen to those that I'd tried on in the first store." She paused to brush the curls of grey hair off her forehead. "And then this young man from Woolco stopped me and asked me what I was doing with the boots. I don't speak English. I tried to explain to him that I just wanted to make a comparison because I'm too old to wear boots on a high heel."

Her voice tended to rise to a singing cadence, but as she advanced towards her story's climax, once again, it ascended irritatingly into a screech. "He took the boots from me and told me to come with him and then I sat for a long time in a room. And then the police came."

She slumped back against the back of the chair and heaved a great sigh of relief, but the fear that I'd discerned from the moment that I'd shaken her hand in the reception area had not dissipated. Her eyes, like those of a caged animal, darted back and forth in their sockets. It was apparent that Mrs. Lukasiewicz had been an attractive woman in her younger years. She was tall for her era, and she carried her slim frame with dignified composure. Straightening her back, it appeared as though she was attempting to alleviate some pain in her neck and shoulders.

"Did you leave the store with the boots?"

"Yes," Mrs. Lukasiewicz answered, definitely. "But I didn't know that I was outside the store! I thought that the store was the whole mall." She pronounced the word "mall" haltingly, struggling with the vowel sound, enunciating it as one might say "mole."

"But you knew that one store was Bata and the other was Woolco?"

"After, yes," she said, nodding. "But not in the beginning."

It seemed far fetched that someone wouldn't comprehend that every store in a mall is a separate business from the next one, but it was also plausible that an elderly person from Communist Poland, where malls were non-existent and everything is state owned, might not have appreciated that Bata was a distinct legal entity from Woolco.

"Did you at anytime try to conceal the boots?"

"I was carrying this same purse," she said, raising it from her lap and setting it down on my desk. "I put the boots inside because I have arthritis in my hands." She stretched out her arms and showed me her twisted fingers. "It is easier for me to carry something on my shoulder." She raised the purse strap and then let it drop.

My spirits plunged. I questioned whether this older woman, only a year older than my own mother, was telling me the truth. "But you weren't trying to hide the boots?"

"No!" She shook her head vigorously. "The tops of the boots were showing."

Glancing again at her purse, I decided that indeed it was not so large that a pair of winter boots could be hidden inside. "Can you describe what the boots looked like?"

Mrs. Lukasiewicz stood up and pointed to her left leg, at mid-calf, to where the hem of her brown woollen skirt extended and explained that the boots were of that height. "Security took a photo of them. They are a chocolate brown colour, and have a decorative fake fur trim at the top."

"You only put the Woolco boots inside your bag to carry them back to Bata?"

"That's right. Please help me, Pani Barbara," Mrs. Lukasiewicz pleaded. "I'm not a thief. I've never stolen anything in my life!"

***

When I entered courtroom 407 just prior to 9:30 on October 22nd, Mrs. Lukasiewicz immediately jumped up from her seat in the front row of the public gallery. The courtroom was already crowded and I knew that it would be a lengthy morning docket. She was very agitated from having arrived much too early at the courthouse. Pointing to her wristwatch, she explained that she'd left her home almost an hour earlier to ensure that she'd make it on time. She looked very tired, dark circles ringed her milky blue eyes, her anxiety about finding her way to the right courtroom had likely kept her up half the night.

I chastised myself for not having arrived earlier, as almost a dozen lawyers had checked in with the clerk ahead of me. Mrs. Lukasiewicz, anticipating her own case being summoned at any moment, would no doubt suffer a mild heart attack every time the clerk called one matter after another.

Outside the courtroom, in the corridor, Mrs. Lukasiewicz immediately asked: "Will that be the judge who will preside over my trial?"

"I don't know," I said, shaking my head. "It could be him. It could be any of the others on the bench."

"Here," she said, handing me two folded one hundred dollar bills. "Please find out who it is and give it to him for me."

Scanning the corridors for who might have seen my client passing me the brown bills, I zeroed in on a couple of unsavoury characters, aimlessly hanging about, waiting for duty counsel or their own lawyers to show up. My imagination getting the best of me, I immediately visualized Mrs. Lukasiewicz on her way home, being stalked to the C-Train station and having her purse snatched. Steering her to a vacant set of armchairs in a quiet corner, I commanded her to sit down. "First of all, Canadian judges do not take bribes. Your matter will be decided on the merits. And, as I already explained last week when you came to my office, you are innocent. You didn't intend to steal those boots, and intent is a necessary element of the offence that the Crown Prosecutor must prove beyond a reasonable doubt in order for the Judge to find you guilty."

"But I'm not guilty!" she protested, her voice again rising into its irritating screech.

"I know that!" I retorted, in exasperation. She wasn't listening to me. I was beginning to understand what some of my older colleagues had said about clients only listening to what they wanted to hear. And my proficiency in the Polish language was limited when explaining legal terminology. I wasn't sure about my literal translation of such concepts as "reasonable doubt" and other evidentiary phrases.

Opening my briefcase to retrieve my Daytimer, I flipped to the pages for the week prior to her scheduled trial date. "I need to meet with you again, Pani Lukasiewicz, on the Monday before your trial. What time can you come into my office?"

"At four o'clock," she answered meekly. "Just like before."

"Okay." I patted her hand reassuringly, before rising to leave. "If you have any questions, please don't hesitate to call me in the meantime."

I came to regret those final parting words. Mrs. Lukasiewicz called me every second day but not with questions; rather, she'd decided on her own that her best defence against the charge was to convince me that she was innocent. After our first telephone conversation, wherein I took great pains to explain, once again, the impartiality of our judicial system, I became resigned to the fact that Mrs. Lukasiewicz would never believe that I didn't have more influence with the judges than I claimed. While she retold her story over and over again, about wanting to compare the heel of the boots to others at Bata, I formed the habit of working on other files at the same time, and consoled myself with the fact that at least she'd have her version of the events down pat by the time she was called to the witness stand to testify on her own behalf.

On the day of the trial, Mrs. Lukasiewicz was attired, as always, in her brown woollen skirt with matching blazer, and a crisp white blouse. I noticed, though that there was something different about her and, upon taking a second look, saw that she'd loosely knotted a bright rust and yellow coloured silk scarf about her neck. The scarf gave her otherwise pale, drawn complexion a little more pigment and detracted from the dark circles that perpetually, it seemed, ringed her weary-looking eyes.

Realizing that the brown suit was likely the only good suit of clothing that she owned, I felt a stab of guilt about the monies that I'd demanded that she deposit with me as a retainer for my services. I'd canvassed her eligibility for Legal Aid, explaining that my proficiency in the Polish language would almost certainly guarantee my appointment as her counsel, but she refused to entertain such an arrangement, stressing that she'd gotten herself in this mess and that she'd pay to get herself out of it.

Despite my confidence that she'd be acquitted after trial, as a precaution I'd inquired about her personal circumstances in the event of the worst-case scenario of having to speak to her sentence. Her husband worked nights as a cleaner and Mrs. Lukasiewicz babysat two small children for a younger, newly arrived Polish couple who relied on their joint income to get ahead. She took her two grandchildren with her so that both her son and daughter-in-law could also work. Both Mr. and Mrs. Lukasiewicz earned little more than minimum wage and, at their advanced age, their future prospects for retirement did not appear promising.

I asked Mrs. Lukasiewicz whether the Woolco security officer who'd apprehended her was in the courtroom. She nodded, turned her head to the left and pointed with her chin behind her. "He's the fellow with the moustache, and he's wearing a grey tweed jacket."

I took a seat at the side bar and studied the security officer for a few moments, hoping to glean some insight from his body language and appearance about what tactic I should employ in my cross-examination of him. Some witnesses reveal more when handled gently; others are apt to contradict themselves when questioned with more vigour.

My surveillance of the security officer was interrupted by John Ceres, the prosecutor, who, I sensed, still begrudged me an acquittal I'd garnered on another theft charge a month earlier. "What's with the boot lady, Barb? I can't see that you've got much of a defence," he said, his eyes darting back and forth over the contents of his open file. "She was caught red-handed with the boots in her bag."

When I didn't say anything in reply, John added: "If you plead her out I wouldn't oppose probation. You might try a conditional discharge but I'll have to oppose such an application. Too many of these immigrants are shoplifting."

Despite my junior status as a defence lawyer, I'd already learned to play my cards close to my chest and remained tight lipped about whether Mrs. Lukasiewicz would even testify. "My instructions, John, are to run this."

"Okay. Suit yourself. But it could be a while. There are two trial matters ahead of yours."

"All rise," called out the clerk, briskly entering the courtroom ahead of Judge Brian Morrison.

A change of plea application, followed by sentencing, was the first matter to be called. I took the opportunity to alert Mrs. Lukasiewicz to the delay in our matter proceeding. I was secretly hoping that

Ceres would run out of time to run our trial, at which time I'd consider disclosing to him Mrs. Lukasiewicz's confusion about shopping malls. Pre-trial discussions of such nature sometimes culminate in the Crown staying proceedings or withdrawing the charge altogether. It was a faint hope though, particularly since Ceres had just suffered a loss in my favour, so I kept my thoughts to myself and gave Mrs. Lukasiewicz last minute instructions to look the Judge in the eye from time to time while testifying.

To my surprise, Ceres decided to push my matter ahead of the other two on his list. Upon the clerk calling out her name, panic washed over Mrs. Lukasiewicz's face. Like a police officer directing traffic, I gestured with my right hand for her to enter the prisoner's box and advised the Court that my client required the assistance of an interpreter. The court orderly promptly wheeled a second chair into the prisoner's box for Mr. Sowa, a lawyer from Poland, with whom I'd become acquainted on the previous theft matter.

The security officer, contrary to my presupposed impressions, was a mild mannered, soft-spoken individual who did not embellish his account of the events. So much for my study of him beforehand!

Ceres ran through the routine questions, concluding with testimony regarding the photograph of the boots that the loss prevention officer had taken, the photo being entered as an exhibit in the proceedings.

I decided to begin my cross-examination, where Ceres had left off, and requested that the clerk hand me the photograph. Seeking the Judge's permission to approach the witness, I handed the officer the photo and asked him to estimate the height of the boots.

"30 centimetres. About 14 inches."

"Would you not agree, Mr. Davis, that it would have been impossible to conceal the boots in their entirety in the purse that Mrs. Lukasiewicz was carrying on that day?"

"Not necessarily."

"But in this instance, the top of the boots, particularly the fake fur trim at the top, were quite visible?"

"Yes."

"And Mrs. Lukasiewicz didn't hide the fact that she was carrying the boots in her handbag?"

The security officer shot a look of bewilderment toward Ceres who promptly rose to address the Court. "Your Honour, perhaps my friend could rephrase the question for the witness."

"Ms Janusz, please rephrase the question."

Nodding towards the Judge, I asked: "You'd already placed Mrs. Lukasiewicz under surveillance?"

"Yes."

"And while she was placing the boots in her bag, did she look over her shoulder to see whether anyone was watching her?"

The witness paused before answering. "No."

"Thank you. The tops of the boots. The fake fur trim were visible at all times?"

"Yes."

"And she was visibly surprised when you stopped her outside the store."

"Objection." Ceres was on his feet again. "The witness cannot testify as to the accused's state of mind."

"Please rephrase, Ms Janusz," the Judge instructed.

"Did Mrs. Lukasiewicz attempt to flee or to conceal the boots once you stopped her?"

"No."

"Thank you. Those are all the questions that I have of this witness."

"Case for the Crown, Your Honour."

"Thank you, Mr. Ceres. Is the defence calling any evidence?"

Rising, I gestured for my client to leave the prisoner's box. "Yes. I'd like to call Mrs. Lukasiewicz to the stand."

The clerk handed her the Bible and slowly, with pauses for the interpreter to translate, averred the oath for Mrs. Lukasiewicz to repeat back in Polish. I noticed her hand tremble as she handed the Bible back to the clerk and then she caught Judge Morrison's eyes and held them imploringly, for a moment.

I launched into my examination-in-chief with the customary questions about her age, marital status, occupation and the date of her arrival to Canada. On being guided through these mundane particulars, Mrs. Lukasiewicz appeared to regain some degree of composure. We had finally arrived at the definitive moment towards which we'd been aspiring since she'd first consulted me three months earlier.

"Mrs. Lukasiewicz, please tell His Honour what happened at the Woolco store on September 10th."

I'd heard her story so many times that I only half listened, and with the other side of my brain I focused upon Judge Morrison. Engaged in the routine task of taking notes of her translated testimony, he paused every so often and peered over his glasses at the witness. Mrs. Lukasiewicz in turn looked away from the interpreter and me from time to time, to make eye contact with the Judge.

Mrs. Lukasiewicz maintained her sporadic eye contact with the Judge throughout Ceres' cross-examination of her. It was only the third time that I'd run a trial through an interpreter, and I realized the distinct disadvantage that Crown counsel faced in attempting to shake the credibility of the accused, testifying on his or her own behalf. The intended biting nature of the questions in cross-examination were largely lost through translation. Ceres' aggressive tone failed to shake Mrs. Lukasiewicz's confidence in her entitlement to an acquittal.

"Redirect?" the Judge asked.

Rising reluctantly to my feet, I felt a gnawing discomfort about Mrs. Lukasiewicz's evidence. Ceres had scored some points, albeit minor ones, about her alleged confusion between Bata and Woolco. Something was lacking. I realized that I'd failed to portray, through her testimony, the differences in retail shopping between here and Communist Poland. "Yes. Just a couple of questions in redirect to clarify my friend's questions about shopping malls."

At no time had I prepared Mrs. Lukasiewicz for the line of questioning that I felt I had no choice but to embark upon. I was apprehensive about how she would answer. "Mrs. Lukasiewicz, if you had to buy a pair of boots for the winter in Poland, where would you go?"

"I would probably go to one of the two department stores in Krakow which carry boots and other items of clothing."

"And can you describe for His Honour how the shoe or boot department of the store is organized?" I sucked in my breath. Mrs. Lukasiewicz had become so obsessed with telling her story, over and over again, over the telephone, in my office and now in court, that I wasn't sure if she could rise to the occasion and switch gears to relate what life was like in her native country.

Her face momentarily lost its colourless pallor, taking on a red hue. She cleared her throat before answering. "Rows of boots would be on display on shelves, behind a counter, with a clerk or attendant."

As Mrs. Lukasiewicz began to speak, Judge Morrison leaned towards the witness stand and turned his head sideways.

She'd begun in an uncharacteristically lowered tone of voice and, as she continued, she articulated her thoughts with increasing vigour and confidence.

"There was never very much choice. Usually one would hear about a shipment of boots for winter and by the time you arrived at the store there would be a crowd of people, demanding the attention of the clerk, giving instructions about sizes and colours of boots. The clerk, if you were lucky, if your size was in stock, would hand you a pair of boots to try on. Then, if the boots fit you, you would hand them back to the clerk, who would give you a bill with the price written on. You then had to take that bill to the cashier who took your money and stamped the bill with 'payment received.' Then you would take the stamped bill back to the clerk who would wrap the boots in newspaper and give them to you."

"And is that the procedure for buying everything in Poland?"

"Yes."

"Even for food?"

"For food it is worse because when I left Poland two years ago we still had ration cards for meat, sugar, flour and other food articles."

"Are there any shopping malls in Poland?"

Mrs. Lukasiewicz broke out into a little laugh and shook her head. "No. There are no such places in Poland. Only small shops with less merchandise than the department stores. And the two department stores in Krakow practically carry the same things."

A hush had descended on the courtroom. There were not many people in the public gallery, but Mrs. Lukasiewicz's testimony, through the voice of the interpreter, preceded by her uncharacteristic youthful giggle, had caught the small crowd's attention.

"It is Communism. The economists calculate many years beforehand how many boots they must manufacture in each year for the citizens. There is very little to choose from. Some people, if the officials grant them a passport, travel abroad to buy clothing and shoes."

"Thank you."

"The witness may step down," Judge Morrison instructed. "Are you calling any more evidence, Ms Janusz?"

"No, your Honour."

"Final arguments, counsel."

Since I'd called evidence, I had the privilege of summarizing my case ahead of the Crown. Opening in the usual vein by stating that the Crown had failed to prove intent beyond a reasonable doubt and that Mrs. Lukasiewicz's testimony had raised a doubt about her intention to steal the boots, I stressed the fact that Mrs. Lukasiewicz

was a new immigrant, foreign to the shopping practices of Canada.
I refrained, however, from referring to my client's age. Judge Morrison, in my estimation, was likely not much younger than her, and
I was loath to imply that older persons are prone to becoming confused in unfamiliar situations.

Ceres, on the other hand, stressed that Mrs. Lukasiewicz had
placed the boots in her handbag in order to conceal them and that
she'd been apprehended outside the boundaries of the store. Arguing that it was inconceivable that she didn't know the difference
between Bata and Woolco, he concluded that, through the un-
contradicted evidence of Mr. Davis, the Crown had proved, beyond
any reasonable doubt, her intent to convert the boots to her own
use without paying for them.

"Thank you counsel," Judge Morrison said. "I found Mr. Davis
to be a credible witness." Pausing to allow Mr. Sowa to translate his
oral judgment, he shifted his focus back and forth between Crown
counsel and myself, but appeared to direct his gaze more upon me.

"He testified that on the day in question he observed the accused in the shoe department of Woolco, trying on boots. And
then putting a pair of boots, the ones portrayed in Exhibit 'A,' in
these proceedings, into her handbag. Mr. Davis followed her past
the checkout where she did not stop to pay for the boots, and then
out into the mall, where he apprehended her."

The beat of my heart accelerated. I visualized myself having to
console a very distraught Mrs. Lukasiewicz, trying to appease her
by suggesting an appeal of her conviction. Commanding myself to
calm down, I tuned in again to Judge Morrison's judgement.

"I find that the accused is an elderly person, who has not been
long in this country. Her knowledge of English is, practically
speaking, nonexistent. She has testified through the assistance of
an interpreter. And as I observed her demeanour in the witness
stand, I too found her to be a credible witness, forthright in her
answers to Crown counsel's questions.

"Given her age and unfamiliarity with our economic system, I find that the accused became confused when attending Westgate shopping mall. I find further that the choice of goods available under our economic system is a phenomenon that could only have compounded her confusion about different retail stores in shopping malls. Having considered the evidence in its entirety, I conclude that I harbour a reasonable doubt about the accused's intention to convert the boots to her own use without paying for them, and I therefore find the accused not guilty."

I promptly rose and thanked His Honour, leaned towards Ceres to thank him as well, and nodded to Mrs. Lukasiewicz as confirmation that her matter had been successfully concluded.

Mrs. Lukasiewicz could no longer hold back her tears. She took both my hands in hers to thank me.

"Dziekuje Pani Barbara!"

"You're welcome."

Releasing my hands, she reached into her pocket. Retrieving two folded brown bills, she placed them in my hands. "Please take this for me as a bonus."

"No," I protested. "You've already paid me for my services." I pressed the bills back into the palm of her hand.

Shaking my head, I turned to leave, walking briskly, as was my habit, towards the C-Train station. Stepping out into the sunlit mid-December late afternoon, it dawned on me that Mrs. Lukasiewicz would never believe that we'd won her case on the merits. Notwithstanding my protestations, my lectures about the Canadian justice system, and despite the Judge's sympathetic reasons for his verdict, I realized that she'd always harbour the misguided belief that I'd used part of her retainer to illicitly sway the Judge.

Letters From Ceinwen*

 ᖱ

Iris Jones (Mulcahy)

IN THE 1920's a teenage girl from Swansea, Wales, immigrated to Canada after the loss of her parents. She was to join her married sister in Dundurn, Saskatchewan. Occasionally, she wrote to her friend, Elizabeth (Lizzie) Williams, later to become my mother, about life in her newly adopted country. When my mother died in 1975 the letters came into my possession, and I brought them back to Canada on returning from my compassionate trip home.

My husband and I had immigrated to Canada too, in 1955, living first in Toronto, then London, and finally coming to Edmonton, Alberta in 1988, bringing the letters back west again, not quite to their original source in Saskatchewan, but to a neighbouring province.

In 2003 we rediscovered the letters among paper memorabilia contained in an antique lap-desk inherited from my Auntie Beck. Once the immigration anthology got underway the possibility arose of including them, not as elements of an essay or story about migration, but by letting them stand alone as tiny glimpses of a young immigrant's life on the prairie in the early part of the twentieth century.

These letters are not offered as literature, but merely as a means of opening a miniscule window onto the experiences of a young immigrant girl, enthralled, and perhaps to a lesser extent, intimidated by her new surroundings. They should be read only for what simple information they provide, and for whatever they might contribute to our ability to imagine the rest of these young women's stories. The grammar, spelling, and particularly the punctuation, have been faithfully reproduced from the originals.

*Pronounced Kine-wen

***

c/o Mrs Hector Bethune
Dundurn
<u>write</u> *soon*   *Sask*
Canada

Dear Lizzie:
Did you think I would not write to you? I would have written sooner only I've been so busy that I've forgotten everything only about having a good time. All throught last Winter I had a lovely time, I took dancing lessons in "Saskatoon" and then I went to "Whist drives" and "Dances" and really I've had a lovely time. I think "Canada" is the next best country to "Wales" as the people are so kind and nice. Well I've done nothing since I've come here Lizzie only learned to be lazy but I think I'm going to "Colegiate" for a year & then going to a business College to take a course in Stenography. I'm going to start next month "August" so I've a whole month to wait yet. I was in Saskatoon Fair last week and indeed I had a good time but it seems one family did not. There's a family living in "Kindersley" about ten miles from here and they went to the fair and left their two year old girl at home with the servant and mind you, they cant find the little girl anywhere. The servant said she went out to the barn and when she went to look for her she had gone, but the saddest

part of it is that last year their little boy was lost and about four weeks later they found his leg and boot outside a "wolf's den" & they think that the same thing has happened to the girl, its awfully sad isnt it. There is an awful lot of wolves around here you can hear them howl in the night and believe me it sounds rather dismal. Well I've nothing more to say now only that I'm learning to drive a car. My sister & Bro has one a "McLaughlin" and I've been trying to drive it but I cant, I go all over the prairie when I try. I'm afraid I'll have to give it up as a bad job. Well, Good night, its getting late and if I don't go to bed now I'll be meeting myself getting up.

Best love from
Ceinwen Clement **x x x x**
remember me to all
& give any girls my address whod like to write to me
I've forgotten some of them

***

c/o Mrs Bethune
Dundurn
Sask.
Dear Lizzie,
Your letter reached me just as I was coming home from school and I was glad to hear you were fine. So your sister is married. I told my sister about it at least, I showed her your letter and she says she remembers her well and she also said you were a good letter-writer. How are the girls over there. Remember me to "Lizzie Mutton" and "Sarah Barkwell" & also "Sarah Winifred Thomas". I suppose you see her sometimes. Did you have your photo taken? I didn't yet, you see its about thirty two miles to the nearest Photographer and so its hard to get there, but maybe "Hector" "Mary's Husband" will run me up in the "car" some day when he's not busy & I'll get it taken then but mind to send yours along I'd love to have one of you. Of course I've got a few snaps of myself I

took with my "Kodak" but they're not very plain. Are you still working at Kardov. You've been there a long time now haven't you & have they finished the "Park" up on "Cefn" and how about the "chip shop" is it still there. I suppose you'll think I'm awful inquisitive but really its good to hear about everything over there. It seems that I'm such a long ways off. I was to a "Pantomime" in a place called "Druid" a few nights ago and there was a dance after it for the Hospital & so I didn't get home till about three-o'clock next morning. I danced till two o'clock. I go to a lot of dances & love dancing, its great fun believe me. Well Mary is calling me. I have to go & Ice a cake. I always have that job but I like it because I can eat some of the Icing. "Ha Ha". I've asked a few girls up to supper to night & they're going to stay all night. Mary lets me have some girls here sometimes and we have a jolly time. We have a piano & Gramophone & little Ethel has put a record on & she's keeping time pounding on the piano so you can guess what a horrid noise is here. Well I guess I'll dry up now.

p.s. remember me to all   Lovingly Ceinwen
x x x x x

Watchful for The Parallels and Overlaps

Romeo Kaseram

IT IS THE time of year now when I look out into the backyard to see the pine trees drooping with fresh snow. I'm fortunate to have a view of majestic trees. There are the ones that lost their leaves early last September and are now stark and wiry against a steel-grey sky; then there are my neighbour's crab-apple trees, the magenta fruits of late summer now wind-dried and dark like faded rubies; and there are those stately pine trees, with branches bowed with snow now as if to modestly hide undergrowth.

After every snowfall I look for tracks from the neighbourhood jackrabbit. Sometimes, I'm fortunate to discern after careful, short-sighted scrutiny, the solicitous trembling of its white coat before it scampers off in a lope, its ears levered downwards and back for speed, the black hole of one eye dilating and swivelling with the dread of pursuit.

And then, over the fences, beyond the tall pines and the steaming vents on roofs, is the sun. I could never stop being surprised at how cold and distant it is in winter. This far north, at such a low angle, the sun becomes a small, luminous speck dully but bravely shining in a sky filled with gradations of white and a harder grey.

"The sun like a ten-cent piece in the sky," a Trinidadian friend once remarked.

"You mean like a dime," I said, my feet too firmly planted here in the Canadian north.

"No, man. It smaller than a dime. It is like a ten-cent piece from Trinidad! That is how cold this place is!" Such was the quick reply. The tone was couched in censure, which was immediately confirmed. "Where you come from? Like you forget how small the ten-cent is or what?"

I pondered my colleague's point of reference. Was it like the inches and millimetres thing—the latter affording more precision for measurements? And so, my friend, in describing the sun and the temperature, had ignored the standard here and had instead reached for an even smaller measure. The Trinidadian coin, with a smaller diameter than the Canadian dime, became the currency of choice to describe the size of the sun in one of the harshest months of winter. The resulting hyperbole was superb; his intuitive rendering of the metaphor was poetic, the iambic pentameter effortless. Many Trinidadians are gifted this way.

I thought I'd run this by another friend whose sum total of experiences could only see the sun as a huge dime.

"What if there was a similar unit of currency but smaller in physical dimension?" I wondered. "Wouldn't an intuitive but comparative approach using both units offer a more dramatic, poetic and perhaps original route for a description of the weather?"

Indeed, it would, we both agreed. We also understood that what we had witnessed was the meeting of two worlds in a confluence of experiences that was as effortless as it was dynamic. This wasn't a case of two solitudes—instead, it was two worlds that could blend seamlessly into each other, working at times in unpredictable ways to both enhance and enrich.

I treasure moments like these because it helps me to better understand the experiences I encounter, and undoubtedly, the world around me. When my friend reproached me for forgetting the size of a Trinidad ten-cent piece, and even worse, for not applying it to the real world, it led to a moment of illumination, which I would have probably missed had I insisted that we use the local currency. I'm constantly on the lookout for these moments that reveal parallels and overlaps between the two worlds I know—the Trinidadian and the Canadian. It also helps me understand who I am and what I'm becoming.

Take a recent experience, for example, at the grocery store. In the fruit section, by the mangoes that thrilled the eyes with shades of rose, burnt orange and healthy tropical yellow, a woman's hands were wandering through the rows, feeling for firmness. At the same time her eyes were appreciating the hues, and her sense of smell was keenly focussed.

My mind immediately found the memory I was retaining, waiting for use one day, of a time on Frederick Street, in Port-of-Spain, Trinidad. There, with the sun blazing downwards on exposed heads, another woman was standing by the back of a van that held boxes of apples wrapped in soft tissue and sitting in trays similar to egg cartons.

"But what is this," she remarked ecstatically. "All these apples have different colours of red. And they smelling nice too, too bad! I feel to eat one right now." She picked up an apple, deeply inhaled its fragrance, and enthusiastically polished it on her loose, open-necked cotton shirt.

"I buying this one, mister," she said with finality to the vendor.

By the time this memory had played itself through, the woman had picked up a mango with the same finality.

I treasure these little discoveries in the parallels and overlaps between two worlds. As it goes, though, it is a currency I'm still learning to use.

Marking Territory

Anna Mioduchowska

"THE CAPELIN MUST be coming," the old man dragging a sheet of particleboard across the uneven road said in our direction. "Just look at the gannets." After two weeks in Newfoundland I knew the difference between a seagull and a gannet. I also understood the expression on the man's thin face as he pointed at the flock of elegant white birds with wing tips that could have been dipped in the tar used for waterproofing fishing boats. As if responding to an invisible baton, they stopped flirting with the wind, pointed their strong beaks down and all together shot into the water of Little Harbour.

Early June is not the best of times to come to *The Rock*. The clouds were so thick when we approached the airport, we saw nothing through the window until the runway literally jumped up at us and the plane landed with an alarming *thump!* The next plane, and all the others that followed that day were turned back to either Toronto or Halifax—standard procedure. Standing outside in the long line-up for a taxi, in rain that came down in sheets, I understood why the talkative Newfoundlander, on his way to his parents' golden anniversary party, had earlier asked why Andrzej and I weren't going somewhere warm, like Florida, the local choice of getaway. What he didn't know was that I had an anniversary of my own to celebrate that week. Exactly 40 years before, the Polish ocean liner *Batory,* carrying my family to Canada, had sailed past here, through the Strait of Belle Isle.

The smelt-like capelin arrive in droves around the middle of June to lay eggs on the high tide mark of the Newfoundland beaches. At least it used to be droves, so that people could scoop them up with their hands. The significance of their arrival is tattooed into the soul of every Newfoundlander. Cod follow this floating buffet, and whales follow cod. The old man's ancestors might have come to the island almost four centuries ago, as the first settlers, or *planters*, a funny name considering how inhospitable this place was and still remains to agriculture.

They might also have come in the 18th century, on one of the boats fitted out by English fish merchants. The crews of these vessels were made up mostly of indentured servants, some of whom had been captured in street round-ups in poor neighbourhoods. They were bound to work two to three summers before they were released, often with empty pockets. Condemned to live on the small boats for months and work around the clock in conditions that boggle the modern imagination—even the dead were disembowelled and salted, like the cod, and brought back for burial at the end of the season.

Many of the fishermen chose to escape before their term was up, and make a life for themselves in one of the communities along the coast. It was a life of work often no easier than the one they were fleeing, but they were free men—at least in theory. The crash course in Newfoundland history I have received since landing at the St. John's airport contains few romantic elements. Whoever they had been, whatever they might have done for a living before arriving here, the old man's blood definitely has a much higher salt content than theirs had.

At thirteen, surrounded by parents and siblings, plus all our possessions in a few wooden crates, suitcases and smaller bundles, I had no eyes to see past the picturesque coastline. Even as late as a month ago, Newfoundland was little more than the farthest possible point on the map from Edmonton, and the poorest province in the country, where icebergs float by in June. Ignorant of its long history of struggle against natural elements, and ordinary human oppression, I had thought it a perfect place to celebrate my anniversary without stirring up too much dust.

As it happened, Andrzej and I spent June 9th, the first clear day since our arrival, exploring what remains of the Colony of Avalon, one of the first permanent European settlements in North America. It is an archaeological dig a short drive from St. John's, and we had made our way along the coast leisurely, stopping often to better appreciate the same landscape that terrified the planters arriving here centuries before; the harshly chiselled coastline and the ocean constantly frothing with annoyance at having to go around this obstruction.

We had a small illustration of what the ocean was capable of, in the form of the ruins of a small fishing village where we stopped to eat our sandwiches. Not much more than outlines of houses were left on the rocks after a particularly ferocious storm in the 1960s. It was hard to believe when one looked down that the waves could climb this high and still carry enough energy to rip up the stone and wood structures. Beauty, as always, in the eyes of the beholder, I contemplated with pleasure the strangely shaped tamaracks and stunted spruces dotting the mostly clear land—the Downs—stretching away from the road. The planters must have wept. As my parents in Edmonton had, the first few years, when they thought they were out of their children's, and each other's earshot, their prospects very much like this landscape, their bodies sore with fatigue.

Strange name, Avalon, obviously imposed on the place by someone *come from away*. The *livyers*, (from "live here"), like to joke that Cabot, who received 30 pounds for discovering Newfoundland, should have got 30 years instead! Avalon conjures up all that the island is not. It is not a sunny postcard. Beaches are lined with boulders, not soft sand, the wind blowing from the ocean is cold, and so fierce at times it is impossible to stand upright—a pleasure we have tasted already—and black flies have sharp teeth. I have not seen any bucolic meadows or pastures. Somewhere on the island a whole tribe of people, the Beothuks, lies buried. Europeans who took their place, went through a Gehenna of their own, and now the island is slowly depopulating for lack of economic opportunities, i.e. jobs.

"I've seven children," an old man fishing for mud trout in one of the numerous ponds along the TransCanada Highway told us a few days later. "Six of them live around Edmonton and in Fort Mc-Murray." I didn't ask about the seventh, when I gathered the man was alone on the island. So many brought into the world, fed and clothed over the years, educated, and still no one left to invite the old father to dinner on Sunday. I did not tell him our only son has chosen to live in the States. ("For now," I always catch myself adding when someone asks.) The pain of absence might be just as real but the circumstances (like our son having other choices), make all the difference. "People are selling nice houses, with all the furniture, for next to nothing."

Taking a break from his fishing, the man pulled from the trunk of his rusting Chev a newspaper supplement with the summer festivals in Newfoundland. "I'd saved it to give to someone like you" —meaning, someone who would stop and talk with an old man. In St. John's, an elderly woman walking her dog invited me to her home for coffee. Her father had been a prominent doctor in the city, and she had received a university education, but her sons were gone from the island.

In Glovertown, a town located by a long fjord, in which the water is so calm it is easy to forget its origins, an exchange of greetings with a woman carrying two bags of groceries home was also followed by a conversation about the absent children and grandchildren. A small, wiry 80-year-old, she directed our eyes to the impressive hill she climbed in the summer to pick blueberries. She was carrying home some salt pork, and, unfortunately, we had to turn down her invitation to come taste her homemade pea soup the next day. The thought that in the near future the homes of these hospitable people might come to be inhabited by summer cottagers *from away* was not pleasant.

If one looks at the map of eastern Canada long enough, Newfoundland begins to resemble a giant kite hovering over the entrance to the Gulf of St. Lawrence. Its nose relatively smooth, the rest is ragged around the edges thanks to the glacier which, during the last ice age, carved numerous fjords, bays and coves in the rocky coasts. They made perfect harbours, where fishing vessels hid from storms, and where fishermen disembarked to salt and cure their catch before taking it back to Europe. Out of poles and branches the men built fish flakes, platforms on which the cod were spread to dry, to which they returned every season.

Originally, no one wintered on the island. The boats came as soon as the weather permitted it, filled their holds, and returned home before the season of storms began. The only drawback of this otherwise good system was that when the fishing boats were gone, crews of other vessels, French, Dutch, or English, often burnt down the flakes. So did the Beothuks, to salvage iron nails, which they refashioned into arrowheads. It didn't take long for someone to decide that the best way to prevent these costly acts of vandalism would be to leave a few men behind to guard the beaches. I doubt if there were volunteers. The prospect of spending several months exiled in this wild place, inhabited by people who painted their bodies red, and who knows what else, with no women to keep house and warm the bed, must have seemed more terrifying than the ocean itself. Familiar demons seem always less of a menace than foreign ones.

Before exploring the Colony of Avalon, we had stopped for lunch at a restaurant that sits just outside the dig. I thought it might be a good day to finally try the *cod tongues and scrunchions*, listed on menus as a Newfoundland delicacy. When men used to come home with their fish, they immediately cut out the tongues, and their children ran from door to door with full buckets to make a few pennies. The tongues on my plate were deep-fried, and seemed *liquidy* inside the crisp batter. This was unfortunate because less than half an hour ago one of the archaeologists working on the Avalon site had told us they were expecting to find the burial grounds in the summer. "Bodies which had been buried in lead caskets will have liquefied, it should be interesting."

The scrunchions were small cubes of lightly fried pork fat, and bore a vague resemblance to a food I remembered from childhood. When available, pork fat was diced and slowly fried in a big pot with salt and sliced onions. Cooled, the rendered fat was poured into glass jars, where it congealed into a white mass studded with crunchy bits called *skwarki*. We used it on potatoes, on pasta; spread on a large slice of bread it replaced the more rarely available ham or sausage. I avoided the waitress' gaze as she took away my plate with most of the scrunchions left untouched. The ghosts of Avalon planters, and of my own ancestors, followed the sweet morsels all the way to the kitchen, and with their sad eyes watched them being scraped into a garbage pail.

George Calvert, Lord of Baltimore, had purchased this land in 1620, from a fellow who knew better, and the following summer sent Captain Wynne with 11 men to start the settlement. After a passage which Wynne described in a letter to his employer as "somewhat tedious, which happened by means of much westerly winds, and not without some foul weather," and which anyone working on the ship would probably rephrase into "we were seasick much of the time and could barely touch the miserly portions of salt pork, mouldy biscuits and stale stinking water, but still had to work day and night," they immediately set to cutting down trees and building the main house, plus lodgings for themselves.

During our '61 Atlantic crossing, in tourist class, I had had my first taste of grapefruit, wild boar and Brussels sprouts, served on a table covered with a gleaming tablecloth. Ironically, *Batory* belonged to a People's Republic, where ordinary citizens could only dream of eating like this, so long as they kept their dreams to themselves. Mostly borrowed money had paid for our tickets.

"For the country and climate: it's better and not so cold as England hitherto," wrote the brave Captain Wynne to George Calvert in 1622. And again, "the air here is healthful, the water both clear and wholesome, and the winter short and tolerable, continuing only in January, February and part of March; the day in winter longer than in England, the nights both silent and comfortable ... Neither is it so cold here that last winter as in England the year before ... I have known greater frosts ... and far greater snows in our own country."

A mixture of half-truth and invention, adding up to a gigantic lie, as Calvert was to discover in the winter of 1628/9, which he actually spent in his beloved Avalon. The same lie which was disseminated throughout Europe in the first part of the 20th century about life on the prairies, where settlers were needed to break the land, and which is often spun in private correspondence, by people who did not want to lose face with folks *back home.* I am not sure I understand Captain Wynne's motives. Was he simply feeding his employer the line he wanted to hear? Did he honestly believe that, sent enough supplies and people, he could build a viable settlement in Avalon, in spite of the harsh climate, lack of agricultural land, and isolation? "Such vegetables we grow in our garden Your Lordship! Radishes as big as a man's fist. Such grains we harvest, and beans. You should see the hay from our meadow ..."

Letters must be the most misleading of all documents, yet again and again people accept the information conveyed in them by the words, and by the spaces in-between, which they mine for hidden meaning and interpret according to need, then use to make life-altering decisions. Photos add to the confusion. Two intelligent people, my parents must have known that, without English, and with three children, they couldn't possibly expect an easy time of it. When I recently found the lame translations of my mother's university diplomas and teaching certificates, typed by my earnest young hands on a portable typewriter, with scratched out spelling mistakes, my stomach did a strange dance. But the photos that had been coming with the letters from Edmonton over the years had showed smiling faces, lovely houses, lawns, cars, scenes from camping trips to the mountains where deer and black bears walked right up to the car.

It did not matter that the houses were burdened with 25-year mortgages, or that the cars weren't paid for. The very fact that an average citizen could take out a mortgage and move into the house immediately placed Canada in a different galaxy than most countries. Not to mention such frills as freedom of movement, access to information through public media and books, and the fact that academic merit alone guaranteed one's children a university education.

Climate and land unfit for agriculture were the main enemies of the planters who landed in *New Founde Land*. But there was also the gold to be had—cod so plentiful at the beginning one simply had to lower a basket over the side of the boat. All the fishermen got out of it, however, was a permanent backache. The gold made its way into the pockets of middlemen, who introduced old ways into the New World. Fishermen fished, their women split, salted and dried the cod, and merchants took it away and paid not in coins but in merchandise, which naturally was so expensive that the fishermen always ended up in debt. The merchants sold the cod for a good price, quickly made a killing, and became prominent members of society, first in England, and later, as the island grew more populated, in St. John's or one of the other centres. This system continued well into the 20th century.

We walked around the Avalon Colony and I tried to see it through the eyes of a woman who might have stepped off a boat in 1622. The men have already put up some buildings and a protective palisade by the time she arrived, so it wasn't as much of a shock as it must have been to them. Still, what business did people have living on a narrow strip of land jutting out into the ocean? The Atlantic had made the crossing so miserable, the very sight of water brought back the nausea, and here she was going to spend the rest of her days looking at it. Rock and dark woods rose up away from the shore. The men looked like savages, the hunger, the *need* in their eyes unbearable just now. How would she build a life out of the few belongings scattered around her in bags and baskets? *"Blessed be you harsh matter, barren soil, stubborn rock, you who yield only to violence, you who force us to work if we would eat. Blessed be you, perilous matter, violent sea, untamable passion, you who unless we fetter you will devour us ...,"* wrote Taillard de Chardin in the *Hymn of the Universe*. I could almost hear the woman cursing.

I plumbed my memory for what I might have felt at 13 when the five of us stood in the Montreal port, surrounded by our crates and suitcases. By the time the customs officers were done with us, we had missed our train to Edmonton. According to the directions on a sheet of paper I found in the small archive in my mother's desk, different coloured labels had been handed out to all the passengers, according to final destination. We were to wait for someone to take us to a hotel; the shuttle bus and hotel wouldn't cost us anything. I do remember the calm, smiling woman in a navy blue uniform and funny bonnet on her head who approached and invited our small group to follow her. After registering us in a small hotel, she left, and we never saw her again. (Once my parents had spare cash again, they began making regular donations to the Salvation

Army, a tradition I continue the way I continue to bake honey cakes for Christmas.)

Another document in the same archive is a six-page customs list detailing everything we were bringing with us. Five warm coats, five sweaters, five pairs of winter boots, warm underwear, woollen hats, scarves and mitts. Obviously my parents knew what to expect weather-wise. Eight cooking pots, a set of china, nine spoons, 21 forks, six knives ... medical thermometer; outside thermometer; 12 hankies. Every stamp in my brother's stamp collection is listed, and every coin in the coin collection certified not to be a museum piece. Books, a few records, a few paintings; equipment for developing photos, which my father never used again; a clarinet he never played again; and a harmonica. Two hammers, a pair of pliers, five files, a table vice, hand-held vice, screwdrivers, a sewing machine, all of them well used in the years that followed.

What I could not find on the list were any of the emotions accompanying the move. Just as I can't unearth anything I might have felt for the next two years. My parents believed children transplant easily, so I suppose much of my emotional energy went into not disappointing them. Even my body obliged, by reverting back to childhood for several months.

So much is needed to build a new life, and most of it one learns on the job. There are no untruths contained in the lists of supplies Captain Wynne asked to be sent from England: Wheels, guns, brewing kettle, clapboards, iron, steel, bricks, "linen for bedding and apparel." He requested masons, carpenters, quarrymen, slaters, a tailor, gunner, a doctor, a minister. I imagine the only thing my parents wanted to send back for was the language, and for old friends to fill the void in which they had found themselves. My mother's letters, written from Canada during the first few years and preserved in another desk, did not lie either. The despair in them is so palpable it is impossible to read more than one at a time. Yet, chained to a thankless job, to her grammar books and responsibilities at

home, she still managed to develop a fierce love for her new country
and kept up to date with politics until the day she died 35 years
later. My father's homesickness never really abated, but he found
an outlet in the wilderness, where he took us at every opportunity.
Few families I knew heated up their Christmas dinner on a Coleman
stove, and ate it on a picnic table by a frozen lake. With time, all of us
became infected with his bug.

Newfoundland, as opposed to Alberta, has the feel of an old
country. Its inhabitants, isolated from the rest of the world, have
made it theirs with generations of hard work and sheer staying
power. Their roots have spread through the shallow topsoil and
penetrated all the available cracks in the rock. In Alberta, a large
percentage of people I know are *from away*, from other provinces,
other countries. They float in the rarefied atmosphere breathed by
nomads, their hearts divided, their loyalties often unclear to them,
they can pack their bags at a moment's notice, and often do. Their
foundations are like those of houses built on rock, yet the old
houses here, sturdy box-like structures made to resist the wind,
and to be dragged over the ice when one wanted to move across the
bay, or even floated on water, know exactly where they belong. No
wonder Newfoundlanders forced to seek their livelihood elsewhere
often suffer from such acute homesickness.

Sandwiched between two generations of nomads, I have stayed
put for 40 years. The only move I have ever truly desired has been
from the outside *in*. My savings from the first year in a full-time
job took me all the way to Quebec City, where I thought Canada
had begun. By the time I was 25 I had crossed the country by train
at least three times. My face glued to the window, I tried to pene-
trate and memorize the kilometres of land rushing by. It wasn't religious fervour that spurred me to walk into Lac St. Anne during the
annual July 26 pilgrimage that brings thousands of native people
to the site they consider holy. I watched the MPs duke it out on
Parliament Hill in Ottawa, and touched the bare dinosaur bones

that stick out of the ground in the Badlands. In Prince Rupert's graveyard, wolves come to pay respects to the dead. Marking my territory like one of those wolves, I took a ferry from Prince Rupert to the Queen Charlotte Islands—Haida Gwai—the furthest bit of Canada to the west, and the last place to be reached by Europeans.

Newfoundland closes the bracket, the whole country more or less mine now. Or so I would like to think, and it seems I am not alone. Chiu, an immigrant from Singapore whom we met at a banquet in St. John's, told us he celebrated his 38th anniversary of coming to Canada by cycling from Victoria to Newfoundland's capital. No van loaded with provisions or TV cameras followed him, he was not raising funds for a cause. He was simply pedalling himself a home. The irony that Newfoundland did not become part of Canada until the year I was born, that it was not entirely willing to do so, and that its status is not quite equal to that of the older provinces, would only strike me when I began to put my thoughts down on paper.

Little Harbour lies outside Twillingate, "Capital of the North," and one of Newfoundland's oldest seaports established in the 18th century, when fishing vessels on the way to Labrador stopped in the Notre Dame Bay to replenish their supplies. Modern Twillingate is really a series of islands in the Notre Dame Bay, connected to each other and to the main island by causeways built about 35 years ago. Previous isolation has helped to preserve the vocabulary and speech patterns of the language which the original planters had brought with them. The *livyers* are proud of what they call their Shakespeare's English. No longer a busy fishing port, and no longer isolated, Twillingate is a favourite tourist destination, and our last stop before leaving the island.

On the way back to our B & B, Andrzej and I stopped to see if the iceberg we had seen earlier was still there. Of course it was, a mountain of ice does not move very fast, but it seemed to have completely changed shape. I double-checked through binoculars to make sure. The only explanation was that it had hit bottom and flipped. Locals ignore icebergs unless they block their harbours, are truly spectacular, or unless they are running boats full of paying customers to view them. In spite of all the local savvy I have picked up, I all but jumped with excitement.

We celebrated our last evening with a glass of golden Lakka, a Finnish liqueur made of bake-apple. The bright yellow berries grow in Newfoundland and Labrador and fetch a good price because like raspberries, they have to be picked one by one. Our B & B host supplied us with ice-cubes which were crushed *berggie bits*, fragments that had detached themselves from an iceberg and were fished out with an ordinary fishing net. Icebergs are composed of compacted snow, and that means zillions of air bubbles. The bits in our glasses melted quickly, fizzing as they released air trapped for 10,000 years. "That's pre-Babylonian times," Andrzej mused, and we bent over our glasses to breathe in antiquity.

According to our host, a few entrepreneurial souls have set up a company in St. John's to export *berggie bits* to New York, where they are served in drinks at upscale establishments. We raised a toast to their continuing success. "And to our safe return home," Andrzej added. *Home* means Edmonton. Although he had come to Canada at 32, alone, with only a suitcase, and no possibility of going back until the fall of the Berlin Wall, Andrzej did not seem to need grand gestures. Simply through working at the same university for several years, and raising a family, he grew a sturdy root system in the new soil.

Avalon Colony thrived until 1698. Its history is like the weather in Newfoundland, *moody.* After just one winter, the somewhat embittered George Calvert, Lord Baltimore, decided to leave Avalon in the care of "... fishermen, that are able to encounter storms and hard weather." Nothing like absolute lack of choice to make you hardy, dear Baltimore! In 1638, Sir David Kirke established residence in the mansion house and Avalon became known as Pool

Plantation. The colony prospered: the lord and his lady could promenade along the cobblestone street that ran through the settlement, that has been partly unearthed by the archaeologists; they had the use of the very first flush toilet, constructed in such a way that the sea came in and took away the waste; they partook of the vegetables that grew in the kitchen garden, and enjoyed milk and meat, compliments of the cattle that grazed on pastureland nearby.

Civil war resulted in David Kirke's incarceration in an English prison, and his subsequent death. Lady Kirke, who stayed on in the colony with her sons, became a successful fish merchant. She survived the Dutch raid of 1673, which saw much of the colony plundered and destroyed, but luckily she did not live long enough to see the final demise in 1696, at the hands of French troops, who looted and burned the entire settlement, took several captives as hostages, and drove the rest back to the English West Coast.

My parents managed to educate their children, and saved enough for a modest retirement. My father paid a few visits to his native Poland, and never stopped dreaming of going back permanently. My mother travelled back once, at 84, and serenely announced on her return that she was ready to die. At their request, their ashes are buried in the Rockies.

***

All the correspondence quoted in this essay comes from a collection of letters transcribed by P.E. Pope, spelling and punctuation modernized. They can be found in "Documents Relating to Ferryland, 1597 to 1726," at www.heritage.nf.ca/avalon/history/documents.

Of Death and The Immigrant: Some Journeys

Michael Mirolla

MOUNT FOREST, ONTARIO, Canada: It's dusk, the late autumn dusk of northerly climes. Through my living room picture window, I watch the shadows of maple leaves in the front yard float gently down like forgotten souls. Some still decked in their finest plumage, verdant and smooth-veined to the end; others as drab as the camouflage outfits of combat troops, as wrinkled as the faces of centenarians. But no matter what their attire, no matter what shred of earthly glamour they cling to, they're alone now as they float by, no longer part of the green world that nourished and held them fast.

Normally, my first reaction would be: "Okay, I'm sitting here, Tim Hortons coffee mug in hand, and I'm watching the leaves fall after one of those flash frosts. The type that finally brings the parsley to its knees. Now, how can I best make use of this observation? This watching? It ought to be good for something, don't you think? Good for something, that is, other than mulch and humus for next year's potato patch. A chapter in a novel, perhaps, undoing pathetic fallacy with a stroke of the mighty pen? Or maybe the setting for a short story, writing what you know reduced to its most minimalist sentiments? At the very least, the theme for a poem?

Ode Upon A Falling Leaf perhaps? Or maybe, *Ode Upon The Last Falling Leaf, Dedicated to O. Henry?*"

Instead, my thoughts are of death. Specifically, of death and the immigrant. And the long-distance telephone call. For the person who, at a tender age, has left relatives, friends and neighbours behind, the long-distance telephone call is the most common signal for death's arrival. To the untrained ear, there's no special ring announcing the demise, a long way off, of someone with whom you may have frolicked as a child. Who may have been the best man at your parents' wedding. Or was handpicked to be your godmother at a time when such duties were taken very seriously indeed. But to the immigrant, used to dislocation, that ring is unmistakable. And it doesn't help that, more often than not, it's a jarring alarm in the middle of the night.

The news is quickly followed by the realization of unbridgeable separation, a split between the source of sorrow and its object that can never be healed, never be made whole—even if one were to take the next flight back. It's almost as if, by mutual agreement (between the living and the dead), an empty spot is designated to take the place of the deceased. A null. A zero. The corpus delicti gone missing. All evidence erased and its existence scrubbed clean. And the mourners weep in a vacuum, denied full catharsis. Or the opportunity to confront—and perhaps come to understand finally —the face of mortality.

✳✳✳

Jelsi, Campobasso, Molise, Italia: *Travelling through the landscape of dreams, you emerge at last in a place that has haunted you since you first formed thoughts. That continues to torment and curse you for having abandoned it some 60 years before. Even if you were but a child at the time. Even if it wasn't your choice. Even if you have often expressed a desire to return. Even if you've rejoined its citizenship ranks.*

The vagueness ... the shimmering ... the undefined unease ... is trouble-
some, product, as you are, of (supposedly) more logical dimensions. Of
the New World where parallel straight lines and clear attitudes are
meant to prevail. There arises a veil, a tangible barrier dividing both
time and space, undermining the very foundations you've struggled so
hard to lay down. That sense of displacement you've tried for so long to
uproot—and the irony of uprooting a displacement always not far from
the conscious surface.

And then suddenly the mist lifts. Suddenly, the town squats high
and solid on its precarious ledge, the impression of age and permanence
marred only by a tangled nest of TV antennae—and the profusion of
grey and blue mini-satellite dishes, expectantly pointing towards the ef-
fervescent sky from tiled rooftops and decorative iron balconies. In the
valleys below, the cross-patched fields, alternately brown and green, fal-
low and cultivated. They've been there forever, it seems, divvied up from
parent to child, shrinking to postage-stamp size, mourned over, greedily
sought after—the result of feudalism, the cause of unending feuds. In
one of those valleys, at the cross-roads, there stands a convent-cemetery,
the disparate rows of tombstones under dappled sunlight. The family
crypts. The ossuaries. There, in the courtyard behind the recently reno-
vated church (courtesy of generous government grants from the right
political party), your grandmother on your father's side lies buried. And
two of her sons. And two of her daughters. Their not quite natural
photos peering out from another world. And you find yourself thinking:
The dead do indeed speak the loudest, adding voice to voice without
cease: Here, you are the mist, the vagrant, the just-passing-through
Giovanni-come-lately. The New World arriviste.

✳✳✳

My grandmother. One longed to kneel before the solid coffin, to
gaze into the waxy face, to write *finis* graffiti-like across all those
pent-up emotions. But it was a listless, unresolved farewell. Truly,

there was no one to say good-bye to. News of my grandmother's long-distance death arrived, not by phone but at our doorstep one morning—literally. In the form of a very distraught and dishevelled Cassandra holding out a fresh pot of meat sauce before her. No Cassandra, in truth, merely a second-cousin relative who would, in the time-honoured Old World tradition, take over the cooking and other household chores that day. As for my parents, they shrank into themselves, weighed down by a sorrow made all the more enigmatic by the lack of a casket (and the presence of a lifetime of unresolved memories and pains).

***

In your dreamscape town, it's Sunday and groups of ancients, their faces mask-like and elemental, sit on stiff wooden chairs in the narrow piazza and watch the ever-increasing, ever more suffocating traffic. Both human and vehicular. Crowds flowing forward like images of the undead. Uninvited. Unstoppable. The eyes of these ancients are a washed-out blue, liquid, brimming with tears constantly threatening to fall but never quite achieving it. The earth beneath them is the dust of centuries, pounded and shaped in the same way as their faces—like somewhat cracked mirror images really. Or in preparation of one soon becoming the other. Flesh into dust. Some stare out at the high floating clouds. Long after they've abandoned the cycle of ploughing and sowing and hopefully reaping, they can't help looking up at the sky in an attempt to predict the weather. Others play vicious games of cards the whole day through, shouting vindictively in triumph, whimpering like feudal slaves in defeat. Still others argue politics, swear at the church and its saints, say their prayers fastidiously. And wait to die. The grandchildren run about carefree, not yet aware of being caught between an ultra-past filled with the smell of freshly-turned earth and a post-modern future of satellite TV and DJ Francesco. Adolescents, dressed in the latest hip hop finery, run up and down the piazza: the girls giggling in dialect over the newest rap idol; the boys in choreographed movements designed to show how cool and unconcerned they are. Their parents, arm in arm, stroll more leisurely, stop to converse with friends and neighbours, and step across to avoid those with whom they've most recently quarrelled.

***

Of course, one mustn't forget the false alarms, when the dark wings swoop down only to mock. Only to make sport. Like the time we received a telegram from Vancouver that a long-awaited relative on his way from Australia was arriving "morte" on the next scheduled train. Dead? But that wasn't possible, everyone kept saying. It couldn't be true. Before leaving Australia, he'd called and the family had gathered round to hear his voice. He'd been in tremendously high spirits and bursting with youth and health, anxious to start his new life in "America". But telegrams don't lie—immigrants know that better than most. So we were prepared for the worst when a coffin was lifted from the baggage compartment. We were prepared to weep and to ask why. Or to weep and not ask why. And then the relative stepped off the train—a little tired but definitely alive. "Dead?" he said, as we gathered around him, touching surreptitiously to make sure he wasn't some sort of ghost. "I don't think so." The puzzle ... that particular puzzle, at any rate ... was soon solved: Whoever had transcribed the telegram had written down "morte" instead of "martedi".

***

The house where you were born: Your father's house. The house he left more than 60 years before, vowing never to return for fear it might rip his heart out. The windows are shuttered. A massive wooden door prevents a view of the courtyard. You look for clues. For marks of distinction. For

*family or clan uniqueness. But there is nothing really to differentiate it
from the other ageless houses along Piazza Umberto Primo. Solid, stoic,
slightly melancholy—like a matron whose chief joy is to reminisce about
when she was young and carefree. Now, the house belongs to the widow
of your father's brother, one of the brothers buried at the crossroads
convent-cemetery, and not even she is in good enough health to live
there. A stable runs the length of the courtyard. This was where, once
upon another time, the horses of weary travellers were housed—while
their riders enjoyed food and drink in the inn your father helped run. In
the night, amid the shadows, you are transported into a world where
gypsy caravans ringed the town. Where their pranks and mischief both
disturbed and made more bearable the orderly and tedious procession of
peasant life. Where, occasionally, revenge was sought for a magic po-
tion gone wrong—or an innocent remark taken as an insult.*

***

My very first memories of death by long distance—death of any
kind, to be exact—came when a young cousin of mine (whom I'd
never met) succumbed to leukemia. She was the daughter of one of
the uncles who lived with us while working to save enough money
for an eventual return home to land and family. One of the men
whose rough-hewn bodies shared our house but whose hearts were
all back in the gold-flecked fields below an obscure town in an obscure region in an insignificant country. Her death occurred at
precisely that moment when the dream imagery of childhood loses
its grip, to sink screaming into the subconscious—and spends the
rest of its time trying to crawl back into the upper layers, much to
the delight of psychotherapists.

I do remember straight-backed wooden chairs placed around
the kitchen walls—but not the familiar yellow melamine table at its
centre. That had been displaced, leaving permanent indent marks
in the linoleum floor. And I remember dour-faced adults attired in

black and sitting very still, handkerchiefs on their laps, eyes rimmed with red. I realized then it was a special occasion of some sort. Why else would I have to put on my Sunday best on a lethargic weekday? And why else would my father be home in the middle of the day, rather than standing before that bakery assembly line, pulling loaves of sliced white bread onto waiting carts? I remember asking myself: Who are all these people dressed in black? Why are the men so close shaven their skins are blue? What are they crying about? Why are all those rosaries rattling and clacking together? Who are they mourning with such painful expressions on their faces? In my youthful unknowing, I looked around, examined the area closely, felt for something out of place. Try as I might, there was no one there I could see that might need crying over.

Three or four other young children who'd been dragged along by their parents also stood around, trying not to giggle or get into mischief. After a few minutes, noticing that the adults were paying no attention to us, we gravitated to the backyard in search of something—anything—to do. Aha, one of the older (and presumably wiser) boys said, pointing up through the light drizzle (itself a poor attempt at pathetic fallacy): Look at that. A flock of blackbirds had strung itself along a nearby telephone line, swaying with the wind. For some reason, those blackbirds offended us. Perhaps it was their simple naturalness. How dare they act as if it were just another day? As if nothing of any particular significance had happened?

We decided, through some unspoken code understood by all of us all at once, that they had to be taught a lesson. Something along the lines of: When humans mourn, the rest of the animal kingdom had better beware. Or at least prepare themselves for sacrifice. So, with slow, measured movements, we reached into the garden, hefted stones and took aim. On a shout from the older (and now not so wise) boy, we fired our missiles in unison. But the blackbirds swaying lazily on the wires were much too alert for us. Even before the first projectile was anywhere close to the telephone wire, they had burst into the sky, scattering in all directions. Into a black blot like spattered ink that I would later identify with other much more subconscious ink blots. But, at least, these blackbirds had the common courtesy to put in an appearance, which was more than could be said for the corpse.

***

Room of generations. Cold stone flowering. Worn-out marble stairway you must have climbed uncounted times as a child. And then it hits you: in this very room, in this room and no other, you were born. And your father before you. And who knows how many before him. A palimpsest of lives peeled away layer by layer. And now you stand there unmoving, riveted. Yet unsure of what to do next. And you fight with all your strength to hang onto your just-regained memories. You push off the tides that want to sweep you away. That will wear you down to dust. That will eventually emerge victorious. That will make of you one more palimpsest.

***

By haunting coincidence, I had my first brush with on-the-scene death when a close friend, barely in her mid-30s, passed away—also of leukemia. In this case, there was no separation whatsoever, no gap to reach across. In fact, it was painfully near, suffocating in its presence like a plastic bag shoved brutally over one's head. And the memories are of the process itself, the premature winding down of life like (for those who still remember) the tell-tale sound of a record on a turntable when the plug is pulled. Or the squeal of a wind-up doll whose batteries need recharging. Still, now at least the lessons can be learned, I told myself. Can be programmed into future tragedies and modes of behaviour. Can be used to ease that constriction. So, what do you learn? Well, you learn that death, in many ways, is the ultimate joke. You learn there's often an element of raw slapstick to it. Of farcical incongruity. That you're the butt of a dark, echoing laughter that seems to be aimed directly at you but never actually acknowledges your presence. You learn that, no matter what the astrophysicists might say, it's the one true singularity on our event horizon, the point beyond which you're forbidden to approach.

In the weeks before my friend was admitted to hospital for the last time, one of the symptoms was a blockage in her intestines so painful she found it excruciatingly painful to sit down. And so she would pace back and forth in our hallway looking a bit like The Little Tramp, bow-legged and wistful, trying to keep contact with our floor—and by extension reality—to the absolute minimum. Or, in desperation when all else failed, she'd stand on her head against the bathroom wall for minutes on end in the hope of dislodging whatever it was she felt had invaded her body. If only it would leave, if only she could flush it out, if only she could convince it to find a more inviting host ... everything would be fine again. And we could all get on with our lives. If only ...

In the hospital itself, there was the harrowing wait; the patter of the doctors as they tried ever newer and more radical treatments; the get-well cards strung along the window sill; the visitors' talk of camping trips and midnight dances come summer; the pile of best-sellers still to be read (can't go without finishing Danielle Steel's or Dan Brown's latest). But inexorably came the morning. And then the afternoon. And then the night. The final tickings of the clock. Objective. Antiseptic. Sterile. The last few seconds. And another ... and another. The thought out of nowhere: Where's that S.O.B. Zeno when you really need him, when you want to make sure the halving will never end? One moment she was alive, gripping a pencil like the good mathematician she'd been; the next ... there was a rustling of sheets, a brief movement of legs—and a letting go. A final letting go. Life reduced to stench, to rot, to fetid smell. A liquid loosening. The remainder coming up zero.

I had to ask myself ... I just had to ask myself: How did it feel to be there, face against the slimy curtain? To peek in as the body spasmed? To be privy to her last sputtering blubbering words: "Please. Just one more second. That's all I ask. One more second"? Was it more "satisfying" than all those long-distance calls in the middle of the night? Did it make more sense than the tersely-worded telegrams that spelled out "death" and "Tuesday" in tossed-salad languages but failed to produce the needed evidence? I had to ask myself ... I just had to ask myself.

***

You stand then in your mother's former olive grove looking back on the town, which appears like a protective fortress across the valley. Everywhere, there are signs of improvement: freshly-paved roads, a new school, new signs welcoming tourists and announcing the village as "Il paese del Grano," a new spirit of revitalization and an air of renewed hope for the future of a place that once lost more than 50 percent of its population to other lands. That once saw an emigration so vast, there were fears it would not survive. Would simply settle back into the ageless dust. Become just one more layer in an ever-buried history that was ancient even when the Romans and the Saniti jostled and jockeyed for position and power. But it has survived and there are town council meetings and agro-tourism bed and breakfasts and even Internet cafes ... There are boisterous youths anxious to practice the latest hip hop movements ... And there are smug faces who now congratulate themselves on not having become migrants and strangers to their own land. Still, what you are left with, what leaves the strongest, most lasting impression, are the voices from the past: the abandoned stables stained by shadows; the original stone cottages settling into old age and struggling to remain upright; the crumbling rural school where, if you listen carefully enough, if you really strain, you can still hear the ferruginous children reciting their additions; the relics from millennia past, recently risen to the surface; and the pockmarked cobblestones pitted to signal the relentless coming and going of centuries.

Soon, too soon, you'll be struggling to squeeze all the gifts into over-stuffed suitcases, and, unable to do so, forced to leave some of them—like a part of yourself—behind. Soon, too soon, you'll be looking back and waving, knowing there are some, despite any wishful thinking, you will never see again. And, soon too soon, the town will be gone once more, vanished into the mist that swallows all in the end. And you'll be left rolling down a parallel-path highway that will surely, without a doubt, and yet miraculously, lead you back from whence you came. To the New World. La Terra Nuova. Where everything is fresh and young and the precarious balancing act between past and future has yet to make its presence felt.

***

The coffee cup emptied, the last grains spilled into the sink, I rise and make my way to the back shed, frosted earth crackling beneath my running shoes. There, I put on a pair of sturdy rubber boots and thick gloves, and rake in hand, begin the task of piling the newly-fallen leaves into neat mounds.

So what if it's now the middle of the night? What better time for this task?

Besides, I've left the answering machine on—just in case.

My Immigration Medical

Carol Moreira

Friday, Oct. 31ˢᵗ

I'm seeing the immigration doctor—it's the final step, after almost a year of moving and other preparations that will allow me to live in Canada with my Canadian husband and children.

The doctor is not particularly friendly. The forms I've been sent by the immigration department, and have arrived with, are not the forms she was expecting. She waves one of her forms at me, demanding to know if I have it. She says the forms the government sends her are numerous and confusing, and now the immigration department has brought out a second form with the same number as one already in existence.

I make sympathetic noises; I imagine processing innumerable faceless strangers must be unrewarding work, but I don't much like being treated like a faceless stranger myself.

I answer her questions about my medical history rather curtly. All at once, I feel resentful of my husband for wanting to come home, thereby forcing me to undergo this indignity. He didn't have to go through this to live in England. He has spent the last eight years in England simply by virtue of being my husband. He has been free to come and go and use the U.K. health service as he pleased.

When the doctor ticks the box for *permanent resident* my heart sinks, even though I long ago agreed to move to Canada for the sake of our children's future.

"How long have you had this lump?" the doctor asks five minutes later as she conducts a breast examination. I am shocked and a little embarrassed, because I hadn't even known I had a lump. I have never had a lump. I feel my breast. She is right. The lump is hard and bouncy and about a centimetre across in the inner/upper section of my right breast.

"Don't worry," she says. "It's probably nothing, but you'd better get it checked."

She tells me to go for my immigration chest x-ray, and says that I'll have to return to the same clinic in about three weeks' time for a mammogram. She asks if my husband is with me, and I say no and feel a stab of self-pity. Now, I'll have to make my way across a strange town knowing I have a lump in my breast.

Outside, it's a beautiful day, and I manage not to panic as I find my way to the hospital on the map, and then navigate the long corridors in the basement depths of the building to pay for my chest x-ray.

I have a gloomy few minutes in the waiting room looking at the anxious faces of women waiting for mammograms. But the chest x-ray is soon over and I stumble back to where I think I left the car. It's still a glorious day and the streets are packed with students. Halifax is a beautiful city. I wonder if my own children, aged ten and six, will ever be students here, and then I wonder if I will be alive to see them as young adults.

I find the car and my way out of the city and onto the road that leads to our new home by the Atlantic Ocean. Thirty minutes later I'm picking up the kids from their new school with a sense of accomplishment—I didn't once take a wrong turn or inadvertently move onto the left side of the road. I'm childishly pleased with myself. I've never enjoyed driving but I'm doing pretty well, and I haven't even taken my Canadian test yet.

Back at the new house the children go out to play with their new friends, and I make dinner alone, thinking how much I miss having them in the house. In England they were usually at home because the streets were too congested and their friends too busy with after-school activities for them to be anywhere else. Here, they are free. Nova Scotia is a kids' own Garden of Eden, but I miss them.

Later, the kids go trick-or-treating with their new friends. I sit by the fire, missing the English friends with whom we always went trick-or-treating. When tiny children knock on the door, I give them candy with a heavy heart. Now, I'm really wondering what is going on in my breast.

At bedtime the wind gets up and hurls itself off the ocean and onto our house. It's so noisy I'm unable to sleep. When I finally lose consciousness, I dream of a small house on an urban street with thick curtains that pull around the windows like a womb.

Saturday, Nov. 1ˢᵗ

Shopping: but first we have to drive for 30 minutes along lengthy highways. The driving is easy, there's not much traffic, but I'm intimidated by the endless kilometres of pine trees. This land is so vast and empty. I don't tell my husband how his native landscape horrifies me, for I'm ashamed of the feeling; I have often said how much I love travel and what fun it would be to live quietly in the country.

The mall is enormous and the wind howls through it. There are no beautiful and interesting old buildings to soften the look of bleak modern stores. I feel a surge of homesickness so strong I feel sick. As my husband drives us home, I weep behind my sunglasses.

My father calls, from Ontario, where he is visiting his Canadian girlfriend. "Perhaps you have a mild case of agoraphobia," he suggests and I laugh, slightly insulted. Later, I acknowledge he is right. I even have agoraphobia in the house.

Monday, Nov. 3rd

Jane, an English neighbour and long-time resident of North America, bangs on the door. I am embarrassed to find that a friendly English face and accent make me weep. I tell Jane about my breast lump and sob on her shoulder and then Jane takes charge. She makes an appointment for me to see her doctor, just to make sure there are no delays in getting the mammogram, and then she brings me books on breasts and a tin full of freshly baked cookies. Jane tells me that, if it is cancer and I stay in Canada for treatment, she will hold my hand.

Tuesday, Nov. 4th

Ploughing through Jane's books on breasts, I discover the five-year survival rate for a 1-cm lump is only 75-80 per cent, which doesn't seem too good. I find I can't look at the line drawing of a full mastectomy. I refuse to think about the kids. I go for a long walk and get chased by unfriendly dogs wandering on their own. I resolve to get a stick to take on future walks. I must walk or I will go mad.

I go to a nearby corner store for milk. There is a strong smell of kimchi, a Korean dish of fermented garlic and cabbage, and I realize the owners must be Korean.

"I lived in Seoul for a year," I tell the man behind the counter. He looks startled and his eyes mist. "It's a wonderful city," I say, lying. He nods.

"How do you like Canada?" He shrugs. It's all right, he means, but it's not home.

I leave the shop. Seeing him has reminded me that I have often lived abroad. So, why should I be so homesick now? It seems being an expatriate is not the same as being an immigrant. Expatriates always go home. I wonder why I hadn't realized this obvious difference before. Perhaps I hadn't wanted to anticipate problems. After all, the reasons for moving were so valid. Southern England no longer offers much quality of life—neither does Seoul for that matter. The Korean storekeeper and I are both here for our children.

I drive into Halifax and go to a bookshop. I see a book on being an immigrant and almost buy it, but the face on the cover is so miserable I resist and decide to muddle through on my own.

That evening, we watch a documentary about British archaeological sites. My eyes drink in the pictures of Britain. In bed, I dream about England. I am stretched out in my mother's garden. My arms are hugging the earth and my cheek is pressed flat against the green grass.

Wednesday, Nov. 5ᵗʰ

Jane brings round more cookies. We discuss the vicious fast-growing cancer her friend has recently beaten. "The doctor dismissed it, but after just a month the bugger was growing," Jane says. "She had a terrible time, but she's all right now."

I read that some breast lumps can be massaged away and attack mine with determined fingers but it keeps bouncing back like a rubber ball on the surface of the sea.

Thursday, Nov. 6ᵗʰ

I get irritated bumbling around the local supermarket because I can't find the things I want, and I'm baffled by many of the vegetables, particularly the extraordinary variety of brightly-coloured knobbly squashes. I can't find caster sugar. It's just fine sugar, my mother-in-law tells me later from her home in Halifax, just look for very fine sugar.

In the parking lot, there is an instant when I think I recognize a blonde woman with twins. Then I remember that the family I know are in England, and I don't know this particular blonde woman or her twins, and my eyes fog up and I resolve to get out of the house more now I have almost conquered my fear of the roads.

Later, my husband gets a movie to distract us from my breast, and brings home *About Schmidt*. I find the dead wife episode depressing. "Sorry," says my husband, "I didn't know the wife dies in this one."

Friday, Nov. 7th

I consider flying home for the mammogram, but the cost is prohibitive. My mother, on the phone from England, sounds almost hysterical with worry, and my mother-in-law in Halifax sounds worse. I resolve to be resolutely upbeat and not to talk to them about breasts anymore.

"The children have lost their English accents," my mother says reproachfully. I agree.

"So soon," she laments.

I agree again. It is startling how quickly children adapt.

"They'll probably end up with those Mid-Atlantic accents," I say and there is an empty silence on the end of the line.

My husband has to go to Boston for the weekend. I read more books on breasts and tell all my female neighbours about my lump. This garners me sympathy, and gets dinner invitations for the kids and me. We spend the next three evenings in our neighbours' houses, and I feel more at home as a result.

Sunday, Nov. 9th

I go to the Korean store. The owner's six-year-old daughter is practising the violin behind the counter. She is producing a nice sound and her father is pink with pride.

My husband comes home with a movie for distraction. *The Life of David Gale* is a very depressing movie and has a woman dying of leukaemia. Sorry, says my husband.

Monday, Nov. 10th

My husband and I go to the hospital for my mammograms and ultrasound. We cough up $440 and hope the insurance company will pay later. The doctor says my lump is probably a cyst that has bled in on itself, but he will do a biopsy to make sure. Reassured, we return to find the kids at Jane's, high on sugar.

Later, I drive the children to basketball practice. First, I drop off my husband and son. My husband is coaching, which our son finds very exciting, as in England my husband was a weekend-only dad, thanks to a long commute into London. Now he works at home and is always available for fun.

Next, I take my daughter to basketball and drive back for husband and son. Altogether, it is two hours on the road in the dark and the rain. Driving along, I yearn for our former easy urban existence in England. I feel bereft.

I feel that I have lost my country and my role at the centre of the family. Now, my husband is the main parent, the fun one who knows the good places to go and the entertaining things to do. I feel diminished by moving to his country. I wonder if stress really can cause cancer. If so, this is my Canadian cancer, the manifestation of my conflicting and repressed emotions over the last year.

In bed, I dream about taking off on my own with a rucksack on my back, leaving home again at forty-two-and-a-half to see what I can achieve. I'm sure that now they are in Canada my husband and kids could manage perfectly well without me.

Monday, Nov. 17th

Due to my husband's work, I have to go for my biopsy alone, but the staff members are very friendly. The lump is close to my chest so I have to squeeze my head, neck and shoulders into unnatural and cramped positions to enable the puncturing machine to do its job and remove five tiny cell samples. I feel like the plump, pink, apple-shaped pincushion my mother had when I was a child. My breast looks vulnerable lying on the cold metal slab and I am surprised by how much it bleeds.

The doctor says that, after all, the lump is solid. This increases my alarm, as Jane's books have taught me that cancer is solid. The nurse reads my face.

"Probably a fibroadenoma," she says.

"But I thought only young women get those? I'm 42."

"I got one last year," she says. "And I'm 41 and my sitter has one, too."

I go home and wait. My mother calls from England; she still sounds desperate. I decide to ignore what the books say about alcohol being a risk factor for breast cancer, and pour myself a very large glass of wine.

"What will we do if it *is* cancer?" I ask my husband. "I'm not even eligible for treatment in the Canadian health system."

"We'll all move back to England," he says, as if it would be the easiest thing in the world.

"But the children love it here," I say. "Perhaps it would be better if I went home alone and stayed at my mother's."

"No," he says. "We'd want to be together."

I feel a stab of self-pity—he would have been treated in the English health service, no questions asked. It seems it should work the same the other way round.

"Perhaps the Canadian system *would* pay," I suggest. "After all, no one has actually said no."

This does not seem very likely; after all, the immigration medical is presumably held to weed out people with expensive diseases. I try to call the immigration department to find out but cannot get through. This is the fifth time we've tried to call immigration and have not been able to establish contact.

I wonder if we were badly advised by all the people who said it is easier to apply for immigration status inside Canada than from without. If this is easy, I cannot imagine what it is like to apply from abroad. I decide to wait and hope for the best. It is probably not cancer anyway.

The wind howls again at night and I have trouble sleeping. I resolve to get some sleeping pills after my daughter comments on my exhausted appearance.

"Mum," she says. "You look so old I'm afraid you might die soon, and I'm only ten."

Tuesday, Nov. 18th

It snows and I have to drive the family to basketball. I've never driven in snow and ice before and I'm nervous at the wheel. My husband offers to drive. I decline. "Seeing as we are now in Canada," I say coldly, "I think I should learn to drive in the snow, don't you?"

Later, my daughter is worried. "Mummy, you shouldn't snap at dad. I'm worried you might get divorced," she says, her voice emerging quiet and reproving from the darkness of the back seat of the car.

The next day, I have to ask my husband how to write a cheque —again. I wonder if he has noticed how stupid I'm being about learning to write a cheque in Canada. In England I managed our finances, so my new incompetence must strike him. I am doing it deliberately, of course. I resent having to learn even the simplest things all over again. I am being very childish.

Friday, Nov. 21st

We still haven't heard about the biopsy, even though the doctor at the hospital said it would only be a three-day wait. I call the local surgery to inquire. The receptionist says she will find out. She calls back to say the laboratory has lost my sample. An hour later, she calls to say the tests are not completed. At 9 pm, a doctor calls to offer words of encouragement. I realize she is calling just because I have to get through the weekend, and I'm struck by her kindness.

Saturday, Nov. 22nd

I visit Pier 21 in Halifax, the former landing point for immigrants to Canada, and now a national museum. The place is wonderful. When I watch the movie about immigrants, I cry.

When the narrator intones: "Can you imagine what it is like to pack up all your belongings, to say goodbye to your family and leave your native land ...?" I start to sob, although I try not to, because I am sitting among a group of teenagers who are far more interested in flirting with each other than in the movie. "It's true," I want to tell them. "It's very difficult, and I didn't even *know* how hard it would be."

Afterwards, I congratulate the staff on the video and, when I realize Pier 21 runs on voluntary help, I offer my services. Then, I start to cry again. Embarrassed and appalled, I promise not to cry every time I come to work.

"Don't worry," the young manager jokes. "It'll make it a more authentic experience for our visitors."

I return to the bookstore and look for the book I saw on immigration, but can't find it. I'm not even sure I'm in the right store.

My mother-in-law takes me to her hair salon. I opt for a new short cut. I haven't had short hair since I was a child. I am not sure if the cut is a sign of regressing or accepting—both my fear of cancer and the need to make a new life.

Monday, Nov. 24th

Still no word on the biopsy. The receptionist at the surgery promises to chase it up. I try to be patient.

Friday, Nov. 28th

Lesley, another neighbour, lends me the novel, *I Don't Know How She Does It*, by Helen Reddy. Lesley has tried hard to make me feel at home; she has lived abroad herself, and I am grateful for the support. But the book depresses me—it's about mothers struggling and giving things up for their kids. I wonder if I have given up too much. I try to continue with the novel I started writing in England, but the words are flat and uninspired.

Saturday, Nov. 29th

I collect my mother from the airport. Alone in England, her nerves consumed her, and she has decided to come to see us.

"You *look* well," she says, tearfully hugging me, and I feel a guilty irritation that I suppress. Look, I'm plodding along okay, I want to tell her, please don't weep all over me.

Sunday, Nov. 30th

The temperature has plummeted. I have never been so cold, and I'm fascinated by the extraordinary weather. I go out to look at the seawater in the bay. It's frozen a glassy aqua green, and mist is billowing thickly over the surface. I realize that the bay has been different every day since we arrived. Urban streets, with all their residents and visitors, don't change as much.

I watch our Russian neighbours tobogganing down the hill near their house. They don't speak much English but they have already told me why they came here. "Peace," they said. Later, my kids shriek with disbelief when they see people walking on a lake.

Monday, Dec. 1ˢᵗ

Mum and I go into the surgery and suggest to the receptionist that we would like to *know now*. The receptionist calls the laboratory and, a few minutes later, the same doctor who called me at the weekend, shows us into her office.

"Good news!" she says, as warmly as if she were treating her own sister. "It seems to be a fibroadenoma. Totally benign and nothing, absolutely nothing, you have done has caused it."

I remember what Jane's book said: 40 percent of women with breast cancer think they have caused it themselves. I've noticed how many *you-have-caused-your-cancer-with-negative-thinking* articles there are in the newspapers. So many women must be suffering terrible self-recrimination.

"What *did* cause it then?" my mother asks.

The doctor shrugs. "Could be caffeine, could be hormones. Some lumps are even caused by knocking the breast."

My mother gasps. "Do you remember? You whacked yourself when you were moving out of your old house."

I grin, slightly embarrassed. I do remember now; it hurt like hell. How could I have forgotten?

Wednesday, Dec. 17ᵗʰ

The immigration doctor calls to say all my tests have checked out and she has sent the papers off to immigration. "How nice of her to call," my mother says warmly.

I join the Halifax Newcomers' Club—apparently there are Brits among their members. I would like to meet some other Brits. I think of the Pakistani women I taught English to in England. I'd been frustrated when I realized that the women were more interested in just being together in class than learning English. It used to annoy me; I was not running a coffee morning after all. But now I understand their need to be together. They were women living with the grief of losing their villages and families. Many of them were depressed. Now, I know I don't want to be like them. I don't want to be one of those permanently wounded women.

Tuesday, Dec. 23rd

We've been unable to contact immigration or access their web site to see how my application is progressing, and my health insurance will run out soon. I feel trapped. When will I be able to work? I volunteer at the local hospital.

We go to watch our daughter play basketball, and I find I am now just as enthusiastic about the game as the other parents. I like basketball; it's so much faster than the English equivalent, netball.

I talk to one of the other mothers about my need to get out of the house, and she asks if I want to come to her running club with her. I flush with gratitude and am embarrassed that the emotion shows on my face.

I listen to the CBC while making dinner. I'm becoming irritated by their politically correct agenda about the importance of multiculturalism and diversity in Canada. It's not so easy to actually *be* diverse here. It's not so easy to be the one diverse element in an otherwise Canadian family.

Tuesday, Jan. 20th

The kids are off school because of a snowstorm, and it's too cold to go out. My daughter says that, if I can't settle in Canada, she too will return to England, although she would rather not.

My husband says he will return to England also, but I have seen the way he watches the landscape when we're in the car. He looks lovingly at the lakes and trees as we pass them, and I feel the same when we're in Britain. He's so happy to be home. The truth is that he wants to live in Canada with his Canadian children and I want to live in Britain with my British children.

I decide that I must stay, at least for a few years. I look out of the window at the bay and realize that I have made progress; I am fascinated by the bay and am no longer intimidated by the landscape. The children are happy, my mother-in-law loves having us nearby, and my mother loves visiting. This is an adventure, as my son remarked last week.

Wednesday, Feb. 3rd

I start volunteering at Pier 21. The staff members are fun and it's interesting work. The place makes me realise what an emotionally complex issue immigration is. Later, I hear my daughter talking to the boy who used to live in our house. They sold to us, and he now lives over the hill.

"I miss my old house," he says.

"You can come round anytime," my daughter says.

"Do you remember when you first arrived you said it was *your* house now?" he asks.

"That's because you told me it was *your* house," she replies. "Anyway, that was a long time ago. That was then, this is now."

Tuesday, April 6th

I keep an appointment to see a surgeon in Halifax. He says he will remove my lump if I want. I say, let's not bother, it's not causing any more trouble, and he nods. "Come back if you change your mind."

As I leave his office, I feel impressed with the Canadian health system. My sister in England has had a breast lump for years. No one knows what it is. Her doctor has told her not to worry unless it grows. She has not had to go through worrying tests, but I think, on balance, I'd rather know what is growing in my breast.

Later, it snows heavily and the children leap with excitement. They build igloos in the garden. "I used to build igloos and snow forts with my father," my husband says, happily joining them.

Thursday, May 23rd

My documents have finally been returned by the immigration department. Soon, I'll be able to apply for a permanent resident's card. All these months of invisibility, during which I've been neither able to leave Canada nor exist properly within it, are nearly over. My breast lump has shrivelled although a new lump, created by the trauma of the biopsy, has emerged and remains obstinately buoyant. I hope that, after the summer, I'll be able to lead a normal life here. And one day, who knows, maybe I'll feel equally at home in England and Canada.

The View of a Writer:
'I am Canadian Enough'

(From *The Globe and Mail*, April 16th 1980)

Jane Rule

RECENTLY, WHEN I visited a seminar on women writers in British Columbia, one student said: "You're criticized for being too American to be considered a Canadian writer. How do you feel about that?"

I was born and raised in the United States. I didn't come to Canada until I was 25. Nearly everything I've published was written after my arrival in Canada, but my first three novels and a good many of my early short stories draw on my American growing up and European travels. Even my fourth novel, set in British Columbia, has some American or ex-American characters. In my fifth all the main characters are Canadian, but two of the six leave Canada for the United States. If readers are looking for a body of work devoted to Canadian identity, they have reason to complain about mine.

Though I have been a Canadian for some years and have lived half my life here, my work will always be flavoured by and sometimes focussed on my U.S. past. In that, I have much in common with numbers of other Canadians who are immigrants, but it is easier for the self-conscious Canadian to accept, as part of Canada's reality, nearly any other past citizenship before an American's. Canadian immigration authorities do not accept "American" as an answer to ethnic background. Even if one's ancestors have lived in the United States for hundreds of years and include not only English, German, Dutch, French, Greek, Italian, but some Indian blood, "American" won't do. "Where did your great-grandparents come from? "Canada," I said. "English" is, therefore, my official ethnic background, for Canadian is no more acceptable an answer than American.

Even though there is great resentment against that giant to the south of us, which controls us not only politically and economically but culturally, the United States is seen as no more real than Canada. The realities are the great and ancient civilizations of Europe and the East, out of which each of us must claim to come. Or what? Be mistaken for a "savage"? Surely one of the shared roots of Canadian and U.S. unease about national identity is that we have systematically destroyed the culture we discovered. I still find it curious that, in so heavily populated a state as California, many of the areas Indians chose to live in are still under-populated wildernesses.

The super-patriotism of Americans, which Canadians find so distasteful, is not the calm superiority of the richest and most powerful nation in the world, but the bragging of an uncertainly young culture, afraid of being mocked for its naiveté and inexperience, its lack of civilization. When Ishi, the last wild Indian, walked out of the Lassen wilderness early in this century, he was amazed by trains, doorknobs, flush toilets. He found himself among immensely clever children, without a wise man anywhere to teach those customs and traditions that make people understand and honour their heritage.

Canadians and Americans still think of going to Europe, to the Orient, to Africa, to find themselves. *Roots* inspired not only U.S. blacks but everyone in the country to take a renewed interest in family history, to find ancestors to identify with and be proud of. We all have to go back to before the crossing of whatever water because we know the people who actually made the journey were mostly convicts, remittance men, slaves and religious cranks, a shaky basis for personal or national pride.

Because Canada did not come into being by revolution, it has evolved slowly into nationhood, with its attendant patriotism. That process is evident in the changing attitude towards Canadian culture. Some 20 years ago when I first settled here, Canadian literature was so little thought of that it was a minor elective in the University of British Columbia English department, taught by one of the few Canadians on a staff made up mostly of Englishmen and Americans. In publishing it was accepted practice that a novel must first find a U.S. or British publisher so that a Canadian house could afford to bring it out by buying pages from the English or U.S. publisher. Because that agreement was necessary, publishers weren't particularly interested in books about Canada, since their appeal outside the country might be too limited to get a foreign edition.

Now, Canadian literature is big business in schools and universities, though I still hear more disparaging than appreciative remarks about it in the academy. (If bragging is a U.S. trait, self-denigration is 100% Canadian.) For the past 15 years not only Canadian publishers but British and U.S. branch plants have brought out books directed at the Canadian market alone. And Canadian writers, if not academics, have become justifiably proud of the literature being written in Canada.

The flowering may be short-lived in our present economic circumstances. Canadian publishers are in serious trouble, and independent book stores are being threatened by the chains, which carry fewer Canadian books. Though the publishing business is also depressed in England and the United States, writers have to look to those markets again for primary support in order to reach, as well, a Canadian market.

The political hostility expressed against the Canada Council, the National Film Board, the CBC, is an indication of how little faith or interest too many Canadians have in their own developing culture and therefore how precarious it is. There is a danger that we will take crucial steps backward, having to rely again on U.S. textbooks for our schools and universities, read only U.S. and British fiction with the few Canadian novels which can compete in international markets.

My books with U.S. settings had British, U.S. and Canadian publishers. When I switched to Canadian settings, the British response was "too remote". So much for the ties of the Commonwealth. My most recent novel, set in Vancouver, has only a U.S. publisher because the one Canadian publisher to express an interest had lost most of its staff and was on the verge of bankruptcy. My "choosing" to be published in the United States is seen as part of my being too American.

It is important for Canadian readers to encounter their own forests and waterways, their own towns and cities in literature. For people who have had to read mostly about other places, there is a sense of surprise and new reality in seeing their own world described and explored, put on the literary map. Only when Canada has a cultural identity can symbols such as the flag be meaningful. Literature is part of what makes a country not only a place to go to but a place to come from.

For the serious writer, contributing to national identity can never be the only consideration. If, for instance, Vancouver is to be put on the literary map, not only of British Columbia and Canada but of the world, books about it must reach the audience of the world. They can do that only if writers' concerns far transcend this new nationalism and concentrate on those questions that concern all human beings.

No American who has chosen to leave the United States and take another citizenship will ever be a passionate nationalist anywhere, for what has turned us away from our own country is precisely that super-patriotism that has led to so many grievous mistakes both inside and outside the country. I will never be a super-Canadian, but in that I feel at home in a country which practices modesty and self-criticism regularly. If, after spending all my adult life here I am still too American, I hope it is in the optimism my ex-countrymen are also famous for. I do not think Canada has to settle for being nothing but an audience for U.S. culture. We can express ourselves and ensure our independence by welcoming the diversity of our voices, sharing the experience in all our backgrounds of being up-rooted, young, still in the process of bringing our country to birth.

The North End

Libby Simon

I ADMIT IT. I'm a North-Ender—a true North-Ender, born and bred. As a first generation offspring of Jewish immigrants who came to this country before the outbreak of WW II, I qualify. I'm not one of those famous North-Enders who drool nostalgia about their North-End roots. I'm not even wealthy, but I share the same pride as the rich and famous. We have reason to be proud. Similar to Montreal's St. Urbain district made famous by author Mordecai Richler decades ago, this small area in the north end of a wintry prairie city produced more than its fair share of scholars, artists and scientists. The 'why' of this interesting phenomenon invites exploration.

Harry, with Mildred Gutkin, in *The Worst of Times, The Best of Times* (1987) wrote that after WW I, the shape of the North End gradually became defined by the Red River in the east, and Keewatin Street on the west side. At the southern tip, it was bounded by the Canadian Pacific Railway tracks on Main Street, and ran northward to the lane behind McAdam Avenue. No more than several square miles, this area developed its distinguishing character as it became the enclave of multi-racial, multi-cultural and multi-ethnic immigrants—mainly Ukrainians, Poles, Jews, Germans, Russians and Mennonites.

I'm not sure when the North End became *The North End*, but it has deep historical roots dating back to the 1880s, when the railway was pushing west. A steady flow of immigrants gradually settled here to escape persecution and political oppression in their home countries. Under the dark cloud of war in Europe in the 1920s, 30s and 40s, many more immigrants, from various places around the world, sought refuge here. It was this particular wave of immigrants that spawned an era of exceptional achievement, disproportionately large when compared to their actual numbers.

Many of these people have recounted stories of literally trekking across Europe on foot to escape brutal regimes in Russia under Lenin and Stalin. My own father witnessed the cruelties and atrocities of vicious men on horseback brutalizing ordinary people on the streets. They pillaged homes and businesses, including his. He fled, penniless, from Russia to Poland where he met and married my mother. Under the new threat of Hitler's rise in Europe, he and his young wife, with two small boys, eventually found their way to Canada and the north end of Winnipeg.

However, there was a quota on some groups, such as Jews, causing many families to be split up. Sisters, brothers, aunts and uncles were dispersed around the world. Members of my own family, for example, found refuge in New York, South Africa and England. Most of those who remained in Europe perished in the Holocaust, or are lost and unknown to us. My father was one of the lucky ones. Under the conditions of the quota system, he was sponsored by the (then) Chief Rabbi of Western Canada, Israel Kahanovitch, with the promise of a teaching position at the Talmud Torah Hebrew School. This lasted for approximately 30 years. Those newcomers from diverse backgrounds who were fortunate enough to be admitted into Canada had much in common. They came with their meagre belongings, with little but a hope and a dream, leaving everything and everyone behind. Without benefit of the English language, they struggled to adjust to a new way of life.

The Depression during the 1930s brought new misfortune to many, in the form of unemployment and economic hardships, my father included, who was laid off despite having five children to support. For a man, the loss of identity derived from work, and the inability to support his family, were degrading and humiliating experiences. Many mothers, including my own, scrimped and saved to keep their families clothed and fed. Even as a child, I sensed her deep embarrassment at having to repeatedly ask for credit for food from the small local grocery store, although our situation was not uncommon then. My father, like many at that time, never owned a car. He went everywhere on foot.

Those were humbling times, I realize, in retrospect, when he had to walk across town to the south end (which even then was regarded as relatively prosperous), to borrow money from a colleague. At other times he would hike several miles, in winter or summer, to the downtown Eaton's Department Store, and back again, to save the streetcar fare; and, if necessary, do it twice on the same day to return something. We lived in modest rental homes and moved frequently, as owners dictated. Although he was eventually able to return to work, teachers were paid poorly then. It wasn't until years later, when my oldest brother was able to loan my father $2000 for the down payment, that he was able to buy a permanent home. They were turbulent times, but immigrant parents stood as good examples of strength and perseverance. Education was paramount. They struggled so that their children could take advantage of all the resources this country had to offer.

They came, these diverse ethnic clusters, bringing with them their customs, culture, rituals … and their prejudices. Seeking social acceptance, a sense of belonging, familiarity and support, they huddled together within their own groups as this self-imposed psychological "ghetto" evolved in this tiny North-End enclave. Their traditions were the glue, the common bond that bound them together. Gradually, this multifarious population, with varying degrees of tolerance, learned to share the same environment. Churches and synagogues were reincarnated in their newly adopted country. Selkirk Avenue became the centre of commerce, with a variety of shops offering holubchi, perogies, gefilte fish, corned beef, strudel, sauerkraut and herring. Oretzki's Department Store provided services in several languages to accommodate this polyglot community. Gunn's Bakery and Kub Bread on Selkirk and Stella Avenues, Jewish and Ukrainian bakeries respectively, still flourish as testament to this special period in the history of Winnipeg's North End.

But the progeny of the first generation immigrants had their own battles to contend with. Poverty was stifling their mostly working class community. Many children worked for pennies after school to help out. Toys were a luxury, compared to the need of winter gloves, so games were created out of sticks and cans. I recall playing Tippy-sticks, Kick the Can or Hide and Seek. Games were never organized or supervised, and all ages played together. School induced acculturation, which could be a double-edged sword. Children quickly learned the new language, but challenges often arose between the two generations as Old World traditions clashed with New World ways.

Racial intolerance too was a fact of life. Inter-school sports games frequently turned into fights among ethnic groups. Leo Yaffe, who became an eminent Canadian scientist, described his experience at Aberdeen School in *The Worst of Times, The Best of Times*, "as being as close to that of Hell's Kitchen as Winnipeg has ever produced, its tensions and deprivations creating a classic breeding-ground for crime" (p. 58). A decade later, my own experience was not much different. As first and second graders at King

Edward School, my brother and I were mobbed and physically and verbally roughed up, accompanied by racial taunting, by groups of older children as we tried to walk home together after school. For safety reasons, we were transferred—to Aberdeen School.

And as young people approached the career stage of their lives they sometimes met with institutionalized discrimination. Many recount the frustration, for example, of rejected applications to Medical College because of quotas on women, Jews and others. Such demoralizing conditions—of poverty, isolation, alienation and prejudice—that could have produced a spate of criminals, turned out instead to be the launching pad for success. Success, not necessarily measured in monetary terms, but in contributions to the welfare of society. Monty Hall, a recipient of the Order of Manitoba, illustrates this well, though not only because of his fame as the host of *Let's Make a Deal*, or as the International Ambassador of Variety Clubs. He was honoured as a person who used his celebrity to dedicate himself to improve the quality of life for disabled and disadvantaged children in our province and around the world.

There are many more celebrities and non-celebrities alike who have made extraordinary contributions to the sciences, the arts and to public service, both locally and abroad—people like John Hirsch, Allan Blye, Billy Mosienko and Benjamin Hewak, to name a few, although one shouldn't overlook the contributions of many other Winnipeggers. It is important that we acknowledge the uniqueness of the unusually high number of individual achievements attributable to a specific time and place in the history of Winnipeg. With so many factors capable of becoming sources of significant social problems, why did the opposite occur? Perhaps poverty and deprivation are not necessarily synonymous. Parents for the most part, in spite of their difficulties, must have successfully shielded their children from the stresses and temptations of the adult world. Somehow, there was always food on the table.

There was no television to bombard us with ads for shiny new "toys." And we may not have had much materially, by today's standards, but we were rich in relationships.

That is not to say that the family was like the one portrayed in *Leave it to Beaver*. Far from it! Parenting skills were unheard of, and they knew little of the issues related to development, either in the home or in the school. Perhaps it was the extreme struggle that challenged individuals, leading them to exceptional achievements. Or perhaps children learned important values early in life, when family bonds were built of concrete and steel, instead of the shifting sands that would emerge later. As Monty Hall notes in *Markings* by A.J. Paquette (1995): "Winnipeggers were stronger for having to contend with economic hardship, the weather and the isolation. Maybe that's why ... the North End produced more than its share of eminent people." The more theoretical reasons "why," however, will have to be left for the sociologists and historians to explain.

And Paquette himself dedicates his beautiful book depicting his collection of artwork in *Scenes and Recollections of Winnipeg's North End* to "... all North Enders, past, present and future ...," and to his wife, whom he refers to as "... a very special North Ender."

The demographics and character of the North End have changed as a new multicultural mosaic has settled here. But the uniqueness of this small enclave, formed in previous eras, is what has given the North End its mystical reputation. As John Marlyn wrote in *Under the Ribs of Death*: "... [F]or not to be swallowed at all is to remain marginalized; and to be swallowed completely is to disappear." (1957, p. 263) These offspring, growing up immersed in the immigrant milieu, found the difficult balance between assimilation and alienation. It was their North-End roots that gave them wings, and I am proud to be counted among them.

***

Post Script

This is a copy of the letter that changed the destiny of our family forever:

#18232
Department of Immigration and Colonization
Winnipeg, Mon. Sept. 7ᵗʰ, 1928
Dear Sir;
Referring to your application for the admission to Canada of your wife's nephew, Aron Kleinman, aged 46, his wife Feige aged 27 and their children, Berel aged 5 and infant 7 months, citizens of Poland, now residing at Wilno ul, Strathuno, 5/4 Poland, I beg to advise that in view of the representation made to the department, it has been decided to permit the entry to Canada of the above named, provided they are in possession of valid passports properly visad by a Canadian Immigration Officer stationed on the continent of Europe, can pass inspection in the matter of mental and physical health, and otherwise comply with the usual immigration regulations apart from that of occupation which will be waived.

This letter is only valid for five months from the date of same and must be presented within such period by the proposed immigrants to the Canadian Immigration Officer by whom they are examined before leaving Europe and from whom visa is to be obtained; also to the Canadian Immigration Officer at the port of arrival in Canada, where the letter will be lifted by the letter official and returned to the department.
Yours truly.
Signed - Thomas Galley
Division Commissioner
Rabbi Kahanovitch
281 Flora Avenue
Winnipeg, Man.

***

Afterword

"At a reunion honouring the seventy-fifth anniversary of St. John's Technical High School several years back, we heard a recitation of all the famous doctors, lawyers, athletes and others who hailed from the North End. They include three Metropolitan Opera singers, a lawyer who sat on the World Court, the doctor who invented the heart-lung machine and a famous nuclear scientist. We also produced a Chief Justice of the Supreme Court of Canada along with show business personalities and hockey players." [Monty Hall in *Markings*, A.J. Paquette, 1995 (p. 10)]. Below is a list which includes these people, along with notable others.

Authors and artists:

Harry Freedman composed music for the Royal Winnipeg Ballet, the Montreal Symphony, and the Toronto Symphony Orchestras. His work was performed regularly on the CBC.

Sondra Gotlieb is a Canadian journalist and novelist whose works include *True Confections*, *Washington Rollercoaster* and *Wife of ...* She is the wife of Allan Gotlieb, a Winnipegger and former Canadian Ambassador to Washington.

Maara Haas, poet, author and actress, is a recipient of an honorary doctorate for her contribution to Canadian letters as well as the Lady Eaton Award for her literary satire, *One Hundred Years of Poetry*. She is also known for her Readings on the CBC show, *This Country in the Morning*, as well as acting in theatre productions.

John Hirsch established the Manitoba Theatre Centre, was artistic director of the Stratford Shakespeare Festival, head of CBC Drama, and directed plays in New York, Los Angeles and Israel.

Jack Ludwig, novelist, essayist, and teacher has a wide range of writing credits, from his novel, *Confusions,* to popular articles on sports.

John Marlyn (pseudonym Vincent Reid), was Hungarian-born but came to Winnipeg's North End as an infant. He became a writer for the Canadian government and taught creative writing at Carleton University. He received a Beta Sigma Phi award for his first novel about a poor immigrant family during the 1920s, set in Winnipeg's North End, called *Under the Ribs of Death*.

Armand Paquette is an artist and sculptor best known for his portraits of western Canadian life, which has earned him a loyal following. His works are found in many private businesses and corporations across Canada and the U.S.

Miriam Waddington, poet and professor of English, has an impressive list of publications to her credit, including her *Collected Poems, 1936-1985,* published in 1986.

Adele Wiseman won the Governor-General's Award in 1955 for her first novel, *The Sacrifice. Crackpot* was re-published in 1974.

Entertainers:

Allan Blye landed his first major role as the singing star on CBC-TV's *General Electric Showtime.* He became a writer and producer for American network shows, notably *The Smothers Brothers, Sonny and Cher, Dick Van Dyke* and *The Andy Williams Show.*

Burton Cummings was born in 1947 but grew up in the changing demographic of Winnipeg's North End as the ethnic mix shifted following WW II. As a pianist, songwriter and lead singer of the 'Guess Who' he achieved fame on the international scene. He received The Order of Canada in 2001 and was inducted into the Canadian Songwriter's Hall of Fame in 2005.

Monty Hall appeared as a guest star on such TV shows as *The Odd Couple, The Nanny,* and *The Dean Martin Show.* But he was best known for 13 years as "America's Top Trader" on the ABC network's *Let's Make a Deal.* He was also the President of Variety

Clubs International and received many awards including the prestigious Variety Club Humanitarian Award, as well as three doctorates, the Order of Manitoba and the Order of Canada.

David Steinberg, comedian, actor, producer and writer began in the first *Second City* on Global TV but his career was launched on the *Tonight Show* with Johnny Carson. Since then he has established many credits as a director in such well-known TV shows as *Seinfeld, Mad About You, Evening Shade, Designing Women* and *Newhart.*

Scientists:

Leo Yaffe was one of Canada's key scientists at Chalk River, the high-priority Canadian atomic energy project. He became professor of chemistry and subsequently Vice-President at McGill University.

Maurice Victor was professor of neurology at the Dartmouth Medical School and Distinguished Physician of the Veterans' Administration.

Louis Slotin was a physicist/chemist who worked on the Manhattan Project, a secret wartime project, during World War II. Their purpose was to develop nuclear weapons in a race with Nazi Germany. This resulted in the development of the atomic bomb, which eventually ended the war. Louis died from an accidental massive radiation exposure in Los Alamos but shielded seven other observers in the same room. This was considered one of the incredible stories of the 20th century, which spawned a 1953 novel, *The Accident*, by Dexter Masters and a 1989 movie called *Fat Man and Little Boy* starring Paul Newman, with John Cusack's character Michael Merriman based on Slotin.

Dr. Morley Cohen was a pioneer in operations for congenital and valvular heart disease, which facilitated the development of open-heart surgery, ultimately made possible by the heart-lung machine.

Lawmakers and public servants:

Lloyd Axworthy, political scientist, author and speaker, was born in 1939 in North Battleford, SK, but grew up in Winnipeg's North End as the ethnic mix and immigrant populations shifted following WW II. He served as minister in several portfolios in the Liberal government including the Minister of Foreign Affairs. He was a Nobel Peace Prize Nominee and the recipient of many awards including the Order of Canada. He is presently the President of the University of Winnipeg.

Meyer Brownstone, social scientist, helped shape the policies of the first CCF government in Saskatchewan, and became national chairperson of Oxfam and head of the Center for Urban and Community Studies, University of Toronto.

Saul Cherniak, lawyer and politician, was a long-serving member of the Legislative Assembly of Manitoba and a cabinet minister in the government of Edward Schreyer. He was also a member of the Privy Council and received the Order of Manitoba and the Order of Canada.

Maxwell Cohen, former Dean of Law, became Emeritus Professor of McGill University and served as a Judge Ad Hoc of the World Court at The Hague.

Chief Justice Samuel Freedman, born in the Ukraine, moved to Winnipeg at the age of three. He became a lawyer and judge of the Court of Queen's Bench in Manitoba and Chief Justice of the Supreme Court of Canada. He was also Chancellor of the University of Manitoba and appointed as an Officer of the Order of Canada in 1984.

The Honourable Benjamin Hewak was the first Chief Justice in the Court of Queen's Bench of Ukrainian descent to hold this position. He served on many Boards and was the recipient of an Honorary Doctor of Laws Degree from the University of Manitoba. He was inducted into the Hall of Distinction of the Canadian National Ukrainian Festival.

David Orlikow was first elected to the Winnipeg School Board in 1944, and was a long-serving member of the House of Commons in Ottawa.

Sylvia Ostry, economist and public servant, became head of the department of Economics and Statistics for the Organization for Economic Co-operation in Paris.

Bernard Ostry, historian, author, public servant and broadcaster, played a definitive role under both Liberal and Conservative governments in formulating Canadian communications and museum policies.

Frank Shefrin, an agricultural economist, was Canada's representative on the United Nations World Food and Agricultural Organization (FAO).

Sports:

Billy Mosienko played hockey with the Chicago Blackhawks and is famous for scoring the three fastest goals (21 seconds). He was a recipient of the Lady Byng Trophy and is a member of the Hockey Hall of Fame.

Inventor:

Dr. Martin Cooper is considered the inventor of the first portable handset, and was the first person to make a call on a portable cell phone in April, 1973. While he was a project manager at Motorola, he set up a base station in New York and with the first prototype of a cellular telephone, the Motorola Dyna-Tac, he contacted his rival at Bell Labs.

This list is not complete. There are many more who have contributed to the arts, sciences and humanities in the local community and beyond, to varying degrees, but the above list illustrates the remarkable phenomenon of achievement concentrated at a particular time and place in the history of Winnipeg.

***

Sources

www.citiesplus.ca/lloyd.html

www.encyclopedia.thefreedictionary.com, http://en.widipedia.org/wiki/
    Louis_Slotin

www.thecanadianencyclopedia.com/index.cfm, *The Globe and Mail*,
    'The Focus,' Saturday, February 1, 2003, www.imbd.com

http://1g.gov.mb.ca/activities/news/2004/eleven.html, The Manitoba
    Historical Society, http://mayberryfineart.com

The Worst of Times, the Best of Times, Jack Gutkin with Mildred Gutkin.
    Fitzhenry & Whiteside, Markham, ON, 1987

I Am an Immigrant[1]

Batia Boe Stolar

WHAT DOES IT mean to be an immigrant? The ontological and existential implications of this question stump me. Let me, then, rephrase the question as follows: What does it mean to identify oneself, myself, as an immigrant? Much better! Let us proceed.

Like a rubber stamp used by immigration officials to stamp a person's papers upon entry at Customs, the word "immigrant" stamps us, labels, us, marks us with an official and permanent impression for all to read and interpret—foreigner, alien, traitor, inferior, exotic, desirable. It is the mark we bear proudly at times, the mark we sometimes seek to hide. It is a personal stamp that is all too public.

I am an immigrant.

Have I recently moved from one country to live permanently in another? Legally I am no longer the landed immigrant I once was. Culturally, however, I still identify myself as an immigrant. I choose to do so, and why not? You do the same when you hear my name or when you detect a trace of an accent. I can pass until I speak. I am not a visible minority; I am an assimilated aural minority who maintains (sometimes willingly, sometimes not) her difference.

To identify myself as an immigrant is to accept and acknowledge the experiences of immigration, or of growing up in one country and entering another, thereby becoming a bicultural subject who learns and absorbs multiple histories.

Identifying myself as an immigrant is a self-conscious act that grants me a degree of agency, allowing me to exert some control over my identity.

If you hail me, "Immigrant," would I respond?

Immigrant. The word is clinical, bureaucratic, void of emotion. I prefer the sound the word "imminent" makes. "Imminent" follows "immigrate" in my dictionary. The imminence of immigration. Did I know our immigration was imminent? Immigration is imminent. Immigration is an event, a series of experiences, always about to occur to someone, somewhere. Immigration is, like imminence, "likely to occur at any moment." The immigrant awaits the signal, that green light in the form of an officially stamped letter, before proceeding with the combined acts of emigrating and of immigrating. The moment is always in the tangible future, always a possibility. The Customs Official, similarly, waits to clear the line of people in front of her or his station. The Customs Official knows that an immigration claim or a plea for refugee status is imminent. The word "imminent" connotes urgency, seriousness, destiny.

The connotations of the word "immigrant" render it a nasty word. To be labelled an immigrant by others is to be targeted, ridiculed ... attacked. Most often inquisitive people *want to know* details about my immigration—*why did you come to Canada*—and in their eagerness to know they often confuse their desire as their legal or social *right to know*. For the immigrant, privacy is a luxury. If I am not forthcoming with my information, my story, my explanation, people want (need; have a right) to know why, implying I am (must be) hiding something. Surely if I don't have anything to hide I won't mind answering a few harmless questions—never mind that I am asked those same harmless questions on a daily basis, sometimes twice on the same day, or that I'm tired, had a bad day, or simply don't feel like making small talk.

Why do my experiences of immigration make such a fascinating and suitable subject for small talk? These are personal, private, stories. Personal questions about my family's immigration elicit in me a plethora of emotions and anxieties, like those I experience when renewing my passport. Do I fill in the name of the country of my birth, or do I check the box to request omitting this information? Is it better to name the country or leave it blank? What are the criteria for choosing one of these two options? One group of immigrants is always the scapegoat. Today it's not me, but tomorrow it may be. History has a tendency to repeat itself.

Memories of a different set of anxieties about renewing my passport well up inside: the hours of waiting in a room filled with people; the smells of people; the hours spent waiting; the counters too high for me to see the official behind stamping papers and photographs. Suddenly I'm lifted onto the counter. Hold out my thumb, a big *rodillo* with black ink makes contact. My thumb is pressed and rolled unto a square on an official form. Then the other thumb follows. The ink would stay in the creases of my fingerprints for days afterward. I would scrub and scrub, trying to get the *mugre* out. In my child's mind I confused going to the doctor's office with going to renew our passports. Both instances were invasive. One meant painful needles. The other meant painless fingerprinting.

I find the self-conscious acts of identifying ourselves as immigrants or self-consciously rejecting the label, intriguing. I choose to pass whenever possible. Passing connotes fear. What fear am I seeking to face here?

The word "immigrant" becomes a tattoo to be shown off or hidden at will; it is a reminder, a medal, a beautiful expression of those experiences we come to associate with the term: triumph, pain, misery, acquiescence, loss, choice, exchange, gain, survival. As we age the tattoo fades into the creases of newly folding skin. Only the Walt Whitmans of the world prefer the beauty of such discolorations; the fading memory of the act over the experience; the aftermath of the event over the raw immediacy of its pleasurable pain. Every day the tattoo changes; or, rather, the tattoo remains the same, stamped onto ever-changing skin.

I am an immigrant.

You find my tattoo in my voice. It is called an "accent," an emphasis of difference. Accents can be beautiful, and especially useful when decorating homes. Bright colour accents are recommended for white, beige, or earth-toned rooms. Bright colours are preferred in small doses; accents connote life, too much of any bright colour is deemed overpowering, uninviting, and uncontrollable. It is best to keep such accents small, manageable, on conditional display. Accents can be exchanged, banished to closets, attics or basements when they clash or overpower.

I cannot banish my accent, but I can be banished.

I am an immigrant, passing, until I speak.

What is your accent?

You found me out. Shall we play? What do you think my accent is? French? *Mais non.*

Where are you from?

Ah, *that* question. Why do you always ask me this? What is it about me that generates this question? Does everybody get asked this question on a daily basis?

Why is answering this simple question so difficult? Sometimes I'm at a loss for words. Where *am* I from? Does having lived in Canada for over two decades and having Canadian citizenship allow me to claim that I am from Canada? I recently started playing hockey. I know who Don Cherry is, and why Tim Hortons is a Canadian icon. I like Tim Hortons coffee. Tim Hortons is now American-owned. Tim Hortons is no longer spelled with an apostrophe. I have lived in three different provinces and six different towns and cities in Canada, making it difficult to answer where in Canada I am from. Do you mean the place where I now live or the place where I lived before moving here? What do you mean, "where am I from"?

Do you want the short or long version? Notice I am offering you control over my narrative; you now have the power to choose and dictate where and how my story will go. I am a text, and you are my reader. The reader makes the text. Are you even aware you have been granted—or have you taken, appropriated—this authorial power?

Where is home?

Well, that question does not help me narrow down my answer. In fact, it complicates it and here is why: You can have more than one home. I have multiple homes—not multiple houses, but multiple places, countries, cities, towns, I call "home." That's what happens when you move from one place to another, and fall in love with or learn to love the places you live in, in the process. Places, like people, claim you. Granted, that's a different topic.

Start at the beginning. Where were you born?

As you will see, that is not really the beginning.

Moreover, if I tell you where I was born you'll want to know how long I've been in Canada and why I came here. You'll ask me how I like the weather. You won't ask me what I think of health care, or Canada's position on global affairs, or even NAFTA. You will ask me, instead, about my native country's social and economic welfare, and about the political and social situation there. You will ask me about our national holidays, exciting vacation spots, the current exchange rate, and expect me to provide you with an authoritative rant on the good and bad political, social, cultural, and economic realities of my birth country. You will want to know about my family then, and about our place within that country. Am I a diplomat? A spy? What did my family do for a living—translated as what class did we occupy and how much money did we (do we) have? Whose side do I represent? Whose interests? Where do I fit in?

I was born in Mexico City. My immediate family moved to Oakville, Ontario, Canada when I was 12. If the move from Mexico to Canada is not startling enough, notice the move from one of the biggest cities in the world to another that claimed (at least then) to be a town (even though its population placed it in the realm of a small city).

You don't look Mexican.

It is not a question; it is an authoritative statement. The reader is writing me. Since I don't *look* Mexican, I can't possibly be *from* there. You *tell* me I'm not *really* Mexican, so where am I *really* from?

What do Mexicans look like? I'd like to point out that Antonio Banderas, who often plays Mexicans in films, is actually Spanish, from Spain. He doesn't *sound* Mexican.

I admit, though, you've got a point. I'm not a "typical" Mexican. The truth is Mexicans question my national authenticity too, calling me *güerita* (even though I'm not really blonde), or speaking to me in English whenever they want to sell me something (even when I lived there and didn't speak any English).

Is your name Mexican? It doesn't sound very Mexican.

Well, you're right there, too. I am named after my grandmother who died long before I was born. She was a Jew living in Kiev. All my grandparents were Ashkenazi Jews. All my grandparents immigrated to different parts of Mexico at different times for different reasons, some because of poverty or persecution, others to eschew unfortunate romantic liaisons. But please don't ask me about them yet—I only have bits and pieces of their stories, and after all, we have only just met.

So you're not really Mexican. Well, I do believe it is possible to be simultaneously Jewish *and* Mexican. Prior to your stating otherwise, I never had any difficulty seeing myself as both. "Jew" or "Hebrew" is no longer an accepted national category for immigration purposes.

My parents, Jews, were born *in* Mexico. *I* was born *in* Mexico. I learned about *La Revolución, los Niños Héroes, Benito Juarez* ("*Entre los individuos, como entre las naciones, el respeto al derecho ajeno es la paz*"), and once thought that *Miguel Hidalgo y Costilla* were two people instead of one. I know about the *Aztecas*, although you have probably heard about them too. Do you know about the *Olmecas*? The *Toltecas* are my favourite—they sacrificed flowers to their gods. I know about *La Coatlicue* and *Quetzalcoatl*. Have you been to a *tianguis*? Have you ever been called an *escuincle*? Do you know why Mexican money features an eagle, standing on a *nopal*, eating a serpent? Mexico's history is depicted in the works of the *muralistas*. Diego Rivera and Frida Kahlo have become internationally acclaimed iconographic Mexican figures. What of Remedios Varo? Or Rufíno Tamayo? Does my knowledge make me more Mexican? Technically, I am a third-generation Mexican. My mother-tongue is Spanish. I like tequila with *sangrita*; I listen to the Mariachis. I went to Hebrew day-school where I learned Hebrew. I eat falafel. Then we moved to Oakville, where few of my classmates knew what a Mexican or a Jew was, let alone a Mexican Jew. I didn't speak English then. On my first day at school I went to French class. My teacher was from the Caribbean and knew Spanish. I loved French instantly. This is somewhat of a contradiction when celebrating el *Cinco de Mayo*.

The truth is, I never thought of myself or my family as immigrants in Mexico. We were Jews, a visible minority, subjected to acts of anti-Semitism. We were practicing Jews who had assimilated into Mexican culture; we ate *Rosca de reyes* (I got the plastic doll in the cake and had to pay for the *tamales*—and I hated *tamales* then); we celebrated *El Día de los Muertos*, without *altares*, and attended friends' *pozadas*. My mother took me with her on excursions to study the art and architecture of churches and cathedrals, to the *Museo de Antropología*, to *Bellas Artes*. Then we moved to Canada, to the land my Mexican friends thought was populated by

Eskimos who lived in igloos. Canadian-Mexican relations had not yet flourished. This was a time before NAFTA. Mexican-Canadian relations are now beginning to flower.

I never questioned why I was treated as a foreigner in the country where I was born and grew up, in the country where my parents were born and raised, in the country I still define as one of my many homes. I never questioned it until I was treated as a foreigner in Canada, the country of my immigration, where strangers authoritatively decide where I am *not* from.

My grandparents were immigrants, but I never thought of them as such. Am I from Kiev, Russia, Lithuania or Poland? Am I from those places were my grandparents were born, where my relatives were made to dig their own graves, exiled, or forced into trains to be later annihilated in death camps? Still, a bio-geographical pull makes me long for these unseen landscapes, for clues to my identity. Will I feel *at home* when in that soil? Even so, Mexico would not cease to be "home." Neither would Canada.

Where is your accent from?

Clearly, because I don't *look* Mexican, I'm not really *from* there. Ergo, my accent must equally have its origins in some other place. I speak Spanish, or *Castellano*, not "Mexican." Hebrew is my second language. English and French dually my third. I seek out languages—Russian, Japanese, Finnish, Italian, Portuguese, Yiddish. I seek to speak like a native of the country, of the town, to camouflage myself. After a week in Scotland I acquired an accent. I lost it after a week in England. It comes back whenever I watch British or Irish TV or films. In Newfoundland I was teased for mispronouncing "sook." It is the telltale word to differentiate the natives from the CFA's. I want, need, to be a chameleon, but I am found out, every time.

I don't even hear my accent, what it sounds like. I try to suppress it to avoid ridicule and adopt the nuances of each region I live in. Relatives always make fun of those who leave Mexico and speak

Spanish with a *gringo* accent. They tell me I don't speak Spanish with an accent, a true accomplishment after all these years. Anglos make fun of people who mispronounce words in English. My accent emerges, unbidden. It is what aurally marks me a visible *other*, more so in English than in Spanish.

Congratulations. You speak good English.

Why, thank you!

I have a Ph.D. in English. I have a tenure-track position in an English Department at a Canadian university. You think it's funny I teach native speakers their own language, not realizing English Departments teach literature. I think of Caliban, although I don't usually teach Shakespeare nor identify myself as a post-colonialist.

It's sad to know that learning to speak English well is my biggest accomplishment as an immigrant. What languages do you speak? What cultures do you know?

Say something in Mexican, sorry, Spanish.

What do you want me to say? Why do you want me to perform for you? You say it's exotic, and sexy. I feel as though money is about to exchange hands. Is that it? Is that what being an immigrant is all about? I don't want to become your object of desire to be acquired, collected, paid for, bought. I am not a commodity. Your wanting me does not legitimize my existence. Remember, mine is not an existential crisis.

You have a beautiful name. Where is it from? What does it mean?

Like my accent, my name has its own identity, its own origin; it is an immigrant too, like me. Should I tell you what it *really* means? Are you anti-Semitic? Am I in danger of revealing all of my identities to you? After all, we have just met. You are a stranger at a bus stop, a clerk at the checkout counter of a grocery store, a student, a fellow traveller in an airplane, a colleague, an employer. I tell you it was my grandmother's name. I tell you where she was from. You nod, as if that explains where *I'm* from.

Sometimes I just want to eat my meal in peace, and join the

flow of the general conversation. Sometimes I just want to pay for my coffee or tea without having to explain where my accent is from or what my name means. Sometimes I want to have a ready-made answer to that first question, where am I from, that will stop you looking at me like I just stepped off the boat. Immigrants arrive in planes too, you know. I did.

Sometimes I want to tell you it's none of your business. I ask you questions about where you come from, but that sometimes leads to more and more questions—about me, not you—like why did I ever leave Mexico? Or how long have I been here (wherever that may be)? And how does one who comes from Mexico City end up in Thunder Bay?

It's simple math, really. It is a joining between points A and B. Point A signals the point of origin, of departure. As we have already established, there is sometimes a discrepancy between the point of origin and the point of departure, and the point of origin does not necessarily signal the beginning. Regardless, the line between point A and point B is a straightforward line that joins the points of origin and/or departure with point B, the place where you are now in. The line between points A and B ignores all erasures, all the pit stops along the way, all those temporary dwellings that last anywhere between one and six years.

How much time do you want to invest in my story, in me? You give me my five, ten, fifteen minutes before moving on to other topics or to other more exciting people. To you it's been an informative conversation, perhaps even memorable. To me, it's been a lifetime—mine.

I must here confess that there is a part of me that sometimes relishes the fact I have a story to tell that others crave to hear. I like the fact that my name and my accent mark me as being somehow different, or *special*. It's something I can draw on to make small talk, something that will draw people to me, make me seem more interesting than I am. My markings open doors and close others;

they generate other stories about other people's experiences too. But in these instances, it is I who am in control over the conversation, and therefore in control over my story—what I choose to reveal, where, when, and to whom. For me, that becomes key—when you unwittingly draw the immigrant in me out into the open, especially on those days or moments when I just want to keep on passing, you take away my sense of control over my own identity. You make me feel exposed, found out, guilty, vulnerable. Eve Kosofsky Sedgwick argues that those who know things about you have power over you. When you ask me about my life you show interest, but you also get my information. If you do not provide me with the same number of details, we are not exchanging information. My cards are exposed. Yours are not. You hold the cards—aces, pairs, or random inconsequential cards—but power lies not in what your hand holds as much as what the cards *could* hold.

I want to have control over when I turn the switch on or off; I want control over my immigrant self. Why do you insist on taking that control away from me? Why is it that silence has become the most efficient way to keep or maintain such control?

I am an immigrant.

I study and teach immigrant literature. I study how immigrants represent themselves or are represented by others in literature and film. I study how legal documents define the immigrant, and how these definitions in turn affect and are affected by the cultural texts produced by and about immigrants.

My work on immigrant literatures in Anglo-North America reflects my search for a critical perspective that speaks to my own experiences as a third-generation Mexican, of Ashkenazi ancestry, who immigrated to Canada. Postcolonial theories, which often deal with issues of displacement and migration, do not reflect the issues I face as such an immigrant in Canada. I have no immediate relation to the English-Canadian history of colonization; as a Mexican, I was educated about the Spanish colonization of the indigenous peoples of pre-Columbian America. As a Jew, however, I feel part of a different history of persecution and of life in a Diaspora that renders problematic any coherent understanding of *a* native homeland and of *a* history of oppression. To what empire do I write back? Of which oppressive empire am I a part? What theoretical apparatuses, then, reflect or speak to my experiences?

In the process of researching writers' and filmmakers' representations of immigrant experiences, my lived experiences as an immigrant surface. I am faced with the choice to either give my memories a voice or repress them. Do I enter that shadowy place and give voice to that which lurks within the spaces of my critical discourse? Do I choose to write myself, as it were, into or out of my critical work? Up to now, I have opted to keep myself outside my work, although implicitly I draw on my experiences as a useful lens through which I can understand the texts I study. Why, then, this silence, this omission (or negation) of a crucial part of my critical self?

The scholar in me easily responds that the critical study of immigrant literatures should not be limited to those who have similar experiences. Emphasizing my own identity as an immigrant or drawing on my own experiences of immigration can provide me with a degree of authority on the subject. But do I want to claim my authority as a scholar based on my lived experiences of immigration? In doing so, do I risk undermining my own scholarly authority and accentuating my immigrant status? Still, establishing a connection between my lived experiences and the texts I study can lead to fruitful critical analysis, especially considering that I already draw on these experiences whether or not I articulate them in my methodology.

Most of us are familiar with a common immigrant narrative I term "heroic," consisting of recurring motifs: an economic or religiously oppressed people in the Old World go through unthinkable ordeals that lead to their decision to leave or to circumstances that render them exiles of their native land. The journey of immigration is long and hard. Traversing countries is a difficult task to reach the port and the transatlantic ship that will roll with the waves, making those in steerage seasick. Hygienic conditions aboard the ships are inhuman: dead bodies among those barely living. Then, paradise. The New World becomes visible—a shoreline, an island, a house, the Statue of Liberty. The processing of the immigrants is another ordeal to overcome, and in the process many are renamed, reborn, into new identities.

The trials in the New World begin as the immigrants fight to survive, realizing the paradise they envisioned is far from their new reality. Nostalgia for the Old World competes with the memories of the atrocities committed in the Old World. The Old World is ever present in the landscape of the New World. Some embrace it, others reject it, assimilating into what they think is the authentic identity of the New World. Assimilation proves to have its limits, but the American Dream, the promise of Gold Mountain, lingers on, hovering just above the horizon that seems to get a little closer with every passing generation.

The heroic immigrant narrative follows the story of a person. It is the story of a journey, filled with obstacles and rites of passage. As readers we identify or empathize with the immigrant sojourner. We applaud and we cringe at the circumstances, the individual characters, the irony, the impossibility of living. We are all familiar with stories of migration. They form a part of our genesis.

Modern stories of immigration still depict people in boats risking everything for a chance to enter the promise of the New World. The Chinese Boat People off the coast of British Columbia. The Cuban refugees who sail in rafts to the Florida shore hoping to outrun the American authorities stationed there to prevent them from stepping on American ground. Stories of illegal aliens stowed in boats, cars, trains abound. So do sympathetic and antagonistic responses. The media portrays these people as heroes, as victims, as malevolent agents of a greater, faceless evil.

My story of a family-class legal immigration seems somehow devalued when compared to these heroic narratives. We left Mexico City on the red-eye flight of August 27. We arrived in Toronto on August 28. It was only a few hours flight, but to me the day difference is symbolic. It makes the passage, the journey, seem quasi-magical. We arrived by plane at the Toronto airport. At that late hour it was almost empty, especially compared to Mexico's airport. Times have since changed; so has Pearson International Airport. We were the only landed immigrants aboard that plane. I felt a rush of anxiety as the Customs official looked over our papers, stamped each of our forms and passports. I remember the rush of joy we felt when we heard his smiling voice: "Welcome to Canada"; on to another office then, and more paperwork, and then on to the Canadian morning. The air felt a little cool, although the sun was shining.

Why is writing in my immigrant voice, about my experiences, so difficult? What control, if any, am I circumventing or asserting by choosing whether or not to position myself critically as an immigrant reading these texts?

Does a person ever stop being an immigrant? Legally, certainly so. A citizen's legal status within the nation can change from that of *landed immigrant* to that of *Canadian citizen.* But the questions, beginning with *where are you from?,* denote the limitations of this civic change. Does a person ever stop being an immigrant? In a sense, no. The experience of immigration cannot be erased, but the experience of immigration need not be the sole or the most defining feature of a person's life.

The act of immigration is an act of interruption. Immigrants face the difficulty of having to "start over." Often they cannot keep or maintain the same positions or jobs they once held. There is an interruption, a break, from the native culture when the immigrant moves. Culture is always flowing, always in flux, and when the immigrant is no longer in a country, she or he cannot maintain her or his immersion in that culture. Conversely, when the immigrant arrives she or he has not been part of the culture of the country of entry. When people reminisce about childhood experiences, I find I am lacking. I do have others, but these are ones they do not share. These cultural and historical interruptions become more and more significant, making me feel sometimes as though I am from no place, for the places I am from are more temporal than geographic. Temporal places exist in memory only, and as such are treacherous places that are constantly shifting. Immigrants are suspended in time. We are often in limbo.

Should a person desire to be something other than an immigrant? To answer this question, we must first consider these others: Why has the term "immigrant" become so objectionable? What does it mean to be defined as an immigrant? What power, or lack thereof, does the term "immigrant" offer a person?

An "immigrant" is sometimes devalued for not being a *real* citizen or *native* of the chosen nation. As such, the immigrant lacks credibility or authority within the nation, albeit she/he can be granted special perspective on the nation precisely because she or he is positioned as being somehow outside it. As such, the immigrant occupies that privileged yet ambiguous space of intermediate status where one is simultaneously inside and outside a nation and its culture(s). That insider-outsider perspective may be valuable and desirable, but it also points to the immigrant's perceived ambiguity about the nation she/he inhabits and about her or his place within that nation. An immigrant is likewise someone who is valued as a foreign, and therefore exotic, commodity to be possessed or enjoyed. When the immigrant becomes commodified, she or he is objectified. The desire for the immigrant can be understood as a desire to possess the immigrant (or whatever the immigrant stands for).

Are we all immigrants, as has been suggested? Have we all gone through the process and experience of immigration? The term "immigrant" is mistakenly entrenched in the word "origin." Hence, if anyone has her or his origins elsewhere, she or he must be an immigrant. This is not the case. The word "immigrant" connotes movement, displacement, choice, and agency. It corresponds to a very specific and particular set of actions and experiences.

I am an immigrant.

What does it mean to identify oneself, myself, as an immigrant?

Perhaps we should begin again. Perhaps we should begin by investigating whether as immigrants we see the world in such a way that is particular to our experiences of immigration. The question is not *what do I see* but *how do I see it*? Is there an "immigrant" sensibility? Beyond the stories are aesthetic nuances. It is these that call out to me, for they tell me that something else exists in the spaces carved out by cultural and temporal interruptions. It is these I seek, in others' texts, in my own.

I am an immigrant.

I'm still exploring what that means.

Notes

1.   Written in 2005.

Between Two Tongues:
Falling at The Speed of Light

∾

H. Masud Taj

URDU IS MY mother tongue and my foster-
mother tongue is English. In post-colonial India I grew up in both.
My mother is a creative writer in Urdu who often rewrites the end-
ings of novels she reads and sometimes even replaces the author's
version with her own. Her daily speech is sprinkled with metaphors and witty turns of phrase. My father, for one unforgettable
year, was an inspired poet in Urdu and turned our staid house into
a spontaneous tavern of Ghazal-guzzlers. My grandmother never
tired of reminding me that I was the descendant of her grandfather
the "the high-sounding Amir Minai (1828-1900) who continued the
Lucknow tradition."[1] In 1873, when Prince Edward Island finally
joined Canada and the ancestor of the RCMP came into being,[2] my
ancestor, concerned more with the state of poetry than security,
published *Intihab-I Yadgar.* It was an anthology of 410 poets of
Rampur, a city near Lucknow that is smaller than Ottawa.

Lucknow was where extreme politeness was the norm, where
passengers missed apocryphal trains while waiting for the other to
board first. The city nurtured Urdu and in turn Urdu was an aural
city in which I lived even in the midst of bustling pre-Mumbai
Bombay. Language was virtual reality: crossing the threshold in

our seafront home was like crossing cities. Later when I crossed the skies in *Air Canada* I encountered an English whose intonation resonated with memories of Lucknow's civility. Canadians end their sentence in a voice that rises upwards. It turns every sentence into a tentative question, as if seeking the listener's permission before speaking further. Though airborne, I had a sense of arrival; I felt intonations were translating geographies, even as I was translating myself to Canada.[3]

I did my schooling far away from my Urdu-poetry-laden home in a school high up in mist-laden mountains of India, where I grew up in English. Both the school Headmaster and its most influential teacher were wannabe-poets who unleashed their compositions on unsympathetic ears. Their passion for English though was infectious, and the disease incurable. Having learnt to write Urdu from right to left, I learnt to write English in the 'wrong' direction: from left to right. One direction cancelling the other and soon my scripts were going where no script had gone before. Poetry led to calligraphy, in both the scripts, and explorations of calligraphic space led to architecture (each time the poet, calligrapher, architect paused to catch his breath he received a new label). I still tend to browse publications backwards which sometimes means, in bilingual Canada, encountering undecipherable French before reverse-engineered English. (Da Vinci would have approved.)

Both English and Urdu are symmetrical; two conditions of the same bipolar disorder. Both tongues are immigrants in alien grammars (Latin and Sanskrit respectively); both have a similar strategy for overcoming their weakness: a voracious appetite for foreign words. Like the monster software AutoCAD and indeed life itself (both versions at 2006), they make up as they go along, disguising their formal inelegance with awesome number crunching, memory and vocabulary respectively. Both English and Urdu are tongue colonisers with their dictionaries metamorphosing into thesauruses. (Webster and Roget face off as John Travolta and Nick Cage once did in an exciting Woo classic.) Both languages also colonise lands, English the world and Urdu the Indian subcontinent and the Indian Diasporas spread out in the world (about 90,000[4] in Canada). They have an evangelical fervour that turns speakers into born-agains, again and again.

With such mother tongues, the opening scene of *Genghis Khan*, when his father is torn between two horses, was destined to freeze, and Papa Khan become, with a healthy dose of multicultural mis-reading and mixed metaphors, Janus forever. For the mirror symmetry of the two tongues borders on the uncanny.

One language has no past tense and the other, no future.

In Urdu, words have suffixes for future tense but none for the past. *Bol* ("to say") becomes *boloonga* for the future. But for the past Urdu takes the present form into past time (*bol raha tha*). Likewise in English, words have suffixes for the past tense but none for the future. "I say" becomes "I said." But for the future English takes the present form into future time ("I will say"). The past tense in one and the future tense in the other are both aliens in disguise forever deceiving the native speakers. Born between two tongues is to not belong to both, to remain outside and in-between twin towers with the knowledge of both unfounded foundations and excess baggage in the sky.

Born between two tenses, one tends to mistrust the past and the future, sceptical of both histories and prophesies, and rely on the ever-present present, the only tense at hand. A fleeting moment that is forever both hyper transient and everlasting (you only experienced, experience, will experience the present). It is akin to dwelling in *Visces Pisces*, an ancient term for the fish-shaped area between two overlapping circles; the only area of the Venn diagram that is in touch with the generative centres of both circles. To dwell in the present is to dwell in the interface, keeping the barbarians of tongues and times at bay.

At the interface, speech turns speechless and time timeless— both inadvertently.

The only way to enlarge the interface is for both the circles to follow the opposing directions of contrary scripts until they completely overlap each other. Past and future then coalesce into present. When that happens, as Einstein pointed out, you are moving at the speed of light while all along remaining motionless. Because then there is no past to travel from and no future to travel to. There is only the present tense: speechless, timeless, motionless.

***

Author's note: Urdu does have a past tense (*kaha*). Only in some fleeting instances is it devoid of it and this essay is situated in those moments. English, though, remains permanently handicapped (sans dedicated verb-form for the future tense, it yet communicates futurity). Hence the symmetry of lacking tenses is only a part-time truth, and this essay is a hybrid of fact and fiction. Urdu's not having a past tense is fictitious; the genealogies of the tongues are suspect; everything else is true.

Notes

1. Schimmel, Annemarie. *Classical Urdu literature from the beginning to Iqbal*. Wiesbaden: Horrassowitz., 1975. p. 222.
2. Northwest Mounted Police. Four years after the death of Amir Minai, it took on the prefix Royal and four years before my father was born it became the Royal Canadian Mounted Police.
3. To translate is to carry from one place to another (Latin *translation*).
4. 2001 Census: Statistics Canada.

A Dozen Reasons This American Is Celebrating Canada Day

Ken Victor

WHEN I FIRST moved up here a little over ten years ago, I was surprised to learn that Canada Day happens just before July 4th. I thought you wanted simply to beat us Americans to the punch. Canada Day might be a few days earlier, I thought, but hey, we'll always do a celebration bigger and better than you. (Thinking like a true American, I was.) Well, after ten years, I've decided it's time to fess up—I love this place. And this year, I'm finally going to focus on Canada Day. July 4th I'll call up the family in the States to say hello, but the party will be on Canada Day. Here are 12 reasons why:

1) Your Electoral Process: At this time last year, the campaign for the U.S. Presidency was already under way. We Americans might be efficient at some things but running election campaigns isn't one of them. Canada, your warp-speed campaigns are a thing of beauty. It's so short that the candidates can practically make a new promise every day, pollsters can go hog-wild, newspapers can add special campaign sections and then—boom!—it's all over. We can get back to our regular lives. You may or may not like the results, but you gotta love the speed. Just like a good hockey game.

2) Your Healthcare System: My third child was born prematurely, weighing 1 lb. 4 oz. I was so scared and confused that I went on-line to find communities of parents experiencing the same thing. The only topic parents from the U.S. could focus on was what their insurance covered and didn't cover. Not Canadians. They wanted to talk about what mattered: prognosis, treatments, risks. Canada, I don't know how much those three months in the hospital and four years of follow-up cost, but believe me, I am forever grateful. You can tax me as much as you want. I'll never complain. I know I'll never pay off how selflessly your medical system was there for us when we needed it. And I have a healthy five-year-old daughter to prove it.

3) The Gun Registry, Decriminalizing Marijuana, Approving Gay Marriages: First, let me come clean here and state my biases. I think it's idiocy to lock people up for toking on a joint, a greater idiocy for allowing everybody who doesn't toke to arm themselves to the hilt, and more than a bit foolish to approve only those committed relationships that have certain approved combinations of genitalia. That said, I'm not celebrating these because I think they're particularly wise, effective or moral. Nope, I name these because—to paraphrase Dorothy—they let me know I'm not living in Kansas anymore. Could you imagine *any* of these taking root in Kansas? Not on your life, Bubba. So Canada, go for it. It make you *you*.

4) Your Lakes And Rivers: If you haven't been in them or on them, can you be Canadian? Your water is what brought me up here in the first place. You've got big untamed rivers swimming with hungry fish, and vast empty lakes waiting for the wind to turn them into a froth of waves. Canada, your fresh water has spoiled me—how many times I've been able to paddle alone on

a sky-blue lake without a cottage in sight. And heck, I was on a river trip where we didn't see another soul for 23 days. *That* is the big lonesome. It's beautiful, it's empty and it's calling you.

5) Your Government Ads: Let me get this straight: federal departments actually run ads on TV about their services and benefits? You must be joking! The first time I saw one I was so baffled I had to ask friends what I'd just seen. Clearly, these departments believe they're part of the solution. I'm for any country that believes government has a positive contribution to make.

6) Your Bureaucrats: Living in Ottawa, I've come to know some of these people. Not what I expected. Some of these folks work awfully hard. Too hard, in fact. If truth be known, they're workaholics. They're a dedicated and conscientious lot. And why? I guess they think they have to live up to the billing in those ads. These folks put in the honest 9 to 5 and then some. Any country would be only too happy to replace their Public Servants with Canada's. OK, I'll admit they're not perfect; after all, money *has* disappeared. But hey, wasn't it one of the bureaucrats who blew the whistle on the lack of perfection in the first place?

7) Your Political Parties: "What," you might ask in shock. "Are you crazed?" Probably, but that's beside the point. It is simply because you have them. I grew up in an either-or world. Either Republicans or Democrats. Here you've got Either-Or-Or-Or-Or-Or (if I can include the Green Party). Now and then a third candidate shows up on the American stage, but everyone knows they're going to be yanked off before too long. The truth is that following political parties in the States is like living with nothing but a 100 years of Bruins-Rangers games. Up here, you've simply got more teams to watch. Keeps it interesting.

8) The Rockies: Maybe the summer traffic slows down in some of the parks a bit too much, but when the cause is people craning their necks to look at what the word "grandeur" was invented for, who can complain? And having to stop because an elk with antlers as wide as your rivers (see reason #4) has ambled into the road is nothing less than a moment of grace. Notice I'm not even talking about what you can see if you get out of your car and head into that immensity! A gift of beauty for all of us to enjoy.

9) Curling: I don't have a clue when it comes to curling. Never saw men with brooms, the movie or the reality. I figure that any country that buries NBA news inside the sports section so it can lead with a curling story has to be in on some important secret. What finally won me over was when you made a national hero out of a woman curler who won the gold medal. Something in the way you then mourned her too-early death was heart-breaking, even for me. Hockey might be your national sport, but something tells me your relationship with curling is about your national soul.

10) Quebec: It's a place apart, isn't it, in the very best sense of that phrase. Is it a distinct culture? You bet. I'm glad I've been a bit around it, married one of its daughters and am having my kids educated in its language. Let's face it: English Canada's more button-down propriety is nicely balanced by Quebec's joie de vivre—good wine, good humour, and you can even light up a cigarette without being banished to the nether regions of Pluto. But what has me most appreciative isn't just Quebec, it's the number of Canadians I've met in outposts far from "the French fact" who want their children to be bilingual, who want to have an immersion program of some sort in their school system. It's

a kind of cultural appreciation that's particularly touching when one comes from a land where Texans and New Yorkers live in separate, parallel universes.

11) Your Introspection: Ah Canada, what would you be without the questions you constantly ask yourself? Questions like: "What exactly does it mean to be Canadian?" You ask that a lot, and loudly. I think you even know you're never going to come up with the answer, mainly because the truth of the matter is that the question *is* the answer. And I love you for it.

12) Canada, I hope you'll join me in celebrating you. I could of course continue with more reasons, but instead I'm going to stop writing, mosey down to one of your rivers with my wife and kids, pop open one of your beers (reason #12) and give thanks I'm up here. Happy birthday!

Definitely Not the Chinatown Field-Trip
To See the New Year Dragon Dance

~

Meguido Zola

When a day passes, it is no longer there. What remains of it? Nothing
more than a story. If stories weren't told or books weren't written,
we would live like beasts — only for the day. Today, we live, but by tomorrow
today will be a story. The whole world, all human life, is one long story.
— Isaac Bashevis Singer

We are not, any of us, to be found in sets of tasks or lists of attributes;
we cannot be defined or classified. We can be known only in the singular
unfolding of our unique stories within the context of everyday events.
— Vivian Gussin Paley

Their story, yours, mine — it's what we all carry with us on this trip
we take, and we owe it to each other to respect our stories
and learn from them.
— Robert Coles

DATELINE: BROOKS JUNIOR High School, School
District #47, Powell River, B.C. My first year teaching in Canada.

"Hey," an exuberant grade 9 asks me as I walk up and down the
rows of desks. "Hey, Mr. Z, you gonna be in church Good Friday, or
what?"

"Well," I say, hesitantly, "well, actually, I'm Jewish."

"Really? Oh. I mean ... what's that?"

"You don't know?"

"Is it like ... like someone from out a' town?"

That was 1967: Centennial Year. Things have changed a bit since then. (If less so in country Canada than in the cities; in smaller places than in big ones.)

Twenty-five years later, I'm driving some grade 5's for a teacher friend. In the back seat, there's Adaan from Somalia, Devi from the Punjab, via Gibraltar, And Lisa whose father is Greek and mother Cantonese.

We're in high spirits and I'm horsing around.

"Why," I ask, "why did the *Canadian* chicken cross the road? Eh?"

"Mr. Zola ...," Lisa says, ignoring my riddle. "Can I ask you something?"

"Absolutely," I say.

In the rear-view mirror, my glance lingers on Lisa's striking face, her smoldering eyes. I have the feeling she's been trying to make sense of the exotic mixture that I present to her, as to many children: The professor with a predilection for big words (I don't talk down to children); the naive and sometimes downright silly questions: (I like to assume nothing and question everything); the slow-witted and vague Detective Columbo persona (to get children to explain their world to me).

"Go ahead, Lisa," I say, "Ask away."

"Well ... like, what ... er, I mean, you know ... What culture are you?"

Aaah, yes ... there it is again—that *big* little 'c' word. Culture. Nearly half a century ago, and a half world away, when I was Lisa's age, at boarding school in Kenya, 'culture' meant ... well, in its everyday sense, it meant (if you don't have it) not knowing how to handle a fish fork, or (if you did have it) being able to dance the tango.

Today, the concept of 'culture' is all pervasive and all-embracing in its popular use. (For instance, 11-year-old Lisa ascribes individual differences to that all-purpose notion. As well as complexity—even opacity—of persona.)

There is an understanding, too, at some deep if unspoken level, that we're all of us, one way or another, *from out of town*. Literally

and figuratively. Each of which presents its own set of questions
—for example: "What culture am I?" "What culture are you?" "And
what is *our* (Canadian) culture?"

For the world has changed dramatically. "It takes all sorts to
make the world," my teachers used to drill into me and my recalci-
trant peers. Today's children hardly need to be reminded of that.
As a grade ten boy said to me in exasperation: "I don't know that it
takes all kinds ... it's just ... we *got* all kinds."

A global education is one response to this new world.

"But," a teacher asks me, "is global education one more thing I
have to do—like flossing?

Last year, we did multicultural education, and before that whole
language, I think ... and the year before ... that it was ... what was
it, now? Who knows?"

What follows is a series of vignettes from teaching episodes with
three classes, in three different elementary schools, in which I ask
myself if a teacher—a white, male, elderly, middle-class, a Eurocentric
teacher—can tell a class of children a story about—of all things—
Christmas? And, if so, in what educationally defensible way? And in
what way that makes it relevant and worthwhile from a global education perspective? And how *that* might differ from, say, the clichéd
Chinatown field-trip to see the New Year dragon dance, on which
some of my colleagues take their student teachers every year as
part of giving them a new global sensibility?

***

We're reading *The Christmas Gift,* a short story by Hugh Oliver.

A story is a good beginning for any education, I prattle amiably
to the class. (They agree.) Come to think of it, a good middle and a
good end, too. ("Neat," someone interjects, "stories all day long.")

Because, I warm to my subject, *everyone* is a storyteller. Every
day we tell stories. Every day we hear stories. Someone has called

this the primacy of narrative: story-telling is a primary act of mind, the basic, pervasive way of organizing human experience. The world, someone else has said, is made up of ... no, not atoms, but stories! And the whole universe, yet someone else has said, is one great conversation, which goes on through the telling of stories. And it is this great conversation that holds us all together!

As I launch into my story, reading aloud, I pause every so often to draw the children deeper into it through role-drama, discussion, and play:

(Synopsis:
Christmas eve. In the loft of a lonely prairie farmhouse, a woman is giving birth. Downstairs, her anxious husband, John, is awaiting the doctor, kept away by the snowstorm that has been blowing all day.

Suddenly, a loud knocking is heard: "Will you give me shelter?" asks the stranger at the door.)

"Will you?" I ask the grade 2/3's, in role.

"I don't think so," worldly-wise Katie says with a smirk.

"Like ... how do we know you're not a *stranger*?" Brad challenges me.

"A stranger?" I ask wide-eyed. "Me?"

And so we dialogue, discuss, debate. We are in role: I am the stranger at the door; the students are John's children in the house.

Out of role, once again the teacher in front of the class, I engage the students in a lively discussion of what defines a 'stranger.'

Now they're better prepared, I turn on my heel, three hundred and sixty degrees, and—poof!—I'm back in role as the stranger talking to John's children.

Back and forth, I move in and out of role: now the stranger, now the teacher, taking the children with me; they follow easily, effortlessly, naturally—without explanations, without directions.

In role, I confront the children with the challenges the story presents. Out of role, I help them process what has gone before, prepare for what may come up next.

The children are struggling. *Wanting* to respond to my appeal to their generosity. But then again weighing what the police officer said in last month's *Stranger Danger* presentation. Yet *trying* to do *something* noble for Christmas.

"Just as I suspected!" I fling at them, as the clamour rises against letting me in. "All those things you said about Christmas and sharing with others—it's all ... just pretty words!"

"Not true!" Tara erupts, stung by my challenge. "We go to the park, my foster mom and me, and we give things to people who ... who ... like ... they're poor."

"Huh!" I say, dismissing her. "Likely story!"

Laughter from the class. (Was I too strong with Tara? Or is the amusement at the irony that, in this class of supremely privileged, Tara—underfed, unkempt and, sometimes, a little grubby—should be the very one talking about helping the poor?)

"It's not funny!" Tara is enraged. "We really *do*. Last Christmas we went to Pigeon Park ... we gave out salami and um ... Japanese oranges."

This time nobody laughs: God, as the artist said, dwells in the details.

"Well, Tara," I say, "that's only one member of this class."

"*We* sponsor an orphan," Emily simpers.

I raise an eyebrow sceptically.

"We can't pronounce her name but ... what I know is all they have to eat is bananas."

"Give them all bananas," I retort, "every orphan in the *world* for all *I* care—it won't help me, will it? *I'll* freeze."

In the end, the girls suggest a vote. A secret ballot—everybody heads down and eyes closed as their teacher counts hands.

***

"Sure, we'll let you in," the grade 4/5's shrug: "No sweat."

I can't stir up a discussion. Everything proceeds smoothly to the next stage. The grade 6's, though, hesitate. They're a different breed, here.

The boys accept the stranger into their midst because, they claim they can handle anything: " ... like with our ray guns."

"We have *no* guns," their teacher quietly interjects from the back, not even bothering to look up from her marking.

"Well ... the axe for chopping wood ... whatever."

This time, it's the girls who are resisting me—the 'pervert', as I become referred to; for the issue quickly links up to abductions and rapes that have occurred in the neighbourhood recently; then to immigrant youth gangs, and their battles in the streets of our city; and the home invasions by yet other immigrant gangs; and the dangers—to a whole country—of carelessly letting in strangers.

At one point, Kenji, in exasperation at the obtuseness of his classmates, asks why the class can't just check out my identity card. In Japan, he explains, *everyone* carries these mini-passports, and crime is consequently relatively rare. The ensuing discussion is rich and wide-ranging.

The impasse is broken only later, when Marie suggests putting me in the barn: "That way you won't freeze or starve ..."

I nod gratefully.

"At the same time," she beams, "you won't get in our way to spoil our Christmas."

"And we won't have to look at you," another voice pipes up.

"Hmm, I wonder," I ask, out of role, "if that is what we sometimes do to some people—immigrants, or the poor, or those with mental illness? And if that was part of the reason Mary and Joseph ended up in the manger?"

"No, no," Jason sets me right. "There was no Holiday Inns in those years, 'member?"

(Synopsis:
The presence of the stranger grows ever more mysterious. His
answers to direct questions about who he is, what is he doing,
where he is going, are disturbingly evasive: "I have much work to
do... I have far to go ..." Soon after, John's mother-in-law comes
downstairs to announce that the baby was born dead. John goes
upstairs to comfort his wife. When he returns, carrying his baby,
the stranger asks to hold the newborn.)

The grade 2/3's readily acquiesce. I sense their intuitive hope in a
deus ex machina resolution through the presence of the mysterious
stranger.

The grade 4/5's, once again, don't care one way or another. Only
Monique objects. She talks passionately about respect for the dead,
reverence for the human body. (Is it because her father is a physician,
I wonder to myself? Is it because Monique—the only black child in the
school—has a different kind of spirituality?). Whatever the reason,
Monique is on fire: articulate and passionate. She carries the class.

In the grade 6 class, Chen vehemently argues the exact opposite: "Is dead body—you just throw away," he exclaims.

Chen is newly come from Beijing. His grandmother recently
gave the class a riveting report on the culture of the old country—
including state-sponsored contraception and abortion to limit
population; and eugenics to improve it.

(Synopsis:
John hands the baby to the stranger, who gives the newborn a kiss:
"He needs to be made warm," says the stranger. "But he's dead,"
says John. Suddenly the baby cries out, eyes fluttering open.
"Why, you have done a miracle!" exclaims the father.
"He wasn't dead—he never lived," says the stranger, preparing
to leave.

"Stay," John begs. "Stay with us forever"—in vain. The stranger hurriedly leaves. As John watches his figure disappear into the distance, he notices that the snow has stopped falling. But the stranger leaves no footprints in the snow. The father's heart is filled with wonder.)

So are the hearts of the grade *2/3's;* wonder and quiet.

"Wow!" Robert, never one to let a good silence last, breaks in.

I recall Vladimir Horowitz once telling us: "It's the silence that matters, not the applause.

Anyone can have applause. But the silence during the playing —that is everything."

And I think about the silence when I was reading ... and about the wonder.

Jeremy—of the SLD ('Severely Learning Disabled') label—asks: "Can Jesus float?"

The children's eyes search my face.

"Can Jesus float?" I echo. "I wonder."

"Why *Jesus*?" Katie asks.

In no time we're in the middle of a theological debate. About the mysteries of a triune God; about the nature of any transcendent power—random? Benevolent? Vengeful? And, of course, about ghosts —TV ghosts, R.L. Stine ghosts, and real ghosts we have known.

"I think," Niels, ever-helpful, proposes, "I really think it might be God in a disguise"—a neat compromise that encompasses all possibilities. That, after some more out-of-role discussion, allows us to move on.

***

Later, with the grade 6's, I offer to read the first, the original Christmas story. "Humph," Nadja, from St. Petersburg, says, tossing her hair before asking dramatically: "Why you call 'original'? Huh?"

"I think," Farid corrects me, "you are meaning is real story only just for citizens of U.S.A." He scrutinizes me: "Isn't it?"

As I move from Luke's narrative of the annunciation to Matthew's account of the finding of the baby in the manger, I emphasize that I am reading not to proselytize, but because we need to get to know each other's stories, and most especially, everyone's myths. "We are not," I quote Vivian Gussin Paley, "we are not any of us, to be found in sets of tasks or lists of attributes; we cannot be defined or classified. We can be known only in the singular unfolding of our unique stories within the context of everyday events." And I am reading because –

"Well, then, just read!" Chen waves me on, hovering over his classmates, stretched out on the carpet of the darkened classroom: "You *not* have to *explain*."

I laugh as I remember my daughter Marah expressing those very sentiments if I interrupted my reading aloud with an aside or even the gentlest of questions. For a good story, I suppose, needs no editorializing—or comprehension check. It surely can stand on its own, as I have been reminded once again with these three classes.

Which suggests to me one answer to my questions: "Why story (even the most unlikely story in circumstances less than ideal)?" "Why dramatic play?" "Why talk and discussion?"

Because, first, talk and play just *are*. In the same way a story just *is*—simply there, like life itself. And because, second, dramatic play and exploration make us pause, and wonder, and question, and, as in this Christmas story drama, we are exploring, "*live* the questions," in the words of Rainer Maria Rilke. And this moves us. And—as we learn with and from each other—perhaps even transforms us.

For what other lesson has prompted us this week in the classroom, in the space of an hour or two, to reflect, and wonder aloud, and share with others, about birth and death; about the body and the soul; about good and evil; about mystery; about magic; about

God; about what we do and don't know; about differences in the way we are, and think, and feel, and do? And what other activity in the class has given us occasion to listen to both our own and each others' lives—or at least certain moments of those lives—for "whatever of meaning, of importance, of worth, there may be in them to hear?" (Buechner, 1992, 17).

***

I recall once watching David Booth question Roxanne, a child with Down's Syndrome, as her class explored John Burningham's *Would You Rather* ... "Would you rather," one spread asks, "your house was surrounded by water ... snow ... or jungle?"

Watching Roxanne make snow angels on the gym floor, but not quite sure of her abilities, David gently asks: "Is your house surrounded by snow?"

Roxanne nods affirmatively.

"D'you like living here, in the snow?"

The child again nods yes.

"Are you ... the Queen of Winter?"

Once more, a nod for yes.

"Then ... what are you wearing on your head?"

"A crown of ice."

Which suggests yet another answer to the question: "Why dramatic play?" Dramatic play is about giving us (or drawing from us) the words—the sublime, creative words—that help us make meaning of (and give meaning to) our lives. And if that isn't at the heartbeat of education, what is?

***

(P.S.: So why *did* the Canadian chicken cross the road? Eh? No, not just for fun (Epicurus). Nor out of custom and habit (Hume). Nor yet because the eternal hen-principle made it do it (Goethe). Nor even to prove it could never reach the other side (Zeno of Elea). And *definitely* not in order to act in good faith and be true to itself (Sartre). *Or* to live deliberately ... and suck all the marrow out of life (Henry David Thoreau). No, no, no. The *Canadian* chicken crossed the road simply to get to the *middle*, of course! I mean, hey! What did you think? Eh?)

Going Back

Three Readings

Roxanne Felix

WHIRR WHIRR WHIRR crrriiiink. Whirr whirrr whirr crrriiiink.

I was certain, now. The throbbing pain on the side of my head mimicked the fan's rhythm.

Whirr whirr whirr crrriiink. Whirr whirr whirr crrriiink.

I couldn't breathe. Was it because of the headache or the heat ... or, maybe the fan? The blade grated against its metal cage in a deliberate attempt to taunt me. It knew I couldn't live without it. It saved me from the stifling air that threatened to choke me. Its hot waves of air felt almost like the blast of a weakened hair dryer, but it knew that was enough for me not to turn it off, despite its irritating grinding gears.

I was full of mixed emotions about that fan. It was how I felt about being in the Philippines.

I had arrived two days before, about to start on a research project. By pure coincidence, my study was in my parents' home country. Before heading south to my research site, I found myself in Manila, visiting relatives who had previously only been names to me.

I had met this particular aunt of mine once or twice before, in San Francisco. She had retired to Manila after practicing as a nurse for over 30 years in the USA. I deposited myself in her darkened living room while she disappeared into the bedroom to fish for something she thought I'd be interested in seeing. I waited.

Strangely then, the traffic noises that incessantly made their way through the open windows of the house seemed to come to a standstill. Usually there was an endless stream of staccato honking and revving, mirroring the "stop and go" flow of traffic. But, now, it was almost … well … quiet. I looked up at the clock and was surprised to be to able hear it tick-tick-ticking away. The pause in the angry, noisy clamour outside seemed to waken a craving for silence within me.

Whirr whirr whirr crrriiink. Whirrr whirr whirr crrriiink.

Should I cry or laugh? It was too much. My muscles gave in to all the tension and I collapsed awkwardly onto the couch, sinking and settling into it. In truth, it was exhausting to be there, representing my father and all that he accomplished in Canada. I was grateful to rest my head for a while on those boxy foam cushions wrapped in their rough fabric.

I remembered then. It was my grandparents' couch, over 50 years old. The hefty, solid couch with its stiff wooden frame looked so out of place with the cool, elegant marble floors. I wondered if my family members looked at me and thought: "*She* looks out of place."

I *expected* to feel out of place, and was shocked when I realized I didn't. In the airport, as soon as I arrived, the porters launched a verbal assault, marketing their services to me quickly in Tagalog. Of course, I didn't understand them—I can't speak the language. Yet, I knew it wasn't rude to dismiss them by pretending I was angry, shaking my head, furrowing my eyebrows violently and avoiding eye contact.

It was as if my body was tuning into something that I had effectively ignored for the past couple of decades. This duality, of feeling like a stranger but also feeling at home, started to pervade everything I did in the Philippines—from expecting a set of slippers at the door, to eating salted fish for breakfast, to bathing this morning with a bucket of water and a tiny hand-sized pail. The dichotomy haunted and exhausted me.

"Ahh, here it is," my aunt called out as she shuffled to where I sat. She was a tiny, wiry lady, still capable of strong, quick movements. Satisfied with herself, she proudly hauled a tottering stack of faded green photo albums in her arms. Over the stack of dusty albums, I could barely make out her ebony hair and intent, dark eyes. I stood up quickly to take the albums from her. She eased herself down onto the couch beside me and hoisted the albums back onto her lap.

My aunt sifted through the photo albums slowly, giving me lengthy descriptions of the different locations, individuals, and circumstances of each picture. Page after page she turned as I watched, distractedly. Finally, she arrived at a stack of brittle, yellowing sheets that had been tucked in between some faded pages.

With delicate movements, my aunt's fragile, almost translucent hands pulled out the sheets and placed them in my hands. The pages were so old they almost fell apart along the two evenly spaced creases where they had originally been folded. In the faded ink of typewritten characters, the first few words read: "The boy was descended from a sturdy stock of pioneers from Paoay, Ilocos Norte."

I felt my weariness lift as my eyes moved to the title at the top of the page. In imposing capital letters, the following words stood out: "BIOGRAPHY OF JUAN FELIX."

It was the biography of my grandfather. He had written it himself, in English.

All of a sudden, I felt very possessive. I really knew nothing of him, except that he died of a heart attack in the 1950s, just before my father had started college.

This cache of my grandfather's words was an unexpected treasure. I wanted to take time to dust off the dirt, examine each nook

and cranny, and discover what secrets it held, without being interrupted. What was only a curiosity a few moments ago suddenly became a basic need. It promised to be something so integral to me,
whose absence, until now, had made it seem just an elusive shadow.

I politely asked my aunt if I could keep the biography to read
later. She nodded absent-mindedly, unaware of the precious value it
carried. I let out the breath I didn't realize I had been holding back.

Later that night, after everyone else had gone to sleep, I put on
my lamp and tucked the edges of my mosquito net securely under
my mattress. I shivered, despite the heat that lingered from the
day. My hands shook as I pulled out the yellowed pages and prepared to read Juan Felix's biography.

My stomach growled and heaved. It was a welcome distraction
from the sudden recollection of rumours that my grandfather
haunted the family home. I focussed on the rustling in the neighbours' kitchen nearby, and the roosters scraping the floor of the
yard with their scaly claws. My uncle's dog dragged his chain back
and forth along the sidewalk outside. I giggled a little. Strangely,
those ordinary sounds seemed to comfort me.

Looking down at the sheets in my lap, I re-read my grandfather's first words: "The boy was descended from a sturdy stock of
pioneers from Paoay, Ilocos Norte."

Pioneers? Images of pitchforks, hay bales and sod houses from
the Canadian Prairies flashed through my head. What did it mean
to be a pioneer in the Philippines? I pushed the question out of my
mind and continued reading, hungry for tidbits of my grandfather's
life. I stumbled over words that were unfamiliar and difficult to
pronounce: *Camiling. Santa Ignacia. Mayantoc.* My grandfather
wrote about being able to exchange a farm for a *bolo.* I didn't even
know what a *bolo* was.

The story carried on, a litany of all his brothers and sisters, his
years of schooling, places of employment, highlights of his career,
and his salaries. I skipped over those details, eager to read about

why he chose my grandmother for a wife, or what he thought of my father, who was his youngest son. How did he feel about the Second World War? Was he glad when the Americans came?

I flipped page after page. I finally stopped, puzzled, when I reached the end of his story. Was that all that it carried? Dates, facts, numbers? I must have skipped a page, or read too fast. I rapidly flipped to the front and started again, studying every word meticulously, searching within those pages for some essence of my Grandfather.

More disappointed by the second reading than the first, I realized there was nothing there to which I could connect. I was confused. He barely even mentioned his family. All the values I respected weren't reflected in his words. He was focused mostly on his educational and employment achievements. No words could be found about tradition, family, or duty.

But then, half-forgotten stories about my grandfather drifted back into my consciousness. Stories about how he worked late and wasn't around much. How my grandmother often cried in his absence. How my aunts used to lock him in the house so he wouldn't go out at night.

I put the sheets down on my lap. "Of course," I thought. "Of course, we wouldn't have anything in common." He was a man of a different time, a different society, a different culture. How could I possibly understand him?

I wondered if he was happy that his children left his home country to forge a better life. Or was he saddened that his son, named after himself, would have to change his name, Juan, to John, so that citizens of his new country could pronounce it? Was he shocked that his granddaughters were working outside the home; disappointed that half of his grandchildren wouldn't be able to greet him in his own language?

And, all of a sudden, my disappointment was eclipsed by sadness. I couldn't bear to think how grieved he might be to discover that his granddaughter, on picking up his biography, wouldn't be able to relate to anything he had chosen to record and share.

My mind was blank, as was my heart. With a sigh, I read over his words a third time. I found a paragraph on how his physical frailty marked him, ironically, as being only good for "schoolwork." I had forgotten that an education wasn't valued back then. How odd. My father had drilled into my head that educational opportunities were the primary reasons that caused my parents to immigrate to Canada.

However, my grandfather was clear that it didn't matter if, in his own words, he was "practically useless on the farm." It was clear that Juan Sr. was proud of his accomplishments, as his "promotions were considered rapid." I found reasons for his resignation ("the director was almost always drunk"); a list of books he liked to read ("Greatest Women of History, Greatest Men Series, Old Italian Painters, Marden Inspirational books, etc."); and names of friends —Tomas Daradar and Candido Prado.

And, then I came upon the last sentence, in which he described himself this way:

Having been very poor, and still poor, and not a be-degreed man, his ambitions consist in having his children go through college and with a life a little different from his with respect to material possessions.

I stopped for a moment and re-read his words. I let out a big sigh then and felt something in my heart lock back into place. What it was, I didn't know. Pride perhaps, of belonging or heritage? It didn't really matter, because I finally felt that I understood Juan Felix a little. I was so glad to have discovered this small fragment of insight, this little something I knew I would always be proud to carry with me.

Excerpts from *'Ireland's Eye'*

Mark Anthony Jarman

*To have an opinion about Ireland, one must begin
by getting at the truth; and where is it to be had in the country?*
—William Makepeace Thackeray, *The Irish Sketch Book*

*And so every anecdote in Northern Ireland
has to come accompanied by its refutation.*
—Will Self

Chapter Twenty: MR. GEARBOX

In the year of Our Lord 1999. Light like porridge pours past our lowering plane and onto the Irish Sea and the pretty land along the water, a frigid, grudging spring yielding a frigid, grudging light. Flying into Dublin once more. Every airport bar between here and Canada is full of Germans with fishing rods, and I appear to be not dating Courtney Love. If I can just arrive, can just crawl to my aunt's house in Ennafort.

A wet cold winter we had of it in Canada, and a very hard winter for my aunt Rose in Dublin since her son Padraic died. My favourite cousin stepped politely into a coma after Christmas, and Aunt Rose caught pneumonia and a big black dog attacked her leg and her leg it gave up a tendon. The dog mauled her on the street just around the corner from her own house, and she made it back to her door but couldn't manage the stairs with her torn leg, thought it was broken.

Her carefree, cosmopolitan son's liver destroyed by a tainted hep C transfusion courtesy of the Dublin hospital. *This won't hurt a bit.* Handing out diseases, as long as you've paid up the plan. A hard winter. No more golf for Rose. Sharkey came over and helped his mother make it up the stairs.

I lean my tired face on a window in a British Midlands plane. The stewardess in her little fold-down seat looks ready to cry, perhaps reconsidering her career choice, and I'm a flying zombie.

Snow fell last night on the Irish coast, dropping on the soft hills and spooky Wicklow mountains. Snow is so romantic, except when it isn't. There's a snowstorm at the end of "The Dead." I'm expropriating the story, making it mine as a squatter might in a Georgian house a door or two from my mother's ruined house on the Liffey. My mother's old house, barely erect in its latest humiliating devolution, has now gone from Island Hotel to Island Motors to Scooter Island to a Mr. Gearbox Mr. Clutch, somewhere down there if you could follow the River Liffey up along the quays. My mother's maiden name the same as Joyce's aunt two doors down. Scholars say Joyce's collection *Dubliners* was about paralysis, but isn't it clear he mostly wrote about me?

I can't find my mother's house on the seagull quays—it's too far away and around a corner—but from the old plane a startling view of the smoking Irish Sea and coastline: ships I'll never know and harbours and snowy fields falling into the sea, and snow on Dalkey and Dun Laoghaire, snow on Clontarf and Howth, and day and night the sooty orange train rushing and pushing past Ireland's Eye to Belfast and Derry, and snowy hills curving like big arms and snowy breasts nuzzling Dublin Bay, surreal snowy breasts dwarfing the city (*only if my love was lying by me*), and soon I'll be walking those cold cobblestones and bricks.

From the air I can't make out individual streets, can't find my mother's tenement house, but I can make out the Royal Canal creeping west in bad weather from Dublin City, can see the useless

18th-century locks and canal that pulled down my grandfather Michael in the green, green water the moment they placed General Michael Collins' bullet-shattered head in the green ground at Glasnevin, and I didn't think of this before, but who, I wonder, who climbed the steps with the jet-black iron rails to my grandfather's high house on Usher's Island, my grandmother's house, my mother's house, who hammered the brass on the big door to tell them that your father and husband and breadwinner is dead as a doornail and may the good Lord preserve ye? My mother in her eighties still remembers the wailing and gnashing of teeth in the house after that knock at the door.

And now my cousin Padraic is dead too, but it's not 1922, so there's no back-story or historical romance, no war and no myths; Padraic's dead just because the hospital that was to help him instead destroyed his liver (the likes of that liver we'll not see again). As I feared, Padraic was HIV positive, but he kept himself in good health. After Christmas he checked himself into the hospital because a platelet count was down, but unfortunately he was given a transfusion of blood contaminated with hep C. Hep C and a lowered immune system is not a good combo, a secret gunman in his blood, a single-stranded RNA virus destroying his liver and sailing him into a very fast coma. Hep C lawsuits stopped this years ago in Canada but it still goes on in Dublin. Padraic awoke once, smiled and told his sister and others that he loved them, and fell back into his coma.

What are your reasons for entering our fair country? I'm back in Ireland, chasing two corpses now and arguing with ghosts. My usual obsessions and lack of clear motives. I want to compare the Ireland living in my head with the real one under my running shoes.

I'm not looking for my roots and I'm not tracing my ancestry or family tree—I just want to see what I see, a bit more each trip, take a drink with my aunts and cousins, go to pubs, ramble around the country. I fly back when there's a chance and the cash or a credit card for airfare. Ireland is my magnet. (What are your reasons for entering my memory?)

And this time I want to ride the cross-country train to the west of Ireland; cycle Dingle peninsula again; tope a pint or two in Tralee, Dunquin, Brandon Bay, Limerick, Galway, Westport; stand at the wildflower cliffs; climb the loose quartz of Croagh Patrick up into the clouds, a wallflower pilgrimage retracing random steps I took when I was younger (*let us compare mythologies),* a lifetime ago when I met and lost the woman at the stone dock.

If only like a crab you could go backwards, interview the dead, walk with them, swim with them. Sharkey the policeman tells me you never get rid of the smell of a decomposing body. Sharkey uses Vicks VapoRub, goes swimming in a chlorine pool, stands in scalding showers, gets blind drunk on black stout, and that nuance of a corpse still way up at the top of his nose and he can't rid himself of that tinge. A different smell from sewage or excrement or other powerfully bad smells. You smell the dead; they stay with you.

It's always women, Sharkey says. Milk bottles or newspapers not picked up at the door, no answer, have to go in. Open a window and recoil. They're often in the bathroom, Sharkey says. Maybe they wake up, don't feel well, gravitate to the loo.

My cousin forces a door or window and finds them. Always women. A man dies, and a woman's there taking care of him. A woman dies alone.

Silently, my cousin and I think about our aging aunts, our mothers, that day down the road and whether we'll be the one who forces the door, the one who finds them in the loo.

The couple next to me on the plane flying in are very friendly, talkative, but I can't form sentences, try to hide my jet-lag face against the glass. They are flying to a friend's funeral in Ireland and seem rather pleased, though they complain that they put the body in the ground too fast in Ireland.

Barely time for us to book a ticket, they both say. They wait longer in England, you know.

The woman tells me that someone offered her a seat on the small airport bus.

"Am I that old now?" she asks me. "It sneaks up on you," she tells me, and I like her.

Their friend is dead and I am dead, not fit to bring guts to a bear, and she feels young still, wants to explain what it's like, how sneaky it is.

My mother remembers the Glasnevin grave diggers and the bumpy wagon ride and the wagon wheels black and the glass bier heaped with white flowers and two men in tall black hats holding the reins formally and two black horses with black plumes and the sound of their hoofs on the streets. Crowds of other coopers and men from Guinness, a cooper assigned to each family child, and she remembers a cooper holding hands with her and the dirt thrown on her father's body and it meant nothing to her then but now she's in her eighties on another continent and no more horses with black plumes and we come in jets and my mother keeps telling me of dirt dropping on her father's body and she dwells on it more now than she did as a little girl in the warm summer of 1922.

I'm three months too late for Padraic's funeral. No one told me. We wouldn't have known in Canada for years if I hadn't called. Sharkey apologized, said he looked for my number in Padraic's effects but couldn't find it. Can't blame my aunt: she had things on her mind. And perhaps easier for older relatives to *not* explain things they'd rather not explain.

Padraic and I e-mailed a few times over the past two years, then in the spring I let him know I was flying there again, but there was no answer. I was e-mailing a dead man. I phoned my aunt Rose and got a shock. I wanted to laugh for some reason, because it seemed so unbelievable.

"I'm sorry to say we buried Padraic after Christmas," said Rose bravely on the phone, though later I found they didn't bury him.

Too late, no matter what. This morning I flew into Heathrow early, a tail wind from Canada, disembarked, breezed through customs, and eagerly ran miles to gate 80 for a 10:50 to Dublin.

Yes! I was so happy, making it to an earlier flight; the passengers all just boarded, and they have seats and I have a ticket.

They say yes, then look at my ticket and say no. This is for a later flight.

So?

Security concerns. My luggage must travel with me.

I plead with the man at the gate (the plane lifts off without me), then plead at counter after counter. There are several flights I can get on—I see them listed on the board: *Dublin, Dublin, Dublin,* where now everyone has bags of money and a new Mercedes Benz, a new Fiat or Lexus or Land Rover. But they won't let me go. I beg, I grovel, I just want to get to my aunt's and sleep. Toss me on a stupid plane! If this was Vancouver to Victoria, they'd say: "Sure, jump on board." Not here. They say I have to wait four or five hours. They worry I'm the mad bomber of Canada.

The Beatles' tune in my head: *I'm so tired.* Trying to stay awake, I walk outside for air, exhausted in exhaust and black British taxis, buses, and pushing past zebra crossings and concrete ramps and tunnels and glass flyovers and tour groups with heaps of suitcases and backpacks and awkwardly flailing skis almost taking my eye out, my exhausted eye. I'm in London and I don't care. ("When a man is tired of London, he's tired of life," said Samuel Johnson.) I give up on fresh air, fresh exhaust, turn back inside the airport limbo, where I must collapse. But what can you do when there is nowhere to collapse?

I walk the wretched airport (abandon hope, all ye) where a tuna sandwich costs you 13 dollars, tea tastes like clay. Why can't I embrace and love this world, and permit it its brute casserole and moronic languages? Just need some sleep and I'll be a good little boy again. Our gruesome obligation to sweetness and light.

I need to move, do something, decide to push deep into the city on the tube, quaff a pint or two of the real stuff in a real London pub, and then turn right back around to unreal Heathrow and catch my flight to Ireland. Still have hours; I'll be okay.

I fall into the airport underground's shunting crowds of post-Asians and post-Anglo-Saxon yobs and blokes bound for Hammersmith and Cockfosters and the Department of Departments, Ealing shopgirls reeling past cricket pitches and bramble ditches and graffiti and Chiswick and council flats and Wren crypts and tombs and magpies and meatpies and *punters agonistes,* humanity hot against the tonsil roar of other blunt trains, blurred citizens yoked and flung in opposing directions in a groaning world that must defeat silence.

On the commuter train I close my eyes, hand on my small pack, exhausted, just close my eyes a minute, fall asleep with the rocking, lovely sleep, to dream I am on a Chunnel train to France, to *gay Paree,* and I have somehow slept through all of London's stops, stayed on the train too long. In my dream a dark train, a tunnel under the straining gin-coloured sea, and people are staring at me.

"I have to go to Dublin!" I shout.

I wake in a train in a dark tunnel, people staring at me in squares of anti-light. Did I just *shout?* That dehydrated panic of half-consciousness, of moving and not knowing where. Am I under the Channel? *I have to go to Dublin at 3:15.*

An older man in a cloth cap slides over, smiling: "Ah sure, Sunny Jim. Don't we all miss the ould sod. Dublin moya, get your nose educated in Moore Street!"

"I mean I want to go to Dublin rather than Paris."

The man exhales loudly. "Well, jaysus, that's all right for some."

A man says with a French accent: "It's Pay-ree, not your mangled version." (All of Europe contributed to Kurtz's making.)

First they won't let me on a plane, now I'm going to miss my fucking flight. Maybe the airport robot is blowing up my backpack this minute.

A woman says: "This train is going into London."

"Oh, thank god," I say.

"Thought it was bloody Dublin you wanted!" the man in the cap exclaims.

"I have to turn around."

Several people make cuckoo sounds, fingers circling at their temples, not caring whether I notice. We stop.

"Mind the gap," says the tape-recorded voice.

"Might as well be talking to the wall," says the older man. It's not the first time he's been disappointed. He reminds me of my uncles.

"I'm from Canada," I explain.

"Mind the gap," says the voice.

"Is Canada still there now?"

I'm in Dublin, asking for stamps in a tiny side-street post office. (At the Dublin airport armoured cars were picking up and delivering money. Coming in from the airport you see Mercedes after Mercedes—20 years ago I didn't see a single Mercedes in the whole country.)

"We don't hear anything about Canada," says the postal clerk. "Now a few years ago you had a fight with Spain over fish. I knew a 65-year-old woman, lived here in Dublin for 30 years but had a Canadian passport. They threw her in jail in Tenerife because she had a Canadian passport. Sixty-five years old and never done anything wrong, never so much as drank out of a dirty tea cup, and five days in a Spanish prison. Well, I hope you make it up."

Ireland always in the news. Canada never in the news. No news is good news.

In my aunt's neighbourhood I say *hi* to a passer-by, branding myself a knobhead North American. Memo to self: I've got to try something else. *Hello, top of the morning, g'day, good afternoon, hark, forsooth.* I try to stop employing the word but can't. Locals reply, "Are ya?" meaning, "How are you?" Or maybe they're closet existentialists.

Sunday noon: restless and walk to get the Sunday *Irish Times* for me and the Sunday *Independent* for my aunt Rose.

I cross over the tracks, bronze church bells chiming, walk a neighbourhood path between bleak cinderblock walls decorated with barbed wire, metal spikes, broken glass, garbage, and sooty evidence of a fire lit last night against someone's garden wall. If it can burn it will be burned, if it can be wrecked it will be wrecked. This is the ugly future, I think pessimistically. Spray-painted names in raging colour: Fingo, Brano, Nixer, Derzer, Toss, Dayvo, and Harmo, the last perhaps an abbreviation of Harmonstown.

Then on this wonky warehouse street I sneeze, and a man pacing toward me smiles and exclaims in a loud voice, "GOD"—dramatic pause—"BLESS YA!" He cheers me immensely; your man makes me glad I sneezed, glad I'm back in Ireland and caught another Irish cold. "GOD ... BLESS YA!"

Writing Home

Monica Kidd

THERE IS A story about my family that goes like this.

One night in the early hours of the 20th century, a group of men, immigrants all, sat around a bunkhouse in a coalmine camp in the southern reaches of the Rocky Mountains. None was long off the boat, and everything was new. The mines had barely begun to open their black, yawning mouths. Alberta was an idea not yet begun.

The men in the bunkhouse passed time telling stories of life at home. Andrew Zak was born a Slovak in the late 19th century. At the age of 14, he had quit school and gone to work selling glass from a sack on his back. Early in his adult years, having already sweated through half a lifetime's worth of work, he learned about jobs in a place called the Crowsnest Pass, where a man could make five dollars a day and have food on the table and a place to sleep at night. He decided—like thousands of others—to go and try his luck.

Andrew had travelled much and taught himself many languages, which would have likely made him a welcome companion on dark nights around a wooden table with a long day's work behind him and nothing but the wind for company. The men passed around photos of their families. A picture of Rosalia Patala came to rest in Andrew's hands. The girl, her uncle explained, was working in New York City, cooking and cleaning for a wealthy family. She was alone and single. She, too, was from Slovakia. She would make someone a good wife. "You, Andrew. Maybe you."

Andrew wrote to the girl and proposed. Rosalia accepted. She left New York and caught a train bound for the Crowsnest Pass.

But that's just a story. If it's true, where is my great-grandmother's train ticket? Where is the letter from her husband-to-be, which she must have read and folded until the paper was thin as a moth's wing? Where is the photo he held between his coal-blackened thumb and finger (already shortened in one of a nameless number of accidents), the photo he might have swapped for a flask of whiskey to keep him company on the last long nights of bachelorhood?

Perhaps it is the prairie tendency to want to wiggle free of history that makes my family disinclined to keep such things as photos or letters. For all I know, Andrew and Rosalia had no desires, took no wrong turns, had no second thoughts; they merely met, married, worked, came north in 1919 to the homestead, then stepped aside for successively noisy, busy generations with their pick-up trucks and complicated families.

Nonsense.

On a shelf in what used to be my bedroom in my parents' house in Elnora, Alberta, I once found a thick blue photo album, with sheets whose plastic had already begun to fuse with the diagonal strips of glue. Among the snaps of my father playing baseball in the field beside the grain elevator, of him standing in his new grocery store sporting snappy plaid gabardine pants and a ball cap matching that of his friend beside him, of my placid grandmother with her cat-eye glasses and her hands folded before a visiting photographer's fake fireplace in a boardroom above the Credit Union, I found a stiff paper photo, the size and texture of a large playing card. Its edges were torn where a scotch tape border has been partly removed; it was bent in places so that the surface was folded and creased much like the skin on someone's knuckle. I have a copy of it still. Four people are gathered outside a finely-boarded log cabin, with snow on the ground, and the cross-bars of a high iron bed visible through the front window. A small girl with thin lips, suspicious eyes, and a head of fierce hair surrounding a plump face wears a black dress that falls below her knees and rises to her chin; she hides her hands primly behind her back. Beside her, on her mother's lap, sits a smaller girl in a white dress, black boots and striped woollen hat; her baby hands curl patiently at her belly, and her dark eyes look distinctly worried. Her mother, sitting heavily in a wooden chair, wears a coarse plaid skirt that gathers on the ground, a high-necked white blouse, and a black jacket with puckered pleats at the shoulders. With the exception of one rogue curl at her right temple, her dark hair is swept high into a neat bun; her strong, knuckle-y hands—they could be my mother's—lie flat along her baby's sides. The baby's father, with his large ears and his long, low nose, stands to the left of his wife, dressed in a grey striped shirt, a polka-dotted tie, and a five-button vest; one hand rests on the back of his wife's chair, the other on his older daughter's shoulder, the first joint of its index finger missing.

The parents are Andrew and Rosalia. Emma Helen is their eldest, their first surviving child, my grandmother. The baby is Annie. Not shown are the first baby, who died at the end of a few weeks of sickly life, along with Susie, Tom and Mary, who would all come later. A 90-year-old photo, one old story, and the sheer presence of their multiplying descendants is all the proof I have that they existed, the blank spaces in their narrative like a long breath held.

***

I am intrigued by Rosalia, my great-grandmother. Haunted by her, in fact. When I was a young girl in the 1970s, my mom worked at the Credit Union and my dad worked at our store, so my grand-mother, Mom's mom, took care of me after school. Helen (Helen Banton by now, for she'd outlived two husbands) was a foreign creature, quiet and stern, impossibly old. She wore housedresses and black-rimmed glasses. She boiled calves' brains for lunch and pasteurized milk in a tall pot on the stove. She fixed me grilled cheese sandwiches, taught me how to bake bread, how to knit, and took me to Lakeview Ladies' quilting bees where I sat underneath with all the knees and ankles and watched the needles come through my multi-coloured canopies. Some nights we'd sleep in her double bed with her wind-up clock ticking through the night and her bottle of Rolaids looming large in the amber streetlight. I loved her with all of my eight-year-old heart.

Later, after my first university degree, I decided to spend a summer at home before moving away to graduate school in On-tario. It was clear that Grandma, now living in a small seniors' home with her television and her budgie, wasn't long for the world. She was losing weight. There was hushed talk of cancer. Her newly apparent mortality and my imminent departure from Alberta made me realize how little I knew of her. I started dropping by her place in the afternoons with a tape recorder.

She told me her father worked in the Hillcrest mine in the Crowsnest Pass while the family lived across the tracks in Bellevue in a house built from logs he had cut with a broad axe. He'd chinked cement between the logs to stop the draughts, and shin-gled the roof. The walls inside were plastered, and underneath the board floor was a space for vegetables. A neighbour had made for them a door out of heavy canvas and a wooden frame; he'd painted it over with all kinds of beautiful designs. Her mother and father shared a bed on one side of the single bedroom; a second bed on the other side held all of the kids. An uncle slept on a cot in the living room. It was warm up in the mountains, my grandmother told me, but when the snow fell, it could cover the windows. One neighbour couldn't open her door when it snowed; she had the kids use a chamber pot whose contents she threw out the window.

After Hillcrest, they moved north to a place called Mountain Park, and Grandma was sent to a convent with the Grey Nuns in St. Albert, near Edmonton. The girls were on one side of the fence, the boys on the other. They went to church every morning before school. There were Indian kids in the school, and while white kids were given a proper McIntosh apple every day, she said, Indian kids were given only crab apples. Everyone was quarantined in 1918 because of the Spanish flu; sometimes a mother would come to visit her child and wasn't allowed in, but was made instead to sit on the porch and speak through a window. Even the mines closed because of the flu. Grandma's little sister, Annie, caught the dreaded virus and became very ill; strangely, after her nose started to bleed, she recovered. Grandma stayed in the convent one year, until her parents decided to try out a homestead in Delburne. The prairie was so different from the mountains, she told me: you could see for miles around and everything was so flat, so windy. Her little brother Tom believed the trees created the wind, and once declared he would cut down all the wind.

Eventually, there was marriage and kids of her own, cream to sell, houses to clean, the team of horses to drive for the community school. Those later days she didn't remember so well. I don't think she liked getting old.

That summer, Grandma and I drank gallons of Earl Grey tea with tiny spoons of sugar while she told me her stories and she taught me (again) how to make noodles from scratch. The next time I saw her, I walked into her hospital room back home in Elnora after a long flight from Kingston and recoiled at the tiny pale body gasping for air. Mom sat raggedly in a chair beside her. Grandma was gone in a few days. Our summer together is precious to me.

As my grandmother has settled into my own history, no longer changing now except through tricks of memory, it has slowly occurred to me that she not only belongs to me, she also belongs to history: the history of women who came to the west with nothing but faith and strong backs, and who proceeded to create their own meaning from soil and sky. Grandma gave me her particular meaning, and I've modified it with my own faith and strong back. As I have realized that I, too, am part of that history, I have come to want to trace our common history back to its source. That source, for me, is Rosalia.

Who was she? Why did she come? Why did the women like her come? Grandma told me the coal camps were a "rough and ready" place for a child to grow up. What about for the women raising those children, drawn (or hurled) from every which direction into rocky jumbles at the base of Crowsnest Mountain? What did they leave behind in their home countries? What did they bring with them? What was it like to watch their only connection to the New World leave every morning to walk into the belly of the mine?

At one time I made my living as a journalist, and I learned that, whereas we know the present is a shifty thing, the past we take —often perilously—as knowable. Trying to retrace the steps of my great-grandmother and so many women like her may be folly.

Perhaps that is why it is so appealing.

***

It is 2:21 by the clock in this hotel room, the little red numbers taunting and violent. I have been trying to reach Dr. Ján Lietava for several hours now and each time I try I get a recorded voice telling me all circuits are busy. The operator was no help, either.

With the exceptions of lecture notes, journal entries and a few poems, I have not written in a year. I can't remember the names and dates and places of this story, and I have no idea what to do with it. I don't know whether it's fact or fiction. I had wanted it to be The Story of Immigrant Women's Experience in Early Coal-Mining

Canada, but instead I'm turning up only a series of anecdotes, perhaps of interest only to me and a few people with whom I share Christmas cabbage rolls. I am flailing about in history. I am chasing sirens.

Now I am alone in a dark hotel room in some industrial region of Montreal, unsure of the way home. In short, I am having a meltdown.

Let me back up a little bit. I am in a hotel room in Montreal because my flight from Toronto to Montreal (and from there to Frankfurt and Vienna) was delayed and I missed my connection. I have not been writing because I began medical school last August, and thus my writing has been lying in state as I have been going through the wrenching process of trying to commit the body to memory. I am trying to reach Ján Lietava because he is a specialist in internal medicine at the Comenius University in Bratislava, where I will spend a week to get a sense of the medical system in a country unlike Canada, and he has graciously offered to drive the hour to the airport in Vienna to pick me up. But I will not be there at noon tomorrow, as I told him I would. I will be lying in this bed, wondering if I should call the whole thing off and catch the next plane back to Newfoundland.

Lately, I have been reading research about the use of writing as patient therapy. The advice one doctor gives her patients is this: *Start writing from where you are. Start in the middle.*

Yes: the complicated, smelly, clamorous middle, where every day begins and ends.

***

I decide to write myself forward.

We touch down in Frankfurt at 6:30 local time, just past midnight to my body. Despite pulling a blanket over my head and contorting myself into a million different positions, I did not sleep a wink on the plane. It is flat here and the air steely. My eyes don't quite work yet, but I can see that the manhole covers are rather artful. As a shuttle bus delivers us across the tarmac to the terminal, I catch myself thinking, *Good God. Why am I here?*

And almost immediately I am thinking, *What if I'd never come?*

Inside the terminal, things are very silver and smooth, all big windows and marble. Past passport control is a long tunnel—the better part of half a mile—outfitted with subtly-placed coloured lights changing with the emotional tone of electronica coming from the speakers. There are no windows, no ads that I recall, just two oppositely-moving sidewalks and a gang plank down the middle, one long experiential portal. (Leave it to the Germans.) The paper towels in the bathroom are green, and airport employees ride bicycles in the halls. I think: so many parallel worlds on this one perfect planet.

I do not expect Dr. Lietava to be here, on this second day of my arrival, but I as I come through the doors from the luggage claim, I cast a furtive glance around the crowd for my name printed on a piece of paper. I see no one, and am slightly relieved that I have not inconvenienced him again. I buy some cash, and figure I will catch a bus to Bratislava and call him from there. Then I hear my name over the intercom.

You've got to be kidding.

I rush out to find the information booth, and standing there is a tall black-haired man in jeans and shirtsleeves. He shakes my hand, picks up one of my bags and walks me out to his car.

I recounted to Ján my horror at not being able to reach him. "I had wondered what happened to you. I stayed in the airport three hours. I waited for all the connections from Canada. I thought maybe your flight was cancelled because of what happened in London." Earlier this week, a group claiming connections with Al-Qaeda bombed the London Underground, killing dozens, injuring hundreds, and stirring up the anti-terrorism rhetoric once again. "We're next on the list you know. We have 500 soldiers in Iraq."

He opens the trunk of his Skoda to throw in my suitcase. I ask him if he's been camping. "No. We have patients all over the country-side. I have to be ready to sleep in my car, if necessary."

On the way home to Bratislava, I mention that I'd searched his name in the scientific literature to find him published on all kinds of topics. He chuckles.

"Before studying medicine, I studied history and archaeology. I still teach in archaeology."

On the way home, Ján gives me a rolling commentary on centur-ies' worth of battles and languages and rulers and conquests, which all took place on this soil. "Did you see *The Gladiator*?" he asks.

"Yes," I reply sheepishly. According to the guy at the place where I rent my movies, shootin'-stabbin'-killin' isn't really my thing. I expect him to tell me it was filmed here.

"It took place here. This was part of the Roman Empire. Around this corner you will see the remains of an old fort."

And there it is, poking out of farmer's field in strange juxtapos-ition to a nearby cluster of huge white windmills. To a prairie kid like me, 100 years is a long time. Roman ruins in a farmer's field is something else entirely.

So far the highway has been flat and fast and, in the succession of villages we've driven through, the streets have been tidy and the plaster on the houses freshly painted. After a time, I ask if we're in Slovakia yet.

"No," he says, "a rapid change in living conditions will tell you that."

Another stretch of empty highway, past fields of sunflowers and wheat, and then, high on a hill appears a series of severe high-rise buildings. Bratislava. We pass through the border control fairly quickly, and instead of taking the straight route back to his place, Ján decides to give me a brief tour of the old city.

Separating Bratislava castle from the coronation cathedral, where, for two centuries, the Austro-Hungarian emperor was crowned, is the main highway and a futuristic bridge. Ján tells me the old Jewish part of town was destroyed in order to put up the bridge, and its traffic now rattles the very stones of the cathedral. Beyond this is more in the way of odd pairings: soft stone buildings with iron balconies and courtyards beside blocky socialist taskmasters, and garishly painted cow sculptures near where early monuments of the republic were destroyed in favour of offerings to the "mother party." It's an odd place: part Prague, part Winnipeg. I'm looking forward to exploring on foot.

We pass the military hospital where Ján's wife, a rehabilitation physician, works. I ask him about the state of the medical system here, generally.

"Terrible. Do you know how much a doctor makes?"

"No."

"Guess."

"I don't know."

"Six thousand Canadian dollars per year. And you have seen the prices here."

"How do people make it on that?"

"I don't know." And he left it at that.

On the way back to his family's house for lunch, Ján drives by the apartment where I am to stay. Last Christmas, they moved into their new home—still under construction, as properly-built houses can take up to two years to cure—but kept this apartment anyway. It is a large concrete block of the socialist persuasion. He gives me a spare set of keys and we go through the outside door to a darkened lobby and push the button for the lift. Through the metal door and into the tiny, airless box bedecked with graffiti, lit by one incandescent bulb, and smelling rather strongly of something that might be urine, we close the door behind us and push the ninth floor button. The lift starts upward with a jolt, and the wall starts sliding away in front of us. We sail past one door, past the thickness of concrete that is the floor, past another door, another floor

—it is all mesmerizing to a lift virgin such as myself. Then, at the ninth floor, we stop with a sudden bang and I wonder if something has gone wrong. But no, it is just the door unlocking, and perhaps my jetlagged nerves. He shows me around the apartment—a bedroom, a bathroom, a kitchen, a big fat couch in the living room—what more could a girl ask for?

Home, then, for lunch. On the way, he asks me if I drink alcohol.

"In moderation, I guess."

"What is moderation? Moderation Slovak-style or Canadian-style?"

"Uh –"

"When my grandfather was working, he would drink one litre of *slivoviče* per day. And I never saw him drunk." I'm not sure what slivoviče is, but I tell him my moderation must be in the Canadian fashion.

Fittingly, then, seated at his living room table, we start with slivoviče—which turns out to be plum brandy—served in crystal glasses of the Moravian tradition. It tastes like something that, at the best of times, could do serious damage to one's sense of gravity; but now, mixed with a bit of jetlag, I decide to approach it carefully. Then comes *Bridzove haluške*—a traditional stick-to-your-ribs kind of Slovak meal prepared from a sharp, soft sheep's cheese, potatoes boiled with flour, and bacon. This is followed by Moravian wine and so many more dishes of food that I stop counting. After lunch, Ján's daughter shows me her pet rabbit and teaches me a few survival words in Slovenske.

At which point, it is time for another road trip. The four of us load into the car to go see a castle some 50 kilometres away. On the way, we pass through small villages with houses set close together to preserve land for farming and to protect against what seems from Ján's descriptions like a constant string of attacks throughout history. The houses are long, squat brick and plaster affairs, some with small crosses cut in the attic walls, which Ján says are to protect the house. The hardwood forest beyond is deep and dark, with vines covering every surface, yet with a clear under-storey, as though green might once have filled the air, but has since settled into a lush mat. There are maples, willows, poplars, dogwoods. A person could be forgiven for confusing it with southern Ontario. Emigrants from here must have been thrilled, if a little surprised, to find that, despite the ocean between them, Slovakia and Canada look an awful lot alike. Except for the castles.

At the top of the hill, a security guard stops us and tells us the road is about to be closed for a car race. "Even the president will race in it," Ján reports. He backs up and points the car back down the hill. Not to worry, there are plenty more castles where that one came from. We'll just go to Devín instead.

Devín Castle can set the mind of one not trained in archaeo-logical metrics to spinning. As near as anyone can tell, people have been living here on this hilltop at the confluence of the Danube and Morava Rivers for 26 centuries. It started in the 5th century B.C.E with the Celts, continued in the 1st century A.D. with the ·Romans, and finally became a proper castle in the 13th century. Napoleon brought it to its knees in 1809, but mere decades later, it was resurrected into cultural prominence by Ludovit Štur, one of the leading figures of the Slovak nationalist movement, who would go there to hold revival-type fires and poetry readings.

"Language is the closest thing to define Slovaks as a people." Ján explains on the long walk to the top of the ruins. "Štur chose a Slovak dialect and made it common. Until then, educated people were not speaking the language. They were speaking German, Hungarian and Latin."

But if no one was speaking it, how was there a dialect to choose?

"The priests spoke Slovak. It was the language people would hear at mass."

Below us, roosters call from their perches in courtyards and wild plums ripen on their branches. The Danube and Morava tumble over each other, both swollen from all the rain this summer. Ján points out another ridge across from us, barely visible, and tells me it is an old road built by the Romans.

What a thing, this lineage. At first, I think: how could you help but be fiercely proud of such a long and intricate story as this?

And then I think: is it possible to feel smothered by history?

How I Lost My Tongue

Myrna Kostash

At nine o'clock the children are already in school.
The children prayed and sang with the teacher. The teacher taught
the children to read and write, to paint and to sing, to draw
pictures and play games. The children loved the teacher.
—From *Marusia*, Ukrainian-language reader
published in Saskatoon in 1947

THE READER HAS fallen apart, utterly, although the pages remain clear and clean, as though I had first read the book only months ago. I leaf through it: the illustrations are acutely familiar to me—the frog, or *zhaba*, the fairies floating on dewdrops like miniature parachutists, Marusia gathering flowers from the garden, the teacher, greeting Marusia and Roman, in a splendid green coat and matching green hat—and even the lessons resonate like fragments of poems once memorized whole and now remembered only for their refrains.

Dzvony dzvonyat', bim-bam-bom. Hen vysoko u dzvinytsi, tam-tam-tam. Dzvony dzvonyat', dzvony klychut', nas-nas-nas. Chy do shkoly, chy do tserkvy, chas-chas-chas. The bells are ringing, ding-dang-dong. From afar in the bell-tower, there-there-there. The bells are ringing, the bells are calling us-us-us. To school or to church, it's time-time-time.

There is nothing remotely ethnic in these lessons, save for a story about lighting candles on Christmas Eve. Marusia and Roman live in Middle Canada, in a suburban bungalow where Mother wears an apron and serves supper and Father appears twice—to eat, and to dandle the baby—and summer is spent at the lake, building sand-castles, and children go to sleep with teddy bears. This is upward-ly-mobile, lower middle class hyphenated-Canada seduced, not by its own difference but by its adaptability.

And yet the little book reeks of that quintessential ethnic pas-time—the mother, her children gathered around her, reading in the mother tongue the stories of little ones in an alien place—for this is how I learned to read *Marusia*, curled up against my mother's shoulder, my sister at her other shoulder, while the book lay open before us and we read out loud, along with her, chanting the text like a trio of cantors in church, and if not strictly *alien* (the bunga-low, the teddy bear) it was nevertheless *other than* everyday life.

For these supremely banal anecdotes, about fairies and frogs, and going to school and telling the time, were told *in the Ukrainian language*, the language reserved for extraordinary occasions and places—church, concerts, speeches, the national anthem, prayers, and those mysterious but clamorous arguments that broke out be-tween my father and grandfather, voices rising, hands slapping au-thoritatively at their respective newspapers—and here we were, this intimate, feminine colloquy intoning the sounds of that very same language.

And how I loved to write out the letters, all the curlicues and whorls and slanted strokes of the Cyrillic alphabet, *drawing* them, for long before the letters arranged themselves into discrete, mean-ingful words, the written Ukrainian language in my eyes was a picture—a design, perhaps, such as one could trace in a carpet or on an embroidered cushion. Pleasing. Like the swirl of my name written in Ukrainian in the front of the reader in my mother's hand.

Yet this sense of otherness is perhaps too self-conscious, and does not belong to the little girl at her lessons, for I don't think I then thought of these sounds and letters as strange or exotic. Pri-vate, yes; belonging to this intimate space in the pool of light in the living room or, later, in the church basement where none but Ukrainian-Canadians would wish to gather to study.

But I had seen the letters all my life—in my father's newspapers, on the envelopes that came all the way from Dzhuriv in the USSR, crabbed and cuneiform on the icons in church. And had heard the language from birth (baba holding me gingerly, her first grandchild, as she stood in front of her root cellar) and had even, so I was told, spoken it babyishly. It was synchronous with my sensory life.

It was, in an important sense, my first language and my mothered tongue. What perverse process alienated it from my mouth?

Kiev, 1984

I stood on a street corner near a group of schoolchildren and listened to them speaking with each other in Russian. We waited together while a battered delivery truck cantered through the intersection, bearing the utilitarian inscription, *KHLEB*. That's Russian, for bread.

In Ukraine, legendary bread basket for eastern Europe, mythologized and memorialized as the Earth Mother cradling a sheaf of wheat in her round, stout arms, as the three-layered and crusty, coiled *kolachy*, they eat bread in Russian.

All my life I had heard about this tragedy—how our kith and kin back home in Ukraine were having the Mother Tongue squeezed out of them, leaving behind a hollowed-out Ukrainian ashamed of a language which in any case he or she could no longer speak with any felicity. The Ukrainian language, as if by some scientific, philological law, was petering out. Russian, on the other hand, belonged to the ages.

I knew all this. I had heard it all my life.

I went to my baba's village. I met with her brother's descendants. They spoke Ukrainian. I didn't.

"Now," intone the elders in Canada, "do you understand why

we send you to language school on Saturdays in the middle of Middle Canada?"

From 1963 to 1968, I studied the Russian language and literature as my major subject at the university. The Russian language was presented to me as a World Language: millions of people in an important country—"Russia"—spoke it. It signified the language of a World Literature: major, canonical, essential. Every literate person in the world knows its writers. As I had earlier come to love the language of John Keats and then Arthur Rimbaud, I now loved the language of Alexander Pushkin. I learned whole poems by heart. I even learned how to sing one to the music scored by Glinka.

> *Ia vas liubil, liubov eshcho by' mozhet,*
> *V dushe moei ugasla ne sovsem.*
> I loved you, and love, perhaps,
> still flickers in my soul.

I loved those words, and rolled them around in my mouth like fruity lozenges, sucking out their hard sibilants, their throaty linguals, as though wooing the poet myself with my flickering tongue.

Screened from us, however, was the official, Soviet state attitude to the Russian language. Because of the undeniable historical fact that the Bolshevik revolutionaries had spoken Russian to each other, the Russian language was deemed more "democratic" than other languages. It was not enough that this should seem to be merely "rational"; it had to be seen as irresistible. The non-Russian citizen was exhorted to learn Russian out of "love" and "obligation" to the Soviet motherland and by this means to gain access to the works of the titans, the patriarchs, the guardians of the revolution which had liberated them all, from the Black Sea to the Bering Straits.

Now, in Kiev, in June 1984, a cold hard rain had been driving down all day from the steely sky and I came back to the hotel room miserable: wet, cold, and disconsolate. All day we had been trying to contact a friend of a friend by telephone in public kiosks but it had proved impossible—broken connections, wrong numbers. I was obsessed with the doleful realization that, had this been a normal country, with normal habits, we would have been able to telephone from our hotel room (here bugged), consult a telephone directory (here classified) or taken a taxi to the address (here driven by a chauffeur on the KGB take). I cursed this society which was frightened even of strangers befriending each other.

I turned to the television set, a bulky console on a table by the window where thin, white curtains barely screened from view the sheets of rainwater falling into the mucky, rubbishy courtyard. The set was turned on to the so-called Ukrainian channel (the other two broadcasting from Moscow). It was late in the afternoon. A children's program. Introduced in Ukrainian. A cartoon, of cuddly bears and fuzzy-wuzzy ducks and tiny, squeaky kiddies. In Russian.

And suddenly, I couldn't bear it: the Russian language vibrating in my skull in sonorous clarity, choleric, harsh and disciplinary. I wept from chagrin, from biliousness. I turned off the television with a savage yank at the cord and turned on the radio.

A concert program. A Ukrainian baritone singing, in exquisite diction, the song by Glinka.

Ia vas liubyl, liubov eshcho byt mozhet ...

Was I now to hate Pushkin, too?

In the fall of 1984, on my return from Ukraine and still smarting from my rude encounters with Russification, I decided to learn to speak Ukrainian. I began where I had left off, 30 years earlier: the Saturday School. No longer held in the church basement, the Saturday Ukrainian language classes—the Ridna Shkola—were now conducted in the church hall, a modern facility.

Together with some 20 teen-agers, I enrolled in the Senior class. The teen-agers radiated a self-confidence in their youthfulness and in their ethnicity that were quite absent from my generation at their age. I reminded myself that these kids were the *great*-grand-children of Galician immigrants, their ethnic baggage carried purely Canadian content and the last immigrant in their families had died quite some time ago.

I sat at the front of the class, took notes, listened attentively, raised my hand to answer questions and did all my homework. I was a model student.

Finally, the day came when I opened my brand-new copy of Taras Shevchenko's *Kobzar*, his collected poems, a book that is in every Ukrainian-Canadian home even if no one reads it (much like Gideon Bibles are in motel rooms). It was my very own copy, just purchased at the Ukrainian Book Store, a Soviet edition, with extensive notes.

I began with the first poem, consulting the dictionary when I had to and underlining words to remember, and so on, poem after poem, until I was a third of the way through the book and reading one of the most famous poems of them all, "The Haidamaky," when I suddenly realized I was not just reading Shevchenko: I was *inside* the language, understanding it directly, the profoundly familiar sounds of it all at once meaningful and carrying a story, a voice, a personality where before there had been only babble.

"Ah," I said to myself, with heated satisfaction, "so this is what they mean by 'Shevchenko'."

And in picturing myself taking my place among the generations who had preceded me in reading these poems, I had another image: that someone had just come along and wiped clean a foggy window through which I had been peering my whole life, nose pressed to the pane, steaming it up with my own breath. For just a few moments I had seen through to the other side, to the company of literates who had known all along the beauty carried by the Ukrainian language and the splendid architecture of its poetry. Soon enough the glass was fogged up again and I was once again stumbling and tongue-tied and overwhelmed by the learning still to be done. But I knew that, once I had been inside the words, without translation.

For at least a generation, since the catastrophic educational "reforms" of the 1960s in Ukraine which gave parents the "freedom to choose" Russian-language or Ukrainian-language schooling for their children, the Ukrainian language had been disappearing from public use—from schools and textbooks, from the mass media, even from road signs, posters and information about trolleybus routes.

Along with this erasure was disappearing the collective remembrance of a language which had produced literature and theology and historiography, leaving many millions of Soviet Ukrainians vaguely embarrassed by this Mother Tongue which lacked status and authority.

I felt implicated in all this.

While for several years I had acquiesced in spending my Saturdays at "Ukrainian school," I had been a reluctant student, made wretched by my dim-witted understanding of what was being taught me and enlivened only by the hour devoted to singing and dancing. (In fact, I was rather good at the dancing, and this was my most successful "performance" as a Ukrainian-Canadian girl.)

Now, as a grown-up, I felt I owed a number of people apologies. To the patient if uninspired teachers, community volunteers who, like me, were spending their Saturdays in the church basement and who tried their best to illuminate for me the secret codes of the Mother Tongue. To my parents who, wishing to enrol the next generation in the Ridna Shkola, committed me to an instruction to which I was miserably unequal, failing as I did to understand not just mere words but the whole enveloping reason for being there. To my Ukrainian kin who were losing their language under the ferocious pressure of state policy while I was losing it from a supercilious disinclination.

To a Canadian-born child, the responsibility for continuing to speak a language imperilled in its own homeland was onerous but irrefutable; imagine, then, the sense of personal, intimate and peculiar *failure* of the child—found wanting before the ancestors—who could not speak Ukrainian.

Now, as a grown-up, I would try again, almost defiantly, daring the ghosts of the martyrs, the despairing teachers, the teen-aged girl, now daring them to say I couldn't do it. I *would* speak, and in speaking be granted membership, if only provisional, in that remote society of the true patriots, the sons and daughters of Ukraine, the Ukrainophiles. I had much to make up for, years and years of indifference and, worse, disrespect. I *would* be forgiven.

I would learn to speak Ukrainian so that, on going back to Ukraine and seeing the relatives again, I could speak with them. I owed this, first of all, to my baba. The relatives were the descendants of her brother, family she had never seen. She would have wanted me to visit them and to speak with them.

But I would learn this language to keep another kind of faith with her—this gentle, pink-cheeked, round-headed old woman who could speak no English but who never, with not a word, not once reproached me for my speechlessness before her. Now it is I who reproach myself, that I have taken up this learning too late.

She died in a state of failed communication with me—her language and memory so much gibberish to me at the time. She was the last person in a long line of generations who spoke only Ukrainian, and I broke the chain, speaking it not at all. Now I pick it up, wanting to hammer back my link in it, so that baba might live again in my broken, stammering syllables.

I Get My Wish

In 1988 I travelled again to Ukraine, this time endowed with the power of speech.

As before, I hear the Russian language everywhere. On the so-called Ukrainian television station, an interviewer addresses his guest, a Komsomol bureaucrat, in Ukrainian and is answered in Russian. In the streets of Kiev, a television journalist chats with a group of very young schoolchildren: he addresses them in Russian, they reply in kind. A little girl even burst forth with a poem by Pushkin.

The Russian language is pervasive, like a gas—in the airport bus, the Customs Hall, the hotel restaurant, on the rock videos, in the boutiques. But, this time, I did not stand by rainy windows and weep.

I revelled in the sounds I was making, even though I often retreated to my hotel room, my tongue swollen with exhaustion, my brain depleted of all vocabulary. Although I often failed to understand jokes, the lyrics of pop songs and the banter of children, there was much, much I did understand—speeches, arguments, manifestos—and although I was often too abashed to do more in conversation than to ask intelligent questions, I was exhilarated by my verve, as though I were dancing.

The Russian I once knew had been filed in some deep archive of my brain; the Ukrainian I was speaking has risen up and inscribed itself on my tongue as though I once knew how to speak it and had only now to remember.

And so I went to the provinces, to the village, met my relatives, opened my mouth, and spoke.

Going Home; Coming Home

Don Mulcahy

WE EMIGRANTS ... IMMIGRANTS ... can never escape the familial bonds that compel us to palliate, if not heal, the breaches created by our departures. Such ties, and the obligations they impose, remain imprinted on our consciences forever. Emotional tattoos, just like the stone-etched reality that it must be *we*, always *we*, who initiate the reconciliation, the reaffirmation and revitalization of those bonds, with return visits—the émigré's inescapable obligation. We are human, civilized, and reason prevails, and we abandon any inclination to deny what is expected of us, becoming comfortable eventually with the admission that it was indeed we who severed connections in the first place by leaving; we who complicated our relationship with our places of origin and all the meaningful others who stayed behind. Yet sometimes, on realizing the true emotional cost of having left, those of us whose departures were genuinely elective might sometimes be heard cursing fate for it all.

But return journeys can be motivated by less poetic, less romantic, more egocentric impulses than stem from family ties and heart-warming friendships. Like wishing to illustrate, to those who stayed, the effectiveness of our autonomy away from the old hearth; showing that we really can thrive beyond the borders of the inhibiting primal terrain. To show, maybe, what we have done with our lives, what we have achieved, materially, cerebrally, basking narcissistically in *the great transformation*, demonstrating who we have become, who we assume we might *not* have become had we remained.

After absences of four, seven, 12-15 years even, we sidle back, audaciously saunter through the old habitat, unrealistically, shamelessly seeking the essence of our vanished youth, and that (*now*) quaintly exotic ambience, dull and restrictive though it may have seemed to us *back then*. And we talk about our life's journey as if it's all been a mere weekend in the country, or at the seaside; a brief visit to Aunt Florrie's or Aunt Agnes's place.

On returning, we await curiosity about our new homeland ... queries that rarely arise ... comforting ourselves with speculation about our explanations having been pre-empted by this 200 channel cyber-cosmos that has insidiously beset us all.

The theme of *returning home* has always fascinated me. Understandable I suppose in an emigrant. Thomas Wolfe certainly knew all about it. *Going back* has formed the basis of countless good books and stories ever since the dawn of literature and before that it must have been prominent in the oral traditions of storytellers, starting maybe with the birth of language itself. Perhaps the transplantation of people, particularly those with an inclination to tell or write, enhances focus in some way, sharpening, sometimes romanticizing, remembered images of places, people, things, events. If the return journey is very long overdue, going home again may even promise the chance of meeting that rare, surreal phenomenon estranged emigrants have been known to encounter: that of experiencing life there, its auras, as if for the very first time. Seeing and filtering everything through near-strangers' eyes rather than our own, as the *locals* we once were.

It would be wrong to imply that journeys home, or their antici-

pation, never invoke apprehension over petty phobias; over concerns which would, at other times, remain innocuous, perhaps
dormant. Like the fear of being viewed as *traitors,* for having left
and transferred our allegiances elsewhere, as Herbert my barber
suggested in order to explain the cool reception he once sensed on
returning. And angst can arise relative to important details in-
accurately recorded, or even overlooked entirely, or about personalities seductively reconstituted from memory with less than
absolute fidelity. And there may be anxiety over an anticipated regret that not all the memories we return with will be positive, the
stuff of future rosy nostalgia. And what about that gut-wrenching
heartache on having to tear ourselves away from our old-country
roots all over again to come back? Or the related feeling of empti-
ness and regret on arriving back in the new country, wondering
why we ever left behind—in our case, all that intense Celtic greenness, and Dylan Thomas' "*... ugly, lovely town ...*" of Swansea, a place
of disparate blessings, the connection to our past. And we know
that once back in our new country that recurring self-recrimination will emerge again, prodding and goading mercilessly about
burnt bridges. Its connotation may seem obsolete nowadays, but
the phrase *displaced persons* would seem to apply to all migrants.
And who, other than someone with the insensitivity of a rock,
could ever escape or deny the ongoing confusion over our ethnicity
and allegiances, old and new; the conundrum that asks who we
really are and where we *truly* belong?

***

For 15 years I balked at going home, because, I lied to myself, the
mysterious lodestone whose magnetism never lets migrants settle
with ease was not yet fully recharged. A truer reason, harder to
admit to, was my dread of all the blank spots over there, the painful
voids in life that were sure to exist in the wake of the departures of

so many loved ones. Could home possibly be the same without the people who helped to define it as *home*?

Ultimately, the electrifying realization that fate can, and does, routinely intervene to destroy plans and dreams, persuades us to rush out and buy two return tickets—Edmonton International to Heathrow and back again.

***

It's June 2001 and the wonders of aeronautical technology have whisked us far away from Edmonton, Alberta. Not to the Emerald Isle, as my old Tipperary surname might suggest, but to its long-separated geological Siamese twin, Wales (or Gwalia or Cymru, land of the Cymry, or Pays de Galles or, reaching back far into history, Pura Wallia). The two countries are a mere 100 minutes or so apart via the catamaran ferries that ply the Fishguard to Rosslare route.

Pembrokeshire, the most westerly county in Wales, has been called *"the little England beyond Wales"* because it seems to have always been an English-speaking enclave, despite being surrounded by the Welsh-speaking counties of Carmarthenshire and Cardiganshire. I see Wales as almost a geographic mirror image of its Celtic geological sibling, Ireland. A common greenness binds the two lands, as do rolling hills, fertile valleys, a rocky coastline and, historically, Catholicism. Saint Patrick may actually have been a Welshman, or Welsh-educated at least, and Saint David was most certainly a Catholic. In the long distant past, in an era that may well unsettle the contemporary, largely Protestant Welsh, at a time when Wales was indeed Catholic, two pilgrimages to the cathedral of Saint David in his tiny namesake Pembrokeshire city was the equivalent of one to Rome.

Many Irish families have happily put down roots in this part of Britain, knowing that their other home is just hours away, feeling secure in their paradoxical *little England* beyond convenient reach of their historical adversaries, the English.

Our current residual family is Welsh by birth but Irish by ancestry and my identity is further complicated by my mother's American birth and probable U.S. citizenship, and by my wife Iris and I becoming Canadian citizens in 1969.

Disregarding politics and (present-day) religion, the Welsh and the Irish are indeed cousins: rugby-loving, addicted to music and the written arts, forthright, pseudo-religious, ambitious—but conservatively so, driven by periodic surges of compulsive creativity, prone to the evils of drink certainly, and acquiescent in the face of wealth, rank ... and sometimes the English. Still tending towards a little hat-doffing, and introspective, sometimes wondering in exactly whose image destiny has really moulded us. And both nationalities share that enlightened Celtic symbiosis of pub and church; of spirits and the spiritual.

***

Coursing the pinched, tortuous country lanes of Pembrokeshire, my nephew Desmond drives his little red Renault with great ease, negotiating the claustrophobically narrow country lanes and blind corners with the confidence and skill of a Grand Prix driver. There are solid, high hedgerows everywhere; dense impenetrable concentrations of both wild and planted foliage. I first imagine them as mute, aligned, inanimate sentinels, but then accept them as the mere delineators they really are. Along with the narrow roads, these densely woven green walls intensify the *enclosed* feeling, magnifying one's sense of speed almost as if in a tunnel. The weather is warm and periodically cloudy today, but bright enough to project ideal photographic light. It's a day that welcomes tourists and those returning, as we are. We reach a T-junction, by a pair of old grey stone farmhouses, still lived in but silent, showing no outward sign of habitation.

We swing left then down a gently curving incline and stop at the iron gate of a parish church, built of local stone in a style that's angular and puritanically plain, its only confection a weather vane, a stylised silhouette of a rooster, on the modest tower. Its walls are green with moss in the damp coastal climate. The doors and windows are boarded up—an ominous indicator of depopulation usually—and there is no sign telling the name or denomination of the church. Desmond says it's 'C of E' (Anglican), and he shows us a smaller, equally historic-looking outbuilding he says was a youth club when he lived in Rhoscrowther with Ma and Pop, his grandparents, my parents.

We browse among the graves, imbibing the latent sadness of the inscriptions on the lichen-covered slabs of marble, granite, cement and common stone, even though there are no relatives of ours buried there. The yellows, greys, greens and black of tenacious, abstract-patterned lichens preside as equalizers now, imparting their badges of antiquity to the headstones of rich and poor alike. Equality for all at last—never in life perhaps, but here at least, in this earth, among these cold stones. Through an opaque patina of grey-green and saffron lichens I read:

> ... *Also of*
> *Elizabeth Nicholas*
> *The beloved wife of the above*
> *Aged 52 years*
> *And of*
> *Hannah Nicholas*
> *Their daughter*
> *Aged 20 years*
> *Who were both drowned*
> *At Bentlas Ferry Feb 8 1889*
> *Also of ...*

We search for the oldest grave and young Amy finds it, dated in the early 1800s. The church is within a walled precinct of locally hewn stone. The walls are densely ivy-covered and look as though they could last forever so long as humans never intervene. Almost imperceptibly, low clouds begin to obscure the sun, a distinct chill engulfing us as moist air from the nearby sea drifts inland. Church and churchyard assume a gothic greyness; a melancholy aura prevails. We all seem to suddenly and simultaneously succumb to the pent-up sadness of the place and we comment accordingly and move on.

As we drive further down the winding hill, I, a retired half-assed-academic nitpicker, begin to suspect that this place may not be aptly named. According to Iris' Welsh dictionary the prefix *Rhos* is Welsh for *moor* or *plain*, making its name *Crowther's Moor* or *Crowther's Plain*. But I see it as a vale or a dell, and although not Welsh-speaking, I suspect it might have been more aptly named *Glyncrowther*, *Pantycrowther* or *Cwmcrowther.* Perhaps linguistically, these *English beyond Wales* may have much to answer for. We pass the original farm property on the right, disused, abandoned but still standing, apparently intact, gripped by a paralytic stillness now, awaiting rebirth or, more appropriately I suppose, re-incarnation. We stop the car, get out and approach the broad welded-iron farm gate. There are seven buildings in all, some lime-washed, others of exposed red brick. It seems absurd to have a farm idle when the soil is rich and blessed with abundant rain in this sheltered vale. But there is more absurdity to come.

We turn and look in the direction of Ma's house, and Desmond points out the ghostly corner, the weedy vestige of an intersection that was once the site of my parents' home. The paving of the streets and sidewalks is still intact, but yielding to the encroachment of coarse grasses, dandelion, strands of rogue cereal escaped from surrounding fields, clover, nettles, burdock and domestic strawberries gone wild. To the right is a meadow where once, while

I was detained in Toronto by pressing work responsibilities, Iris had photographed Julia and Lynne on poor Stanley the horse, now long gone. My mind readily conjures up Pop then, hosing down the green Hillman Minx on the street in front of their neat newly-built bungalow, polishing the car meticulously as though it were rare silver. Cars were not so easily acquired in those days.

From the farm gate we get the best view of the hamlet that used to be. The bus shelter still stands over to our right and beyond it is a red mailbox. We walk across to the mailbox, on which is a notice that informs of the weekly mail schedule. "Shades of the Canada/Quebec linguistic debacle," I comment to Desmond, briefly explaining the festering Canadian bedsore called *bilingualism.* The unequivocal mail schedule is bilingual, in a predominantly Anglophone county, in a principality that is now officially bilingual but where only around 25 per cent speak Welsh—all this within an Anglophone island:

> *Amserau casglu—Collection times*
> *Llun-Gwener—Mon—Fri*
> *8.30 AM & 4.30 PM.*
> *Casgliaed olaf Llun-Gwener—Last collection Mon.—Fri*
> *4.30 PM ...*

In the 19th century, the Welsh language, which is claimed to be the oldest *unchanged* language in Europe, was banned in Welsh schools. A child heard speaking their native language on school property would be made to wear a sign dangling from their neck, reading, ungrammatically: "WELSH NOT." Welsh place names and street names had been purposefully anglicised, causing young hot-blooded nationalists in the post World War II era to superimpose the correct version in green paint in the dead of night. The correct Welsh names were officially re-instated once the Plaid Cymru Party eventually gained meaningful support. The Anglicisation of names was so deliberate, that in some instances only a single letter of the name would need to be changed … but changed it was.

Desmond says that a small convenience store existed next to the mailbox, and as we walk in that direction the paving of the parking spaces in front of the shop becomes evident through ubiquitous weeds. Beyond that there had been a neat row of purpose-designed lock-up garages. The swan-necked street lamps still stand, though they no longer intrude upon the inky blackness and solitude of night in the still, sheltered dell.

Iris and Kassy amble up the slight incline of the weed-invaded sidewalk in front of Ma's home-site. They pick wild flowers. After a few silent minutes of searching intently for something … anything … recognizable belonging to the Mulcahy household, Desmond says he's quite sure that a copper-beech tree at the one-time rear property-line actually belonged to Ma. I wade through the waist-high weeds to the sidewalk and return to the farm gate and look back. Amy and Lucy stand in an area where the Mulcahy living room must have been and Desmond, awestruck, continues his search for souvenir trash in the backyard. I finger the three marble-sized pieces of crumbled sidewalk I've placed in my pants pocket, wondering about the number of times they may have been beneath my father's heels, wondering too about the countless occasions when the Hillman's tires left their black signature on the concrete curb that contained these pieces. Today the small pieces of concrete rubble reside in a glass pin-tray in our dining room, sharing space with seashells, also from Pembrokeshire.

Desmond joins me and we walk part way back to the church, passing a rear yard, weed-dominated now, but with its trellis rose-arbour still standing. The arbour is aflame with the potent, brilliant red of domestic roses, not having reverted yet to the feral state. I look up then at the crest of the hill behind which the oil refinery is located and see a slender stack reaching for the sky, emitting nothing today, except perhaps invisible toxins.

I become incensed by the assault on the human aesthetic that has occurred here; by the fact that the tentacles of American anti-culture should have reached even this bucolic backwater, cutting a swath through the way of life here as effectively as if it were the 8th Army replete with tanks and napalm. I resent the third-world implication of Wales selling off the countryside to avaricious Americans just for tenuous jobs and a few more litres of over-priced gasoline. In 1944 affections here could be bought with Wrigley's gum, Hershey bars, packs of Lucky Strike, nylon stockings, K-rations, free beers; nowadays it takes jobs and oil to manipulate wills.

Desmond elaborates: "There was an explosion just over the hill there one day, followed by the release of toxic gases, and Rhoscrowther and the surrounding area had to be evacuated. There were no casualties but the oil-company and the local authorities both became concerned about the potential fate of the locals should '*the big one*' occur." I think of the Bhopal tragedy in India. "After long discussions the company agreed to pay the county enough for the land and houses to enable the inhabitants to be settled elsewhere. Eventually the oil people razed all the homes completely." Clearly, he doesn't enjoy relating this story. He removes a tin from his pocket and rolls a cigarette out of the duty-free tobacco I'd bought for him in Edmonton before we left. Silent, looking off into the distance, he lights his hastily made, loosely packed caricature of a cigarette.

Iris and Kassy are picking intensely red roses from the trellis arbour, the labour of love of some anonymous gardener. I can't resist speculating as to whether or not his dissatisfied spirit might still linger next to it, at night, or maybe only on certain nights when the appropriate juxtaposition of forces exists.

The church, with its watchful tower, whose inert clock persists in deceiving with the mute assertion of *eleven thirty-two*, seems to confer an atmosphere of spirituality upon the place. I'm tempted to fantasize about the little hamlet clinging to the church, drawing abstract sustenance from its ancient spiritual well.

I comment to Des that I'm glad Ma and Pop eventually moved back into Haverfordwest, even though inwardly saddened by the mundane little tract-house that they ended up in, surrounded by near-strangers. I find it hurtful, and embarrassing in a way, to admit to my father's myopia and egotism in believing it appropriate to move from the Swansea Valley to West Wales at their age. How could he have failed to recognize that Ma was a near recluse who would never be able to establish an adequate circle of friends in a new location? Eventually, she ended her days watching the world go by from her armchair in front of the TV set, her swollen, mis-shapen feet resting on a pillow atop an old leather hassock.

This is my first visit to the hamlet of Rhoscrowther. I remem-ber Iris raving about it, extolling its unspoiled beauty when she got back to Canada that time when I was unable to go with her. Perhaps because of a reluctance to admit to being *industrial refugees,* the reasons Ma gave for moving into town from this idyllic place were twofold. She claimed it was too remote, which made her lonely when Pop was at work or slopping around in his boat, and, also, she resented a few undesirable families who had moved in.

On the drive back into town we're all quiet, but I can't help tak-ing the annihilation of the little hamlet very much to heart. I im-agine an oil-company executive, explaining, in a Texan drawl, to the bewildered householders: "… nothing personal yuh understand folks …", then taking off hurriedly in his limo for the nearest air-port from where he'll embark soon in the company's luxurious jet for a quick return to Heathrow and, eventually, New York on the supersonic Concorde. I hear him telling boastfully about the sani-tary nature of the operation: "… not a single shred of collateral damage …" His virtual phraseology causes me to suspect he may have been an officer, with daunting responsibilities perhaps, in Vietnam. I feel angry … then relieved … then almost happy, over not having acquired U.S. citizenship at their Calgary consulate, as I believe I most likely could have done on account of Ma having been born in Cambridge, Massachusetts.

***

Another week passes before we depart for Canada. In the 767 somewhere over the southern tip of Greenland or Baffin Island, I shoot my last three frames of film—porthole shots of low, snow-capped peaks, frozen shoreline, and open turquoise ocean with icebergs afloat in it. If the plane were a little higher and had a more panoramic window we'd be able to see the curvature of the earth's surface.

I'm Lilliputian up here; dwarfed, overwhelmed and powerless in light of the scale of things. An undiagnosed phobia, a nonsensical panic takes over, and it's much worse than that elicited by the recall of a fearsome nightmare upon waking. Similar perhaps to the more immediate sense of alarm experienced when standing on a quay-side next to an enormous ocean liner, its great bulk and its divergent sides towering over you menacingly, seeming to *lean* right over you. And you're terrified suddenly by this monster with buoyancy and mobility, that almost seems alive; this *giant* with the potential to run amok. Somehow, it all seems to be related to scale, and proportions.

Colossal entities, by their inherent nature, certainly dwarf lesser things, sometimes rendering them miniscule, insignificant, vulnerable—impotent even. Accordingly, this infinitely dimensioned universe dwarfs everything too, making America a mere flyspeck and causing Rhoscrowther to disappear altogether. That pretty well describes the state of affairs; that's about how it is when you stand back and look at the bigger picture. That's how it is throughout this world—in Europe, Canada, the U.S., Wales, and in Rhoscrowther, too. That's just the way it is. And it makes no sense whatsoever to fret or agonize over the plodding immutability, the sometimes relentless, crushing, jack-booted heartlessness of fate.

Eventually our aluminum leviathan touches down, with a benign bump and a series of shudders, onto Edmonton's terra firma again amid muted sighs of immense relief. In retrospect, I visualize our completed journey as being bracketed by the symbolic parenthesis of the trajectory of our ascent three weeks ago, and this landing. I talk, about trivia, like an excited child suddenly relieved of accumulated stress, realizing it's merely euphoria at having completed another transatlantic crossing without mishap. We sit and talk, waiting for the congested aisle of the plane to empty. Despite mixed feelings, the near-schizophrenia of emigrants' conflicting loyalties, there's great satisfaction and a certain sense of conclusion in being back ... dare I say it? ... *home* ... again.

Acknowledgements

Henry Beissel's "The View of an Outsider Inside" is from *Canadian Pluralism: The View of an Outsider Inside*, an address delivered to the Couchiching Conference on August 11th 1985 on the topic *Who Needs Canada?*.

Dana Borcea's "They Left Their Homes with Nothing, and Made a New Life with Hard Work" appeared in *The Edmonton Journal*, page A1, on Tuesday Sept. 7th. 2004 and is reproduced here with permission.

Roberta Buchanan's "Come from Away" won a prize in the Newfoundland/Labrador Government Arts and Letters Competition.

Ursula Delfs' "A Simple Wedding" is an extract from her published work, *To a Brighter Future* (Trafford, 2005), which chronicles the story of the Pankow family in Canada from 1928 on.

Vid Ingelevics' "Attention Mr. Ingelwick" first appeared in *Descant*, # 124, Vol. 35, Number 1, in Spring 2004, and appears here with permission from the author.

Biographical Notes

Henry Beissel, poet, playwright, translator and editor, lives in Ottawa. He taught English and Creative Writing at Concordia University, Montreal, becoming Distinguished Emeritus Professor in 1996. His poetry publications and plays are too numerous to mention, and his work has been translated into many languages. He has produced translations of Bauer, Huchel, Ibsen, Mrozek and Dorst; a book on Canada; two anthologies of plays for high schools, and the literary journal *Edge* (1963-1969). He won the first Walter-Bauer Literaturpreis in Germany in 1994.

Dana Borcea, who lives in Toronto, is a newspaper journalist who has reported for the *Toronto Star*, the *National Post* and the *Edmonton Journal*. She currently works the police and crime beat at the *Hamilton Spectator*. At six years of age she immigrated to Canada from Israel with her Romanian-born parents. She is sensitive to the rewards and challenges of the settlement experience and has always been drawn to the stories of immigrants, both through her writing and her volunteer work with settlement agencies.

Roberta Buchanan was born in South Africa, educated in England (B.A. Hons., Keele University; PhD Shakespeare Institute, Birmingham University), and immigrated to Canada in 1964 to teach English literature at Memorial University. She helped to establish Women's Studies at Memorial, later becoming Coordinator of the programme. Her interests are in the area of editing, and autobiographical texts, and she is a poet, memoirist, and active in the local literary and feminist scenes. Her publications include an edition of an Elizabethan satire, *Ulpian Fulwell's Ars Adulandi, or The Art of Flattery* (Universität Salzburg); *The Woman Who Mapped Labrador: The Life and Expedition Diary of Mina Hubbard*, with Anne Hart and Bryan Greene (McGill-Queen's University Press; short-listed for the Winterset Award for Excellence in Newfoundland and Labrador Writing); *A Charm against the Pain: 29 Voices from Newfoundland,* co-edited with Georgina Oliviere Queller and Geraldine Chafe Rubia (Flanker Press); and a book of poetry, *I Moved All My Women Upstairs* (Breakwater Press). Her historical research into women's autobiography has been extensive. Her latest publication is on the Inuit diary of Abraham Ulrikab, recruited with his family to be exhibited in a Berlin zoo. She has been an editor, founder of and an official in various Newfoundland writers' and women's groups, and was an initiator of the MUN Pensioners memoir group in 2003. She acquired Professor Emerita status at MUN in 2005.

Anton Capri was born in Czernowitz, Romania but has long been a Canadian citizen. He is a theoretical physicist with a B.Sc. from Toronto and an M.A. and Ph.D. from Princeton. He has been Professor Emeritus, University of Alberta, and Adjunct Professor of Physics, Athabasca University, since 1998. He has been a research physicist for Kimberley-Clark, Senior Research Fellow at the Max Planck Institute in Munich, and has been visiting professor at universities in Austria, Italy, India, Germany, and

Japan. He has authored 73 research papers, three book-chapters, four books, and has co-edited one other book. He has an interest in creative writing, and published a book in 2006 which dealt with physics for the layperson.

Laurent Chabin was born in France and has lived in Calgary for the last 11 years. He has published over 50 young adult and children's books as well as novels and short stories for adults, including *La conspiration du siècle, L'assassin impossible,* and *Misère de chien.* Several of his books have been translated into other languages.

Chung Won Cho is Professor Emeritus of Physics, Memorial University of Newfoundland. Born in Seoul, Korea in 1931, he is a graduate of Seoul National University. He immigrated to Toronto in 1953, eventually earning an M.A. and Ph.D. at the University of Toronto. His first faculty appointment was at MUN in 1958, where he taught until retirement in 1996. He was Chairman of Physics from 1976 to 1982. Visiting faculty posts: Penn State University (1966-68); Institute of Space and Astronautical Sciences, Tokyo, Japan (1984). He has been President of the Federation of Korean-Canadian Associations (1989-91), Executive Committee Member, Canadian Ethnocultural Council (1990-2000), and Asian Cultural Advisor to the Premier of Newfoundland and Labrador (1994). His wife Joyce is a Japanese Canadian, and they have two daughters, Carolyn and Rosalyne.

Joan Clayton received her Ph.D. at Western University, and is a Clinical Psychologist and Trauma Expert who has been in Private Practice for thirty years. She came to writing at the age of 48, and is primarily a poet and playwright. Her historical story presented here has appeared onstage twice: in *Perhaps English Isn't Your First Language*, which premiered at the McManus Studio Theatre, London, Ontario, in December 2009; and in *Displaced* *by God*, in the London One-Act Festival in the spring of 2010. Dr. Clayton received the Kobzar Scholarship from the Shevchenko Foundation in Winnipeg in July 2012 to attend The Humber School of Writing's summer workshop.

Thuc Cong was born in South Vietnam in 1953, where she was a language teacher from 1975 until 1985. She and her husband immigrated to Canada in 1985 and their gifted daughter, who is now studying medicine, was born here in 1988. Since 1993 she has been an educator and immigrant writer. She has had many letters and articles published in the Edmonton Journal and her work has appeared in the U.S. anthologies, *A Break in the Cloud* (1993), and *Dance on the Horizon* (1994), and in the Canadian anthologies, *Dawn's First Light* (1998), *The Story that Brought Me Here: To Alberta from Everywhere* (Brindle & Glass, 2008), and in *Lotus Petals in the Snow: Voices of Canadian Buddhist Women*, (Sumeru Books, 2015). In addition to writing, she is an avid reader and swimmer. She retired from library work in 2009.

Antonio D'Alfonso is the author of over 30 books. He founded Guernica Editions in 1978, where he published over 900 authors and 475 books. Since selling Guernica in 2010 he has worked primarily as a literary translator and teaches, when possible, in the fields of creative writing, script writing, film studies, and Italian, at various universities. His novel, *Un vendredi du mois d'août*, won the Trillium Award in 2005. His feature film, *Bruco*, won best director award and best foreign film award at the New York International Independent Film Festival in 2010. He has a BA from Concordia University, an MSc from Université de Montréal, and a PhD from the University of Toronto (all in film studies). His latest books are *Un ami, un nuage* (Noroît, 2013) and *The Irrelevant Man* (Guernica, 2014). He has translated the work of poets from Italy, Quebec, Belgium, France, and Switzerland.

Ursula (Pankow) Delfs was born in Alberta to parents who emigrated from Germany in 1928 and homesteaded in the Peace River Country. She grew up experiencing the hardships and poverty, as well as the community spirit and sharing of rural pioneer life. She is a farm wife, mother, grandmother, retired teacher, writer, amateur horticulturalist, chronicler of the Pankow family history, and community volunteer in and around Woking, north of Grande Prairie, Alberta.

Roxanne Felix resides in Edmonton, Alberta, where she was born and raised. By day, she works in the area of workplace health promotion; by night she struggles to finish her fantasy novel. She has been published in *Canadian Living* and in *Howling at the Harvest Moon,* a *Five Coyote Ink* prairie anthology. When not writing, she enjoys spending time with her family, kickboxing and heading off for hikes in the nearby Rocky Mountains.

Irene Gargantini Strybosch, a native of Milan, Italy, obtained the degree of Dottore in Fisica from the Università degli Studi di Milano. She held positions with The European Atomic Energy Community (Ispra, Italy), the IBM Research Laboratory in Rüschli-kon (Switzerland), and the University of Western Ontario, now known as Western University. She immigrated to Canada in 1968, and currently lives in Strathroy, Ontario. After her retire-ment she fulfilled the long-time wish of being a storyteller. She writes under the nom de plume *Rene Natan.* Her nine novels and several short stories have met with an enthusiastic recep-tion, earning her several prizes.

Vivian Hansen's poetry has been published widely in Canadian journals. Her fiction and nonfiction have appeared in many an-thologies, most recently in *The Madwoman in the Academy* (Uni-versity of Calgary Press, 2003), and *Writing the Terrain* (University of Calgary Press, 2005). She has been the ghostwriter of four murder mysteries. Her chapbook of poetry, *Never Call It Bird: the Melodies of Aids,* came out in 1998. Her first full-length book of poetry *Leylines of My Flesh* was published by Touchwood Press in 2002. In 2004, she published *Angel Alley*, a chapbook about the victims of Jack the Ripper.

Vid Ingelevics is a Toronto artist, independent curator, occasional writer and a teacher at the Ontario College of Art and Design. His artwork and curated projects have been seen across Canada and Europe. His reviews and essays have appeared in numerous magazines and academic journals, including *Canadian Art, C Magazine, Blackflash,* the *Journal of Material Culture* and *Descant.* He was a founding member of a preservation group that won a 2003 Community Heritage Award for their work to save the Wychwood Car-barns. He has participated in talks and panel discussions on many occasions in Canada, the U.S., Latvia, Sweden, Switzerland and Denmark. He has taught at The Nova Scotia College of Art and Design, Sheridan College, and Ryerson, and is currently an Associate Professor at the Ontario College of Art and Design in Toronto.

Barbara D. Janusz, a University of Alberta graduate, has degrees in both the arts and in law, and has published poetry, short stories, essays, book reviews and editorials in numerous literary journals, newspapers and anthologies across Canada. A contributing writer for *Alternatives Journal, Canada's Environmental Voice,* Barbara has given readings at various literary happenings, and has appeared on CBC's *Newsworld.* She has instructed in law at Mount Royal College and The Southern Alberta Institute of Technology in Calgary, and in technical English at the Universidad Catolica, La Paz, B.C.S., Mexico. In 2001 she was a runner up in the John Whyte Memorial Essay Contest, and in 1999 and 2005 won awards from *Synchronicity Magazine.* She is author of the novel, *Mirrored in Caves,* and her home is in the Crowsnest Pass, Alberta.

Mark Anthony Jarman was born in Edmonton, Alberta. He is the author of three short story collections—*Dancing Nightly in the tavern, New Orleans Is Sinking* and *19 Knives;* a poetry collection, *Killing the Swan;* the travel book *Ireland's Eye*, and the hockey novel *Salvage King Ya!*, which is on Amazon.ca's list of 50 Essential Canadian Books. He edited *An Ounce of Cure*, an anthology of alcohol-related stories and has been published in *Best Canadian Stories, The Journey Prize Anthology,* and many literary journals. He has won a Gold National Magazine Award in nonfiction and his stories have been nominated in the U.S. for the Pushcart Prize and the O. Henry Award. He attended the Iowa Writers' Workshop, has taught at the University of Victoria and the Banff Centre for the Arts, and presently teaches at the University of New Brunswick. He is the current fiction editor of *The Fiddlehead*. His latest publication is *Knife Party at the Hotel Europa* (Goose Lane Editions, 2015).

Iris Jones (Mulcahy) is from Pentrechwyth, near Swansea, Wales and is the wife of Don Mulcahy, They married before migrating to Canada in 1955. She is a retired dental assistant-cum-technician, an avid reader, a world-class knitter and crocheter, a proud mother of two daughters, and grandmother to three exceptional grandchildren. *Letters from Ceinwen* is her sole publication, to date.

Tchitala Nyota Kamba is from the Congo. She is founder of Apapi Film & Theatre, and her first collection of poems, *L'exil*, is currently with a Canadian Publisher.

Romeo Kaseram was born in Trinidad and now lives in Edmonton, Alberta. He has worked in Trinidad as a newspaper editor in both dailies—the *Trinidad Guardian* and the *Trinidad Express,* and has worked as a journalist in Canada. In addition to being a graphic artist, working in the printing industry, he continues to write as a columnist and editorial consultant for the Toronto bi-weekly newspaper, *Indo-Caribbean World*. His published work has appeared in the *Toronto East Asian Review.* He is presently working on a novel, and on his first book of short stories.

Monica Kidd grew up on the Alberta prairies. Her literary works include two novels: *Beatrice* (Turnstone Press 2001) and *The Momentum of Red* (Raincoast Books 2004); a book of non-fiction, *Any Other Woman: An Uncommon Biography* (NeWest 2008), in which a version of *Writing Home* first appeared; and three collections of poetry: *Actualities* (2007), *Handfuls of Bone* (2012), and *The Year of Our Beautiful Exile* (2015), all published by Gaspereau Press. She has worked as a seabird biologist and as a reporter for CBC Radio, where her news items and documentaries won numerous awards. She presently lives in Calgary, Alberta, where, as well as writing, she works as a family physician and tends to her young family.

Myrna Kostash, of Edmonton, Alberta, has authored seven books, radio dramas, radio and TV documentaries and theatre cabaret, and her work has appeared in various Canadian magazines and literary journals, in *Literatura na swiecie* (Warsaw), *Stozher* (Skopje), *Mostovi* (Belgrade) and in nine anthologies. She has been writer-in-residence at several locations in Canada and the U.S., Visiting Professor or Teaching Fellow at various Canadian universities, and sessional instructor in the English Dept., University of Alberta. She has conducted writing workshops at various Canadian and U.S. locations and has given readings and lectured extensively in Canada, the U.S. and Europe. She has been President of the Writers Guild of Alberta, Chair of The Writers' Union of Canada, Alberta representative to the Board of Governors of the Canadian Conference of the Arts, and is designated "arts spokesperson" on the Executive of the Parkland Institute, University of Alberta. In 2002 she was awarded the Queen's Jubilee Medal and an honorary lifetime membership in the CCA. She was co-founder of the Creative Nonfiction Collective (2003), and served on the first jury of the Shevchenko Foundation's Kobzar Literary Award in 2005, on the jury of the 2005 CBC Literary Nonfiction competition, and on that of the Writers' Development Trusts' Pearson Award for Literary Nonfiction. Her most recent book is *Reading the River: A Traveller's Companion to the North Saskatchewan River* (2005).

Christopher Levenson was born in London, England and came to Canada with his family in 1968 after spending four years at the University of Iowa working towards a doctorate in Comparative Literature. From then until his retirement in 1999 he taught English and Creative Writing at Carleton University, Ottawa. He has published ten books of his own poems, most recently *The Bridge* (Buschek Books, Ottawa, 2000), has edited two anthologies, including *Soundings: An Anthology of the Ottawa Poetry Group 1973-2002,* and has published two books of translations from 17th-century Dutch poetry. In 1978 he co-founded *Arc* literary magazine, which he edited until 1988. In 1981 he started the Arc Reading Series in downtown Ottawa and in 1995 co-founded and was Series Editor of the Harbinger Poetry Series, an imprint of the late Carleton University Press. He now lives in Vancouver.

Ian Mah was born, raised and educated in Edmonton, Alberta, where he eventually attended the University of Alberta, gaining a B.Sc., with specialization in Microbiology, in 1988, and a

D.D.S. in 1992. He currently practices dentistry in Sherwood Park, Alberta and teaches part-time at the U. of A.'s Faculty of Dentistry. He has a pilot's license, and also has a passion for cars, motorcycles and shooting sports. His grandmother's story is his first published work.

Anna Mioduchowska, poet, translator, author of stories, essays and book reviews, has lived in Edmonton, Alberta most of her life. Her most recent work has appeared in *Edmonton on Location, River City Chronicles,* published by NeWest, Edmonton; *Writing the Terrain, a poetry anthology,* University of Calgary Press; and *Dance the Guns to Silence:100 Poems for Ken Saro Wiwa*, published by Flipped Eye Publishing, London, England. Her own collection of poetry, *In-between Season,* was published by Rowan Books. Anna is also a freshly baked grandmother, and if you like, has a bagful of photos she can show you.

Michael Mirolla, author of a clutch of novels, plays, and short story and poetry collections, describes his writing as a mix of magic realism, surrealism, speculative fiction and meta-fiction. Publications include the novel *Berlin* (a 2010 Bressani Prize winner, translated into Latvian and French); *The Facility*, which features among other things a string of cloned Mussolinis; and *The Giulio Metaphysics III*, a novel/linked short story collection wherein a character named "Giulio" battles for freedom from his own creator; the short story collection *The Formal Logic of Emotion* (translated into Italian); a punk novella, *The Ballad of Martin B.*; and two collections of poetry: *Light and Time*, and *The House on 14ᵗʰ Avenue* (2014 Bressani Prize). His short story collection, *Lessons in Relationship Dyads*, from Red Hen Press in California was published in the Fall of 2015, while the novel *Torp: The Landlord, The Husband, The Wife and The Lover*, set in 1970 Vancouver, was published in the Spring of 2016. Born in Italy and raised in Montreal, Michael now makes his home in the Greater Toronto Area.

Carol Moreira, born in the UK, has worked in journalism around the world. Her work has appeared in the *Globe and Mail*, the *Toronto Star*, and the *South China Morning Post*, among many other newspapers and magazines. She won a magazine feature writing award in 2009 and another in 2011. Her first novel, a young adult story called *Charged,* was published in 2008 by James Lorimer. Her second novel, a young-adult fantasy titled *Membrane*, was published by Fierce Ink Press in 2013. She is currently working on a novel for adults. Carol has earned a degree in English from London University and a post-graduate diploma in Modern Chinese (Mandarin) from London's Ealing School of Languages. She is a co-principal of the start-up news site www.entrevestor.com.

Don Mulcahy, born in Clydach, Wales, and a Canadian citizen since 1969, lives in Strathroy, Ontario, where he writes poetry, prose, book reviews and newspaper articles following an academic career in dentistry. His work has appeared in 5 countries: in dental journals, newspapers, The *CHS Newsletter* (Wales), *The Prairie Journal, Matrix, Coffee House Poetry* (U.K.), *iota* (U.K.), *Verse Afire, fait accomplit, blood ink, Tower Poetry, Antigonish Review, Vallum*, in the anthologies *Butterfly Thunder, Sounding the Seconds, Ascent Aspirations, Voices Israel 2013 Poetry Anthology, Ekphrastia Gone Wild* (U.S.), "*Writing After Retirement*" (U.S.), and online at www.blueskiespoetry.ca, Cyclamens and Swords (Israel), www.prairiejournal.org, and at www.magazine.utoronto.ca/writers-circle. In 2014 he published a political critique titled "*Bogus Democracy*". He has written occasional columns for a rural newspaper, and is a book reviewer for *Ninnau,* the Welsh-American quarterly.

Susan Ouriou is a Calgary-based literary translator, fiction writer and interpreter. Two of her translations—*The Road to Chlifa* by Michele Marineau and *Necessary Betrayals* by Guillaume Vigneault —were short-listed for the Governor General's Award for translation. Her first novel, *Damselfish*, was short-listed for the WGA's Georges Bugnet Best Novel Award and the City of Calgary's W.O. Mitchell Best Book Award.

Theresia M. Quigley is a retired professor from the Université de Moncton where she taught Canadian Comparative Literature. She is the author of two collections of poetry and a collection of literary essays on the child protagonist in Canadian adult fiction. Her latest book, *I Cry for Innocence* (DreamCatcher Publishing, 2002) is an autobiographical account of her family's experiences as German refugees in Japan during World War II. For more information one can visit www.tquigley.net.

Jane Rule, born in Plainfield, New Jersey, graduated from Mills College in California. She came to Canada in 1956, ultimately becoming a citizen. She taught intermittently at the University of British Columbia until 1976, when she moved to the Gulf Islands. She is a novelist, short story writer, essayist and author of a dozen books, including *After the Fire* (Toronto: Macmillan Canada, 1989), *Memory Board* (Toronto: Macmillan Canada, 1987), *Hot-Eyed Moderate* (Tallahassee: Naiad 1985), *Contract With the World* (Tallahassee: Naiad 1982), and *Lesbian Images* (Trumansburg: Crossing, 1982). Her awards include C.N.I.B Talking Book of the Year, 1991; U.S. Gay Academic Union Literature Award, 1978; Canadian Authors Association Best Story of the Year, 1978; Canadian Authors Association Best Novel of the Year, 1978. Ms Rule passed away in December 2007. Her article is produced here with permission.

Libby Simon, MSW, RSW, is a freelance writer and retired school social worker. She worked for several years in child welfare, and for 20 years as a school clinician and parent educator with the Child Guidance Clinic of Winnipeg, in the public education system. Her articles and publications deal with social/educational issues, personal narratives and humour. She has been published in newspapers, magazines, anthologies and scholarly journals in Canada and the U.S. Her most recent project is a violence prevention program for K-3 called *Don't Fight, It's Not Right*, available through the Manitoba Textbook Bureau.

Carrie-Ann Smith, originally from Sault Ste. Marie, Ontario, is a graduate of Dalhousie University's School of Library and Information Studies. She started working at Pier 21 in 1998, and is now Manager of Research at the Pier 21 National Historic Site in Halifax, N.S. She contributes regularly to the *Panoram Italia* magazine, and joined other Canadian writers of Italian descent in the 2004 ECW Press book, *Mamma Mia: Good Italian Girls Talk Back*. Her 2005 story "Pecan Logs and Leonard Cohen" formed part of Madeleine Lefebvre's *The Romance of Libraries.* In 2006, the much respected U.S. periodical *Library Science* called her one of this continent's *"... movers and shakers."*

Batia Boe Stolar is an Assistant Professor in the English Department at Lakehead University, Thunder Bay, Ontario. She is currently working on a book-length manuscript on the photographic and cinematic visual constructions of immigrants in Canada and the United States.

H. Masud Taj is an architect and poet who lives with his family in Ottawa. He is the architect of the War Memorial for the Indian Navy. His written work was featured in the Penguin India anthology of contemporary Indian poets, *Reasons for Belonging* (2002).

Ken Victor, originally from Boston, Mass., lives in the Gatineau Hills of Quebec with his wife and three children where, most nights, around the dinner table, you can find him pretending to understand French. When not being dad or husband, he moonlights as a poet (for which he has received a National Magazine Award) and as a consultant in leadership and organizational development. In August of 2003 he finally became a Canadian citizen.

Meguido Zola is Director of Professional Programs, Faculty of Education, Simon Fraser University. He is a storyteller and an award-winning writer for children and young adults. Apart from scholarly writings, he has compiled anthologies of Canadian writings for children and has edited a language arts series for schools, a young adult novel series, a writing process series and a poetry series, as well as children's newspaper and magazine columns. His own writings for children encompass picture books, novels, poetry and biography.

Printed in June 2016
by Gauvin Press,
Gatineau, Québec